APEX TO ZULU A2Z!
The History Of The Most Feared Multi-Racial Football Firm In Britain

Written by David C George

TRAFFORD
PUBLISHING

USA • Canada • UK • Ireland

© Copyright 2006 David C George.

All rights reserved. No part of this publication may be reproduced, stored in a retrieval system, or transmitted, in any form or by any means, electronic, mechanical, photocopying, recording, or otherwise, without the written prior permission of the author.

Note for Librarians: A cataloguing record for this book is available from Library and Archives Canada at www.collectionscanada.ca/amicus/index-e.html
ISBN 1-4120-9422-4

Printed on paper with minimum 30% recycled fibre.
Trafford's print shop runs on "green energy" from solar, wind and other environmentally-friendly power sources.

TRAFFORD
PUBLISHING

Offices in Canada, USA, Ireland and UK

Book sales for North America and international:
Trafford Publishing, 6E–2333 Government St.,
Victoria, BC V8T 4P4 CANADA
phone 250 383 6864 (toll-free 1 888 232 4444)
fax 250 383 6804; email to orders@trafford.com

Book sales in Europe:
Trafford Publishing (UK) Limited, 9 Park End Street, 2nd Floor
Oxford, UK OX1 1HH UNITED KINGDOM
phone 44 (0)1865 722 113 (local rate 0845 230 9601)
facsimile 44 (0)1865 722 868; info.uk@trafford.com

Order online at:
trafford.com/06-1177

10 9 8 7 6 5 4 3 2

Dedicated to my mother Lyn George, and all Birmingham people who are in the know. Dedicated also to Alton Manning and family as you are not forgotten.

Special thank you to Ben Green, Tony from Cool Print, Coo–Coo, Morph, Justin at ID Create, Tony Graffiti and also Jim Morgan over in Italy, who got the ball rolling with his vision. Much respect lads from myself for everything. Special thank you to Adrian King who came up with a vision that changed our lives.

Contents

Introduction to the A to Z		5
Brief Birmingham History		11
Club History		15
The Experiment		26
Chapter 1	Wedge Head	48
Chapter 2	The Apex & The Townies	68
Chapter 3	The Wimbledon Tennis Addiction 80	83
Chapter 4	The History Of Aston & Villas C-Crew	101
Chapter 5	Brummy Characters	128
Chapter 6	Junior Business Boys	134
Chapter 7	The History of British Fascism (Northern & Southern Racists)	177
Chapter 8	Millwall Rivalry: Millwall Vs Birmingham City 1971	186
Chapter 9	Middlesborough Away 84 The Mighty Few	207
Chapter 10	Yids Are Kids	245
Chapter 11	The Cardiff Stronghold	258
Chapter 12	The Pompey Estate	271
Chapter 13	The ICf Situation	279
Chapter 14	World Cup France 98	301
Chapter 15	Leeds United Madness	320
Chapter 16	Different Grade	343
Chapter 17	Operation Red Card	372
Final Word		384

Introduction to the A to Z

THE CASUAL WAY OF LIFE is not a new phenomenon, although some of you will be able to understand totally if you are, or, ever have been involved in any of the previous decades youth cultures, fair enough. But it's to the everyday man, who has never thrown a punch in anger. I'd like to inform you of the story so far.

Challenge your beliefs, whatever your constitution. It doesn't demand a leap of faith just empathy. So please indulge me!

If you too, could of stood there, shoulder to shoulder, with a gathering of like-minded souls and shared moments forging fantastic new ideologies which would shape and define through profound and privileged experience your very everyday being. Thus laying down the blueprint of the person you would become.

Whether be through oppression recession or in the face off aggression, you reacted and rebelled. Gave em a dose of their own medicine.

To some the only things left after family, are football, fighting music and fashion.

Some manage it staying sober. Some ignore prohibition and administer their own prescription.

Be it in a ballroom at the end of a pier, with the powder mostly on the floor. A D.I.Y. Punk do, letting the youth and the un-waged in through the back door. Whether in a pill popping bingo hall, or a disco where the crowd screams out for more.

On to a hazy smoke filled dancehall, or a laser beam and light show flooded warehouse. Dogs barking! Drowned out by the twenty K. turbo sound-system, that the collectable flyer was advertising. Then the sirens sound out the criminal justice bills warning.

A basement gathering, on invitation only, dressed to impressed with that smug look of the informed on your face. The Tribal Gatherings only differed due to Biology and Time. Where else would you find Spiraling Tribes out of place and out of line?

I say stand and be counted for you were the few. The rest although not there whether scared or un-prepared or unaware needed you. Whether they approved or not it was always a contentious issue, either recalled with pride or a stories integrity jealously denied, from myth to legend false or true.

I actually believe it was important, it did define us, you did see the light, get an insight, you did get in tune it was unique, there wasn't a time like it whatever the time was, but after close inspection it was the same reaction to the same situation by the same searchers. The only difference being the climate, whatever!?

It was out of our hands. Dictated by whichever oppressor had hold of the reigns. Policy makers were rarely righteous mostly misguided and hopelessly out of touch with intuitive youth. They had an alternative agenda. The point of this book is brutally honest so hear us out before you shoot the messenger.

When your population is bordering sixty million it becomes a numbers game, The Empire used to divide and conquer and I believe they used the very same regime in their attempts to tame.

In England the borders between each community were defended in the same way. It became inherent to hate your neighbor if he wasn't the same. Color, or class, or religion, were all used as reasons to lay the blame on someone else. Who you thought was better off than you and better served by your country.

The point isn't to patronize or glorify, but to speak truthfully.

Being a Clan, a Tribe, a Club, or a Firm. Bye the very nature of the loose lips sink ships, and secret handshakes mentality necessary to organize and exercise the events of an era. If you didn't have a clue a sociology degree was no good to you. That's why the truth about your youth has always missed the point. So regarding the modern British terrace incarnation of the voice of treason.

APEX TO ZULU A2Z!

I testify.

But you must appreciate although a right royal turn out on match day we may bring. It is only five to ten percent of the paying attendance on the day, which thinks this way. Therefore. Too do the math. Although an impressive one million marching for the cause it leaves twenty-four million who don't know or don't care, and why should they?

The struggle of everyday life in any town, or city, even village although appear totally different and alien to the generation before.

Are, after closer dissection just a manifestation. Of political, and, or social reactions to the previous times weaknesses.

Paying the bills and taxes, feeding, clothing, housing, educating and protecting are the paramount responsibilities of any keeper.

Whether it be a one-man band, a family or a community, indigenous or immigrant, whatever the decade or postal address maybe.

I do think it deserves some attempt to inform though, for by the very nature of you reading this you must in some way or form be somewhat interested, and this books contributor's set about to pay some attention to the complexities of this culture that the individual's who witnessed and became immersed in felt.

This will be assisted by comparison with other youth cultures of the times. From the early Teddy boys, who rebelled against the fifties standard issue collar and tie. Flat cap, Bowler, or Pork Pie and Sunday best.

The way previous generations had dressed. Fed up with the first soundtrack of radio broadcasts by the BBC. Big bands and subway singers sending their mothers nervous souls floating off over the reassuring white cliffs of Dover.

From Rudeboy, Skinhead, Mod and Rocker, Punks, Soul boys to Ska and Two Tone. New Romantics to your modern day Raver, then comes Clubber, post Hip-Hop, Trip Hopping amongst a Junglist massive, or Garage heads, Brit popping as they swagger, draped in the couture of the day.

Listening to life's soundtrack that would dare baffle any Ethnomusicologist of his day. But some would drift off nonchalantly to it, in transit on the way back. From a memorable Glastonbury exodus, as they contemplated, they'd been sacked.

Never pondered, never wondered?

Maybe the comparison to underground movements, ironic yet metaphoric started with these wartime communities. Displaced and finding sanctuary after a preplanned well executed exodus to shelters, and there hugging each other finding solace and reassurance in their creative members courageous but not thankless attempts to calm frayed nerves and instill some camaraderie with their artistic endeavors.

In uncertain times, a bit of music hall comedy, social club classics or heavenly voices soaring. Resonated, momentarily drowning out the grim realities that were waiting above and were greatly appreciated and warmly received.

Realizing once the sirens sounded and they returned over ground. Too there damaged homes and displaced communities, to pick up the pieces of their lives.

When the returning heroes were repatriated and the war stories started on their transition from myth to legend, and we stood in remembrance for the fallen and the unknown. Whether they were battle hard soldiers or cowering everyday men. We moved on, put it behind us. Laid it to rest. United in two minutes silence. What else could you do?

Some things change some things stay the same.

So don't believe the hype!

The revolution will be televised!

But the one percent will be snug as drugs in a nuclear proof world many miles underground while the other 99 percent.

The Minions, Serfs, Underlings, and Slaves. The Blacklisted workforce who don't own, just rent. Let alone save for a rainy day.

Party on and scatter as they embark on another mission, portrayed by the media as rioting minors, poll tax partisans and heinous hooligans.

When the wind blows, the Metropolis rumbles, stumbles.

Civilization crumbles, acts of her Majesty to keep us humble.

Four meals away from anarchy, no matter what messiah you serve.

Or way of life you needed to preserve. Only then one realizes the ascent from precious lament to complacent neglect when the tide turns.

APEX TO ZULU A2Z!

Do we ever learn?

Did we evolve from animals through survival of the fittest? Early days on newly built housing estates the length and the breadth of our land only stand to back up this.

Some were rational compassionate men who were noble and had righteousness on side. Some were mongrels and preyed on innocent folk, profiting from bad mindedness and their aggressive ways. Mugging people off using fear and a blade for their own selfish aims. Taking away people's ideas, hopes and dreams.

We all get knocked down but you brush yourself off and start again, that's how we survive. That's how we first came to realize

If you treat a man like a dog for so long, after a while he will think fuck it and bite. A Pit-Bull lock's jaws that can only be opened when he has died in the fight!

Individuals break free, rise above the herd mentality and search out the bastards who enforce inequality. As a result unions form. People come together. Helping each other out, to weather the storm.

My hopes and dreams rest on these casual shoulders! Modern day moral soldiers! They surely are our next evolutionary free-runners!

This story, a matter of fact account of the life and times of an evolving second cities people, is a local tale but is relevant universally.

What your about to read isn't pretty. The benchmark raised with arrogance. Disregarding the watershed with belligerence.

Shamelessly documenting the nitty gritty.

A true tale told with some help, by his friends to the end, from the pen of Junior Georgie.

Tip your hats blood and brethren.

His balls and his word are broken for no one.

Laid out naked on the page, by a chronicler of the 21st century.

About the rise and the risks of the Casual nation! From notoriety to immortality,

When we're all gone it will live on in the library.

A tale of two cities has already been penned,

But Shakespeare never had the privilege of standing on the Tilton or the Railway End.

The bastard offspring of Socrates maybe, or just a figment of my

DAVID C GEORGE

imagination, am I digressing?
    Or? Or! Am I comparing the Casual to a pavement philosopher?
    Future revolutionaries! Don't slouch watching Sky on the sofa!
    All together now! 'Their coming to take me away ha ha hee hee, their coming to take me away haa haa,,,,'
    Welcome to the story, the story so far!
    The reason for my parables is because we are still at war.
    The pen is mightier than the sword.
    The minions rattle the cages of the lords.
    Once more into the fray the call!
    I'm not a preacher or a dictator.
    Make your own minds up.
    That's the only freedom they can't take away from you.
    Now read on,
    As we journey on!
    Kingy.

Brief Birmingham History

THE NAME BIRMINGHAM IS derived from the Anglo Saxon name Beormaham, ham meaning hamlet or village and Beorma possibly the name of a local Saxon tribal leader.

Just after the Norman conquest of Britain, the De Bermingham family owned the area known today as Birmingham. They established a small farming estate and Birmingham at the time was recorded as a minor village.

In the Domesday Book of (1086) Birmingham was said to consist of land for six ploughs, but only three plough teams were used. There were also five families of villeins and four borders. Woodland covered half a league by two furlongs, with no mill nor meadow to its name. Birmingham was valued at just 20 shillings. It had a long way to go with regards to becoming a wealthy city. But "From little acorns, mighty oaks do grow."

In 1154, Lord Peter de Bermingham obtained a charter for a brand new market. It was called the Bull Ring and was located at the crossing point on the River Rea. This helped attract skilled craftsmen to set up business in the area.

The name Bull Ring came from the many slaughterhouses that were in operation in the centre. Bulls were chained to the ground in preparation for slaughter then taken inside to be butchered.

Birmingham became one of the leading centres of trade and market innovation, and in the 1200's developed from an agriculturally insignificant village, into one of the greatest industrial cities in Europe.

DAVID C GEORGE

It had now earned a reputation as the city of a thousand trades.

1641 saw the birth of the Roundheads, parliamentary supporters during the English Civil War. The name referred to their short haircuts worn by Puritans of the time in contrast to the fashionable longhaired wigs worn by many of the supporters of King Charles I, who were called Cavaliers. Birmingham City was made up of Roundheads, with the name Puritans coming from followers of the Church of England, while in neighbouring wealthy Aston, they were called Cavaliers. By the 1700s, Birmingham already had a broad cultural mix of people from Europe and beyond.

In 1760, a large network of canals was built to transport raw materials and finished goods.

Mathew Boulton, a leading businessman of the time was expanding his empire from toy making to buckles and buttons. 1765 saw Midland intellectuals set in place a society that would assist in the foundations of the Industrial Revolution. The Lunar Society brought chemists, scientists, engineers and theorists together discussing inventions and ideas. Watt, Erasmus Darwin, Boulton, Priestley and Wedgwood all contributed to the vision and ideas of the time.

The Priestley riots erupted in 1791, which resulting in Joseph Priestley having to leave Birmingham after his home was trashed and ransacked. He had upset local church leaders and the establishment with his radical ideas, but religious and political disputes were common in these times.

In the 1820s, the canal system had been extended, giving Birmingham more miles of canals than Venice. 1834 saw the Birmingham Town Hall opened and it attracted visitors over the years, including Charles Dickens, Cardinal Newman and the Midlands home grown composer, Edward Elgar.

Birmingham's first railway arrived in 1837, and was called the Grand Junction Railway. This linked Birmingham to every corner of the UK. New Street Station opened in 1854 as a joint station with the Grand Junction. This was closely followed by the Great Western Railways/Snow Hill station.

The Industrial Revolution saw many businesses prospering, including the area known as the Jewellery Quarter. To this day it is still the largest concentration of jewellers in Europe, with a third of the UK's jewellery made in the city. Birmingham also has a Gun Quarter, which was once the foremost gun manufacturing community in the UK. William Powell & Sons, have manufactured high quality firearms for over 200 years, including the Napoleonic Wars and the American Civil War. In 1864 the Powell patent Snap Action appeared and enjoyed long popularity and many guns employing this system are still in use today. William Powell & Sons established themselves as Master Gunsmiths 50 years before Smith & Wesson of America.

In 1889 Thomas Atwood a leading politician of the time, helped pass the Reform Bill of 1832. Birmingham had now become a City.

In 1939, Birmingham had in place four aircraft factories and skills with which to produce any aircraft needed in the event of war. 400.000 of Birmingham's population were involved in war production, and it could be said that without the industrial skills of Birmingham, Britain could well have lost the Second World War. Spitfires and Hurricane aircrafts poured out of the cities factories. Shells and ammunition, armoured vehicles, motorcycles, amphibious crafts, engine parts and trucks were supplied to the British war effort. Birmingham is now known throughout the world for its innovation and manufacturing, the once proud home of the motor industry, but still boasts companies such as Dunlop, Lucas and (British Small Arms), to name but a few.

During the Second World War, Birmingham suffered heavy bombing and was redeveloped during the 1950s and 60s with many concrete ring roads and office blocks. It was described as an ugly concrete jungle. Large-scale immigration after the Second World War enriched the city, with an influx of people from the British Commonwealth and beyond taking jobs that British people thought were beneath them.

With a huge amount of bars and clubs across the city, Birmingham is a vibrant place. The oldest Inn/pub is the Old Crown in Digbeth built in 1368. The Anchor Inn, is also in Digbeth, was built in 1797. 1945 saw Abdul Aziz open a coffee shop in Birmingham's Steelhouse Lane selling curry and rice. Later this became The Darjeeling, which was the first Indian restaurant in the city. The world famous Balti, and Chicken Tikka Masala were both invented in Birmingham and have received gastronomic acclaim for the "Balti Belt" of restaurants situated in Balsall Heath, Sparkbrook and Ladywood areas. Brylcream is also a Birmingham product in origin.

Famous food brands to come from the city are HP Sauce, Typhoo Tea, Birds Custard, Blue Bird Toffee, Bournville cocoa and Cadbury's chocolate.

Birmingham's music scene is not as prolific as that of Liverpool or Manchester, but it still has a varied history of over half a century. The 1960s "Brum Beat" saw bands such as The Moody Blues, Traffic and The Move. Birmingham is often described as the birthplace of Heavy Metal music, with Ozzy Osborne's Black Sabbath and Judas Priest coming from Brum.

The founders of Led Zeppelin, Robert Plant and John Bonham lived in nearby towns, and played gigs in local Brum Beat bands before forming Led Zeppelin.

The 1970s saw members of Idle Race and The Move form a new band called the Electric Light Orchestra and also Wizzard. The rise of reggae and ska in the late 70's introduced the masses to great bands such as Steel Pulse and UB40. Musical Youth and The Beat, also Joan Armatrading, had many chart hits.

The 1980s brought us the most successful new romantic group, Duran Duran, along with Dexy's Midnight Runners, Fuzzbox and the Fine Young Cannibals. 1990s, Birmingham bands were The Charlatans, Ocean Colour Scene, Electribe 101, Bentley Rhythm Ace, Echobelly, singer Ruby Turner and the group Dodgy. In 2005, we had Editors, Jamelia and the true bluenose Mike Skinner from The Streets. Underground House music, Hip Hop and Dance Hall sound systems such as Goodwill International, Now Generation, Wasifa Showcase, Observer, Romantic Bubblers, Radics, King Ally, Luv Injection and Immortal have, and some still do, entertain the masses with upbeat, lively, underground black music.

Club History

BIRMINGHAM CITY like so many clubs, has its origins within the church. Formed by a group of cricketers from the Holy Church in Bordesley Green in 1875, its first home was Munts Street which was rented from the Gressey family in 1877 for £5 a year. At the time, Blues went under the name Small Heath Alliance and the first ever game played against their future rivals Aston Villa was won by Small Heath Alliance 1–0. Just goes to show that some things never change.

The club turned professional in 1885 making an agreement with the players whereby they received half of the gate money and in 1888 became the first club to adopt limited liability. The share capital of the club was £650. The club then changed their name from Small Heath Alliance in 1905, to Birmingham City football Club.

In 1906 the growth of Birmingham City FC meant a change of ground was necessary so Blues moved to St Andrews and played their first game there in December attracting a crowd of 32,000.

The first goal scored at St Andrews was by Mr Benny Green, who was rewarded for his efforts with a piano, which he then sold.

During the First World War, Birmingham City were asked to help out by offering the use of St Andrews as a rifle range to train soldiers heading off to fight the Germans. The 1925-26 season saw the first foreign visitors to St Andrews, Real Madrid. We beat them 3–0 in a friendly.

On 15th May 1956, Blues were the first English team to play in Europe when they drew 0–0 with Internazionale. In 1960 Blues reached the Fairs cup final, losing to Barcelona 4 – 1 on aggregate. The biggest ever attendance at St Andrews was in the FA Cup tie on 11th February 1939 against Everton. 67,341 spectators packed in to see Birmingham draw the game one – one, only to be knocked out in the replay 2 – 1. During the war years, St Andrews was heavily bombed by the Germans and took a number of direct hits, forcing Birmingham City to play their home games at Aston Villa's ground.

When St Andrews was being rebuilt, the players had to dress and get ready in a nearby factory. In 1946, Birmingham had their most successful year to date by winning the Football League, also appearing in the F.A. semi final. In 1947, Birmingham won the Second Division title, conceding just 102 goals in 126 league games. In the 1954 – 55 season, Blues gained promotion from the Second Division to the First Division. 1962 – 63 saw Blues' F.A. cup-tie against Bury postponed 14 times. A game was also abandoned, and a replay, which brought the total of attempts to 16 before the match was decided.

In the league cup competition, Blues beat their local rivals Aston Villa 3 – 1 on aggregate at Villa Park. A young Trevor Francis appeared in 1970, and in years to come would evolve into the first million pound player being bought by Brian Clough at Nottingham Forrest in 1979. The 70s saw Birmingham become a stable and steady top-flight team, enjoying seven seasons in Division One.

Alberto Tarantini moved from Argentina to the Midlands to play for Birmingham City, and was one of only two players to receive a World Cup Winners medal who played for the city; the other was Frances, Chistophe Dugarry.

The early 80s saw Birmingham promoted and relegated, doing a yo-yo in Divisions throughout the decade ending with being relegated to Division Three in 1989.

In 1991 Birmingham reached Wembley in the Leyland Daf Cup final and won the game 3 – 2 with the Chelmsley crew including Neil Wilf Williams RIP, Dyson, Noel, Myself and Scotty having the time of their lives.

Two clashes with quality opponents Blackburn Rovers and the mighty Liverpool, proved that Birmingham have the tenacity and gaul to succeed against tough opposition. Birmingham lost 3 – 1 over two legs in the Coca-cola Cup against Blackburn Rovers, who went on to take the premiership title. Also, after a replay against Liverpool in the F.A. Cup, Blues lost on penalties, with Andy Johnson missing our chance to beat top opposition and go into Europe.

Birmingham also went on to win the Auto Windscreens Shield Competition at Wembley Stadium, attracting a 76, 663 crowd.

My name is David George nickname Georgie. I was brought up on a rough working class council housing estate in Birmingham called Chelmsley Wood, where I and a number of my friends from Alcott Hall Primary School used to hang around one of the most notorious pubs in Birmingham, The Happy Trooper. This council estate in North Solihull, South East Birmingham, was not your run of the mill due to its characters and size. The population of Chelmsley Wood alone is approximately 40,000 and it is located near Birmingham International Airport, which is right on the edge of south Birmingham. From growing up in Chelmsley Wood, I learned the essence of being a man and knowing right from wrong. When you are educated into an environment such as Chelmsley, you have to learn about survival as soon as possible. People who stood out on the Wood in the seventies did so for many different reasons. Some had strong personalities compared to the average individual, but what they had in common was an edge with regards to their personal lifestyle choices, such as music, fashion and experiences. Six secondary schools were in walking distance, so you can imagine that when the kids came out to play, they really did like to play. The main schools that had gangs of kids ready to fight at the drop of a hat were Simon Digby, which had the majority of good lads in the seventies; Whitesmore which also had good lads but took over in the eighties; Kingshurst, some good lads, but also a number of racist skinheads; Archbishop Grimshaw, had a few good lads; Smiths Wood, also some good lads, but not as prolific as Whitesmore & Digby; and a few from Park Hall, which had one or two good chaps. Forrest Oak was a special school at the time, for people who couldn't read or write very well, or just enjoyed killing small animals. Forrest Oak also had its fair share of kids who enjoyed starting fires, particularly in their own homes or someone else's.

With "Knock a door run," to "Kick the can," "Ackee one two three" and "Feet off ground" and Tracking, it wasn't all fighting and mayhem on Chelmsley Wood, as the Brummie sense of humour and character kept most people in good spirits.

The working classes of the 60s were experiencing separation with regards to sub-standard housing and they were feeling ignored by their political representatives. A lot of middle class youths at the time could afford the new fashions popularised by such bands as the Beatles (haircuts) and Carnaby Street clothing. These were classed as Mods, who were a subculture known for its consumerism and admiration for style, music and scooters. The youths, who had lesser means, such as factory workers and labourers improvised and came up with a style that suited their employment. Hobnail boots, straight-legged denims with checked shirts and braces. With money being tight, the working class man would only spend good money on garments if he were having an evening out at a dancehall where he would be enjoying the new sounds of ska, reggae and rock steady beats. I was the Rude boy of the West Indies and also the Mod, with the music and the style that has given birth to the skinhead, which has evolved, into so many different movements. These were exciting and experimental times to be involved in fashion and music.

Bammo

When the coal strikes and unemployment-hit Birmingham in 1972, The City suffered a great deal as a sizable amount of homes were fuelled by coal at the time. The strike hit and the coal man was no more, and at the time when this was all happening we had this little gas heater that we used to keep the house warm.

There was a big meeting down at the Saltly gas works and this man appeared who turned out to be Arthur Scargill who explained to the frustrated working classes that he was going to put things right. Even though I was ten at the time, I knew this was important to every local workingman. I watched the news all the time and was pretty clued up on the political situations in Britain.

I made it my business to go down to Saltly gate to see what was going on, and all the local workers were gathered together hoping this person could find a solution to their plight. The local men were all standing there in their overalls with their donkey jackets and they were inspired by Scargills speech.

There were lots of banners from all over the Midlands. They marched from Saltly gas works to Saltly gate. Crossing over the viaduct towards Saltly gate and resembling a sea of human ants. They sang of all for one and one for all. Scargill did make things happen for the workingman back then, and it was the first time I had experienced what it is like being with like-minded people who all believe in the same dream and the same goal.

The Johnny Heron Interview

Sitting in a pub in Cotteridge having a pint of Guinness talking about the old days at St Andrews and getting a feel for the changes that have taken place over the years with the mentality of Midland football supporters, was quite an eye opener. Johnny Heron enters the pub with a warm smile on his face while I'm sitting down with some old school chaps who have followed Birmingham City since they were children. Johnny is a proper stand up bloke with a warm personality and his friends who were also fellow blue noses welcomed me into the their pub. My first question for Johnny and his friends was.

Q How did you become a blue nose?

A I used to live in between Westheath and Northfield, Chattersley Road. Everybody was a bluenose; there wasn't any Villa at all. I must have been around 7 – 8 years old at the time. We used to jump onto the back of an Asprian Madley van getting a lift off this guy who used to drive us to the games. He used to drive us through Ballsall Heath down Vana Road, and all the brasses would be hanging out of the windows. He would take us to the game and at the time, it was a tanner in and it was absolutely brilliant. And you wouldn't see that much of the game cuz you were that small, but you knew that this was the place that you wanted to be.

Malcolm Owen

Same as Johnny really, I used to live on Tickers Farm Road in Northfield and all me neighbours took me down there. Johnny Scofield used to

DAVID C GEORGE

play for blues when I was there.

Q What year are we talking?
A 1961.
Les Newman and Mike Owen are also sitting with us, and Mike says, "Funnily enough, I've got a Staffordshire bull terrier called Shearer, and my surname is Owen. If I was to tek that up to Newcastle and breed it, I'd mek a fucking fortune.

Q What was it like going down the football in the early 70's?
A My own recollections, I'm still at school and the date is 1967–68 season.
March 30th sixth round of the FA cup. We are all a load of urchins on the Tilton Road; Tilton Road was full of greasers and Hells Angels. We used to stand on the Tilton, and that was the main end. The Tilton held 1200, I believe. There was no crew at the time, but there was hundreds and hundreds of these greabows everywhere. The Cossack chapter, the 69ers, was the second biggest in Britain at the time. March the 30th changed my life forever 67–68 season. 51,576 attendance, we beat Chelsea 1–0 and Fred Pickering scored and I'd never seen anything like it.
The Chelsea skinhead hordes that come in on that day were absolutely unbelievable. They had the Doc Martins, Jeans; I didn't see any stay press. And jean jackets. The were proper jeaned up. Wrangler jackets. Police soon got into the middle of the fans, and there was raw violence throughout the whole game. We went to school on the Monday, or you did what you had to do and you know, you wanted them fucking Doc Martins and you wanted to be a part of this fashion. Got the head shaved at the continental barbers down to a quarter of an inch. But we couldn't get hold of the Doc Martins, as they weren't in Birmingham then. So we had to go to Riders, the army and naval store to get hold of the big hobnail-fucking boots. An when it went off, sparks used to come off the bottom when you slid onto your arse a lot, as the bottoms were covered in metal dome like studs. Give it to near the end of the season; we started wearing Doc Martins then, turning your trousers up with the big gap an stuff. But then obviously we knew that the

greabows, the Hells Angels for some reason, were the enemy. We were clean cut, so we fucked them out the Tilton, didn't we. Started battling them, there were bloody hundreds of em. Smallheath was greabows. And after many a game in 67–68–69 season, the Double Zero club down by the old bus depot on Cattle Road was attacked.

> So we raided the Double Zero one Saturday night
> There was many an Angel and we won the fight
> So listen all you Angels with your Nazi wings
> Don't come up to Birmingham where skinheads are the Kings.

The day when violence started to change at Birmingham City was when Chelsea came to Birmingham 67–68 season dressed in all the skinhead gear, and banged it right off in the ground. After that game, that's when St Andrews put up a fence around the ground to stop any troublemakers getting onto the pitch. It took about a season to get rid of the greabows, to get rid of the Hells Angels. You know we would go down the game and you would have these dirty bastards everywhere. And the start of the new season was the start of the new era, and it started with what you were wearing.

There was a shop in Smallheath where you could get your Doc Martins on St Oswald's Road called Greenways. £5. They also sold Monkey boots in 1969. Pillar-box red was the colour before oxblood polish, and you know the best thing about coming from an away match especially, your stay press would be covered in red. It was the original paintballing really. If you got loads of kicks up the arse, people could tell you had run away. The worst shoe ever to wear down the football was the Loafer. I was fighting a Millwall fan by the clock in the ground, this was the promotion year, I've gone at him right, and my fucking shoe has sailed out of the ground, gone. So like a fucking pratt, I haven't thrown the other one away, and I'm hobbling around all night in town. What's going on? I was born in Ireland by the way, ha ha ha.

Q What pubs were moving and shaking in the early 70s?
A The Greenway Arms with a big horse trough outside across the road from St Andrews, but we were 15 years old then, and we weren't

piss heads. The Greyhound was at the top of Holloway head. Basically town consisted of The Gilded Cage, The Mulberry Bush, The Demon strip club, Tavern In The Town, The Crown, The Eagle, which was all ZZ Tops. And we never moved out of that square mile, "Did we?" But the greatest club in the 68–69–70–71 era was above the Co-op, Brian T the DJ. Playing every single reggae & soul record that came in. The Rainbow suite up in the lift, every single tune I heard there, you went down to the Bullring market to Bailey's records in the actual market and bought your tunes. And when you started to get more knowledgeable about your reggae and your blue beat, there was another place to go which was the blue beat shop in Digbeth by the coach station. You had Don Christies on Ladypool road. Toots & the Maytels were absolute quality. But in them days you had Desmond Decker, The Pioneers, I've seen Laurel Aitkin at the Mayfair suite, and in two minutes, the row went off and he went off stage. Styles and flavours formed which meant that Laurel went on to form Symarip, which led to other bands such as Joe the Boss and Judge Dread.

Q Name the areas in the 70s that had good mobs?
A Well the early 70s that I know, Quinton always had a firm regardless of who they supported which was mainly Villa. Northfield had a good firm. And then you had Townies, people who were called townies because that's where they hung about. Dave Curtis, people like that. Chelmsley Wood wasn't even there then was it. There were individuals from many other areas of Brum, and you would put the word out there for a meeting, and if you missed it, tough shit. We had no mobile phones, and most people didn't have a house phone.

Q Who could you rely on back in the day in the early 70s?
A Well I mean my firm was Jayo, Genocky, Jamie, Steve Matterson, Danny Quinn who came a little bit later, Nigel Hamilton, cuz the fact is that there was such a euphoria of the feeling that we didn't even think of running in them days. It was just so fucking high wasn't it? The buzz was incredible.
You talk to a criminal, and he'll say. Me mates put me in, he's put me in, he's put me in, and probably the worst worst thing ever, is to

say that Heron run. When we run, we all run together. I was the cross-country champion so I could fucking run like a gazelle. But I had to go back for fucking Chunky, the fat cunt. Remember him? He'd come off the fucking burger van outside the Blues ground, starts a row, and we would have to go back for him wouldn't we. The lads used to all wagg school to come and hang round with us. But we were influenced by the reggae weren't we? John Holt and stuff, I could fight like fuck to that music. What you would have is Trojan done club reggae one to about five, and the Tighten Up volumes.

Coo-coo-Remember Moon stomping? I want all you skinheads to get up on your feet, put your braces together and your boots on your feet. I give me some of that old Moon stomping. Johnny H.-We used to smash the old village hall up didn't we?

Crafty-Remember Kevin Braid? Around 1976, he gave me all of his Tighten Up albums and I've still got em, I bet he wishes he never gave me em now.

Q What sort of clothes was popular in the early 70s?
A It was only a few years that we were proper boneheads. 1972 we were just growing our hair then, suede heads, and smoothies. But your original style was your Harrington, Doc Martins. Gibson's, Loafers, Nobles shoes didn't come in till around 72–73. Crafty/Coo-coo Major Domoes were similar to the Docs, but we couldn't get hold of them in the mid 70s, so we had these Major Domoes that were squared off at the ends. They were air wear, but square at the ends. Johnny H.-The average skinhead would have his Doc Martins on, your stay press or his Levis.

And then he would have, whether what you could afford your Ben Sherman, Jaytex, and Arnold Palmer, also your Harrington or your jean jacket. And I remember robbing granddad vests off washing lines; we used to wear granddad vests and our braces, jeans and boots.

Old Birmingham Classic Songs
If you go down to the woods today
You're sure of a big surprise
If you go down to the woods today

DAVID C GEORGE

You'll hardly believe your eyes
For Jeremy the Sugar Puffs Bear
Has got big boots and cropped his hair
Today's the day that Jeremy joins the skinheads.
* * * * *
We want the whole wide world to know
The blues are going up
With Trevor Francis and the lads
And just a bit of luck
With Freddie Goodwin and the boys
Division One bewhere
With Lactchford Hynd and Taylor to
We'll soon be playing there
Oh what a city Oh what a team
Oh what a city Oh what a team
We'll beat em down at Stamford Bridge
And White Hart Lane as well
And when we get to Old Trafford
We'll give old Besty hell
Oh what a city Oh what a team
Oh what a city Oh what a team.

Keep Right Who – From The Brummie Mod

Name; Mack The Mod
Born; 1960 Kingsheath Birmingham
First season at St Andrews; 1967 – 68
First season home and away; 1978 – 79
Grounds visited with Blues; 82

The best pubs to VISIT before the match in 1978 were, The Roundabout, Teddies, Temple Bar, Shakespeare, The Glue Pot, The Parasol, and The Crown, then up to The Greenway near St Andrews ground.

First heroes at St Andrews; Fred Pickering, Jimmy Greenhoff, Trevor Francis, Bob Latchford, Bob Hatton, Kenny Burns and Roger Hynd.

Fashion of the late 70s; Doc Martins, Army trousers, T-shirts in Royal Blue with white writing on the front – David Nivens Fridge.

Mod Revival 78 season, people were dropping second hand suites, white shirt and dark tie with Jam shoes.

79 season people got into tailor made suits made from Press Burgers in Brum.

A funny incident at Forrest away was when Mike Sefton wrote on a St George's flag (Godzilla Vs The Smog Monster). When approached by the police in the ground, they wanted to know what the flag meant as they thought it was a code in order to cause some trouble. The Forrest fans were not happy either as the police told the Birmingham fans to take down the flag. As the police left, the flag went straight back up in the air to the disgust of the Forrest fans. The reply to the policeman's question was, "It's a giant man eating carpet." This baffled the police who walked off none the wiser. Mack is still slick and his clobber is proper retro mod classic with his shirts tailor made at Stephan's in Cyprus and his shoes from Rackhams. This man is a true bluenose with a big personality.

Keep Right On!

The Experiment

IN THE LATE SIXTIES there were a number of families who came from many other areas of Birmingham to start a new life in Chelmsley Wood, as this brand new housing estate was designed to deal with the overspill that had been created by the increasing population of Birmingham City. Areas such as Small Heath, Saltly, and Alum Rock Handsworth and Nechells were very run down and deprived, so the idea of moving to a brand new housing estate with all new facilities with comprehensive schools that had heated swimming pools was pure luxury. On paper you could say everything was in place for a huge catastrophe as the area created was brand new, and the police, with the police station being fresh and virgin like, had no real idea how to deal with the new residents on this large multi-racial estate.

Chelmsley Wood was a social housing experiment by the then Birmingham City Council, then being taken over by Solihull, to supply cheap affordable housing in abundance for the working classes of Birmingham. Very similar to what the Americans have in their country except they call them the projects. At first it was fine, and everything ran smoothly, until young police officers eager to make a name for themselves started to bully and harass local youths on a regular basis. This is where instant problems arise, because you are from an area such as Chelmsley Wood that from its conception has all have the trademark reasons why crime would flourish. The local youngsters have a stigma attached to living in such a concrete jungle. When you are pushed about by authority, and told you are nothing and will never amount to anything in life, it should be no surprise that some kids turn to a life of crime, believing this is the only thing they can do to be respected and earn a living. From my short time on the planet, I now know that a combination of the two is what makes you successful. Working full time and also having extra curriculum activities is what makes you your real cheddar in life, and if I'm wrong, then I had better start watching Walt Disney movies around the clock and sucking my thumb. If there were any way I could truthfully say people actually earn everything they own in their lifetime, I would be a liar. Throughout history, corruption and deception have run hand in hand in all areas of society, especially those who have the power to oppress and persecute the local community. The people who control most of the information we get, i.e. the media/politicians/Government, are also the same people who always seem to be knee deep in one sleazy underhand scenario after another. Life on Chelmsley Wood was like a roller coaster ride, full of ups and downs with people who come off the rough tracks, and people who were well and truly strapped in for the bumpy journey into adulthood. I came from a strong Christian background like a lot of other black families on Chelmsley did, and my brother Gary and sister Jaqui used to attend Sunday school every week to make my parents happy. I wasn't really into religion, but I did believe in God. I was more into the deep fried chicken that was cooked by the short wide black women who attended the church meetings on Bosworth Drive. They could make an old sock taste like a meal at the Ritz, and it was fantastic.

Through the Punk and Skinhead scene, through the Mod and the Rude boy, New Romantic and the Trendy or the Dresser. Through Roller Discos and Dancehall- Sound clashes, Jazz-fusion and Soul, Hip Hop to House music and Warehouse parties, and on to Acid house and Rave in 88. I have seen all these changes and laughed and cried throughout my thirty-seven years on the planet. My story starts on Chelmsley because that is where I'm from, and not because I think Chelmsley Wood is the be-all and end-all. I write what I know to be true and also give you my opinion and many other people's views of what life was like living through these sometimes colourful and turbulent times.

DAVID C GEORGE

I can remember numerous occasions when young unemployed people were followed home late at night after leaving friends houses, and stopped by the police and arrested for anything that had happened that night. When attending Solihull Magistrates Court and explaining that you are unemployed and from Chelmsley Wood, you were instantly found guilty in their minds of whatever crime, whether it was vandalism, robbery or whatever. The surrounding areas of Chelmsley Wood are made up of more affluent middle class communities who looked down on the workingman and would at times make him feel unwelcome if he or she ventured into their idea of middle class heaven. On occasion, this would lead to violence outside public houses or in local clubs, resulting in Chelmsley Wood people being classed as troublemakers and undesirables, and sometimes they were. It was always easy pickings for the young police officers to get a name for fighting crime. In fact, I would go so far as to say the police had made thugs out of just average people who had had enough of gangs of police officers jumping out of police vans and goading the youths to lose their temper in order to arrest them and beat them up. This happened on a regular basis throughout my childhood and also to a huge number of my friends. It was common knowledge that at least 90% of the Chelmsley Wood police force was racist and very young, and would provoke trouble with most of the local youths and sometimes the parents in order to get a violent reaction. Some police would stop a black man driving a car with his wife and children, and ask him to get out of the car, then blatantly tread on his foot and spit in his face in front of his children. Now because a percentage of our parents were more passive than their children, the fathers would go home and then react to being treated like a wild dog on the streets out of sight from the police, but we as the children felt our parents pain and frustration. Stop and search was out of control in the seventies and for both black and white youths, it wouldn't be unusual for the police to stop you and search you while you were on the way to school wearing your uniform.

Most human beings if they are honest, will admit to having a dark and a light side to their personality or character. When put into situations of conflict or making a decent amount of tax-free money, humans will make their own choice on the route that's best for them. The Luke Skywalker Route? – Or The Darth Vader Route?

Depending on what profession you choose, a large majority of the country will decide on your character. Whether you are a good person or a bad person. E.g. Doctor = Good – Used Car Salesman = Bad.

This however is total stupidity to think that a person's vocation is a mark of his character, as some of the most depraved and evil people ever to have walked the planet have had a very high standing within the community, with a dark side that would shock the world. To name just a few.

The Marquis de Sade, Josef Mengele, Ted Bundy, Harold Shipman.

Casuals are mainly working-class youths who will look after their own and don't take kindly to being pushed around by anyone, including the police or other casuals. Even though the media claims that the hooligans are to blame for violence in and around football matches, I would say the most evil firm I have ever seen on numerous occasions at matches up and down the country are the police.

For instance, they are the only ones who always come to the ground tooled up, they are always looking to provoke a fight, and they have the capability to kill you and get away with it, as well as being funded by the Government.

Before the Trooper mob had evolved into anything, Chelmsley Wood had gangs such as The TC mob i.e. the town centre. They used to congregate around the chip shop on the shopping centre on Friday and Saturday evenings before the Happy Trooper was built, and used to frequent our one and only nightclub called the Hard Rock, which used to be where the Bingo hall stood but has now also gone. The Hard Rock was shut down after a fight took place outside the club, and a guy from Acocks Green was thrown from the town centre bridge and killed. The Alder Hall skins were also a gang, which had a reputation on Chelmsley Wood but would really only keep the rep in-house.

In the Seventies The Happy Trooper public house was built and produced a local gang of youths called the HTBB, the Happy Trooper Boot Boys who were one of the most active gangs connected to Birmingham City. They were also one of the armies that travelled in and around Birmingham sometimes fighting and invading punk and

DAVID C GEORGE

skinhead gigs in the city, fighting and sometimes causing mayhem at football matches home and away. Other not so well known pubs had mobs that would join up with the Trooper when travelling to foreign territory such as The Friendly, The Prince Hal, The Roundhouse, The Southern Cross, The Greenwood, The Trustee Servant and The Marston Green Tavern. The Trooper public house also had another gang called the Trooper who were older than the HTBB and would handle things in the pub. Situations that would develop into confrontations around the pub would usually be dealt with by the HTBB. The youth! Who congregated outside due to their ages?

Some of the Trooper members had a band that used to rehearse locally called Excretion 2000. They played punk music and at one time were looking for a drummer to join the band, and one of the guys knew Roger Taylor before he joined Duran Duran, and was going to ask him if he would be interested in playing the drums for them. It never happened due to the band not having a mixing desk. The rest is history, Lucky Roger.

Famous Trooper Songs
For you're tired and you're lonesome
And your heart has skipped a beat
You're sure to get your head kicked in
As you walk down Greenland's Street
Cuz when you reach the Trooper pub
You'll hear a mighty roar
So fuck off everybody, we've killed you all before.

Trooper Loopy
Trooper loopy nuts are we
Him and him and me and me
We'll show you what we can do
With a baseball bat and snooker cue
Hit him on the head with a baseball bat
And pick up the cue hit the cunt with that
What's it like to be a screw?
When you're National Front and a bastard too

APEX TO ZULU A2Z!

If you walked through Chelmsley Wood back in the mid seventies you would undoubtedly see sprayed on numerous walls; Glen R, Trooper Skins – Ste – Coo – Baz & Gibbo – Morris – Trout. They must have been the most well known youngsters around those times, even though most people didn't know what they looked like. An interesting character from back in the day was a guy called Deano who would entertain the youths outside the pub by eating pint glasses and scaring the locals. On one occasion, Deano was trying to befriend a stray dog when it bit him on the hand. He now chases the dog through the housing estate for at least a mile, and corners it in an alleyway. He grabs hold of the dog and bites off half of its ear leaving it yelping uncontrollably. From throwing people out of second-storey flat windows onto their faces, and steaming into ludicrous amounts of rival skinheads at the concerts all over Birmingham, Deano was a very well known lad on Chelmsley Wood. Asked what was the best fight he had against rival supporters, he instantly said Bristol City in Birmingham. Just over by where the old King Kong statue used to stand in the Bull Ring in the late 70s, Bristol City had it with twenty Trooper even numbers and it was absolutely fantastic. Proper fighting fist-to-fist, feet to feet. People were getting banged up with good body shots and the lot was going. Lumpy bruises and split lips were everywhere, but it was a proper full on brawl or bit of knuckle, not what you get now.

After the row, we all stood there looking at each other smiling and shaking hands with the Bristol City lot and said, "Fucking sweet that was lads, nice one." Bristol went on their way, and so did we, all looking the worse for weather on both sides. Fucking great it was, I'll never forget it.

The Trooper in the mid seventies was a no go area for anyone who did not know somebody from the there. You were standing on dangerous ground if you did not hear the warnings banded all over the rest of Birmingham City. If you know somebody and you're doing business, sweet. If you didn't know a soul and you entered the pub, then you would be given a chance to leave, but if you did not here the warnings, I'm afraid you would have to pick up your teeth, then leave. What would normally cause problems on Chelmsley at the time would be when a few local promiscuous skinhead girls would invite skinheads from the other side of town, with the inevitable consequences. A gang of skinheads from Northfield were invited to a party in Chelmsley and decided to pull up outside the Trooper public house. The thing was these people thought they where safe because they were also skinheads. Wrong! If people say don't go up the Trooper pub uninvited, then don't go.

Everybody would stick together in those days and if you came to fight up the Trooper you would be fighting the whole area, not just the people in the pub. That's why nobody ever came up the Trooper.

No matter what gaffer they had at the pub, it was still classed as their pub. They didn't smash it up at all, but every gaffer who ran the pub knew he didn't really run it except for pouring drinks. When police officers entered the pub, they would only come in if they were mob handed and tooled up because they also knew it was highly unlikely to arrest someone in the pub if you hadn't got the numbers or were unsure of yourself. Ambushing the police was the only way some youths could get their own back in the late seventies and eighties, and this occurred a number of times when youths had been assaulted and beaten up by the local constabulary. This was implemented by calling the local police into a cul de sac, and explaining that there was a burglary, and getting a police van or car to drive into the cul de sac, then introducing them to a hail of house bricks and bottles, while sliding a number of planks of wood with nails sticking out into the road to puncture the tyres when they started to reverse. Many police at the time were evil and some still are to this day. In the seventies they used to drive around in Black Maria vans; they were called the SPG. (Satan's Pig Gluttons)

Mid seventies fashion was varied, but a popular look at the time was the checked lumberjack coat with the large fur collars, Wrangler jeans and a pair of black & white Adidas training shoes called Samba, Mamba or Bamba. Any of these three pairs were very popular, also Adidas kick. A number of people in and around Birmingham were experimenting with different styles of dress from Mod to Skin to Soul Boy, and were mixing and matching garments they felt suited their personality. Long black three-quarter length nylon French Gabardine macks were also a favourite, as you could hide an array of weapons under your jacket with no bulges. The Trooper mob had seen Chelsea come to Birmingham in 76 and was overwhelmed by the style of the Londoner. They had on Harrington jackets and checked shirts with Levis and desert boots or dock shoes. Chelmsley Wood embraced this London style, and they were the first casuals at St Andrews to change the frequency of fashion in a big way. Half Skin & half Mod, this new style was very recognisable down St Andrews football ground. White cricket trousers purchased from Harry Parks, and Fred Perry T–shirts were very popular and made it easy for a number of lads into this style of clothing to make the crossover. Fred Perry evolved into Chemise Lacoste, and your white cricket trousers turned into Farahs. The James's at the time were a well-known local Irish family with style that many people across Chelmsley Wood would talk about. The youngest brother, David, was one of the best dressers in Hatchford junior school with his black & white Adidas and his black bomber jacket or Gibson shoes. Local girls would drool over this young mans style and his attention to detail. Donald also had on mint clobber and his sister Sonia also had an eye for style. Eugene the older brother was the Ace Face on Chelmsley, make no mistake. This guy was cool as fuck. Black Lamberetta and the slick clobber were always in this man's corner. People would talk about his style at school and would stand and stare anytime he went past on his scooter.

Alcott Hall also had a number of youngsters who stood out with regards to early style. In 1978, a local lad called Richard Douglas was dropping Adidas kick and Levi jeans when most lads were wearing Whiz kids or black slip ons. He was also the lad who was good at football and had girls talking about him for the right reasons. Warren Rose, who also went to Alcott, was a John Travolta fan and would wear the black bomber jacket with the parallel black slacks with the white T-shirt to school and had the moves at the school discos. Windy Arber was the school that had a lot of the early Trooper lads attending it the early 70s and spawned a group of chaps that would wagg junior school in order to follow Birmingham City home or away. St Anne's and Lowbrooke junior school also had a handful of youngsters who were switched on to the new style of clobber coming through. A lad called Brains, who used to travel to football matches with the Trooper as a skinhead, had now changed his style, and was now wearing kickers, with tight Adidas jogging bottoms and a flying jacket. His style was noticed across Chelmsley Wood, but most lads our age didn't really know anyone from Arran Way, which is the other side of Chelmsley. I was the lad who tried to be a shoplifter at the age of ten in Rackhams Birmingham, with Chames & Evs, and didn't quite make the grade, so while sitting on the 98 bus from town back to the Wood, had the piss taken out of me till I burst into tears. Those were the days.

Through the infant, junior and senior schools in Birmingham, the word used for the toughest person in school was the cock. Regardless if they were male or female. It was the term always used, the cock of the school. When fights used to occur between local schools, you would be looking for the cock of the school you were facing to be there. If they were, then the rival school, if they were any good at what they were doing, would try to rush the cock, and overpower him/ her. From attacking the cock straight away, this was an indication to the other school that you had come to take no prisoners.

If you saw an SPG van pull up, then any sane person would run away as fast as possible, because the police had a reputation for torturing youths who hung around the pub or were known to be a bit lippy. The police were the most feared mob on Chelmsley Wood due to having the power to beat you half to death, arrest you for assault, then get you sent to prison on jumped up charges. A lot of the guys from Chelmsley Wood only started getting into trouble from defending themselves from other gangs or the police, but seemed to have a reputation when many were just average guys who looked after their own.

At the time the older Trooper mob had many battles with most of the surrounding areas including Castle Vale in the early eighties where a number of people were chopped with axes in a fight at the Tradewinds public house on the Vale. – Lea Hall was also an area that had a number of run-ins with the Trooper, and there are numerous accounts of fights taking place at the Mackadown and also at the Meadway public house and the Red Lion in Shirley. The Mackadown was the venue in Kitts Green, which everybody who was anybody from our side of town used to frequent. From the Skins and Punk days through to the late 80s, the Mackadown has seen its fair share of goings on. I can remember standing outside on the car park at the back as a young lad and watching the bouncers beating people up and throwing them out of the doors onto their faces, while inside the venue, everybody was dancing to Monkey House by Devo. Due to the reputation of the Trooper, it was sometimes necessary for them to travel to these places to seek and destroy people, sometimes for reasons as minor as having too much red meat in their diet. Sheldon was also a place that felt the Trooper's hands, only after the Trooper were chased across the Marston Green golf course, with Aston & Troganite taking a hiding from Sheldon. Chelmsley then took 400 up to Sheldon to cause absolute mayhem and devastation, but were stopped by a huge number of police – Shard End – Kingshurst and The Timberley all knew who the Trooper were, and at the time none of them would even entertain the idea of taking them on if they had the full crew out. One night at the Timberley in Castle Brom, a number of local people didn't take too kindly to Tony G and Clifford dropping some dance moves in the pub that evening. The local disco was in full swing with comments being made about the local white girls dancing with black lads from another manor. It all went up in the air with a few Chelmsley males and females, getting battered, as the numbers attacking them were large, including locals and the bouncers who were from Shard End. Chelmsley then came up with their firm on a later date, and messed up numerous people who tried to have a go on the car park outside the Timberley pub. Special shout out to the original Happy Trooper firm who got the job well and truly done including over thirty arrests all from Chelmsley on the same night. Got to give a shout out to Serena Chashmore and Karen Barry who at the time were two Chelmsley girls with fire and spirit. When you se the a Chelmsley lad bowling through a pub with a hunting knife snarling with red eyes and froth coming out of his mouth then, to be fair, this would give most people an indication that it's probably time to leave really quickly. The Trooper could assemble in no time at all with one phone call that could be made to a phone box across the Greenland's Road from the pub, and land in an area such as the Solihull Civic Hall Centre where there would be pitch battles in the road against skinheads from Shirley and Acocks Green and surrounding areas when live bands and discos took place in 1978–79. Sometimes the Solihull mob would attack Chelmsley when they turned up in small numbers, and they would have to make a hasty retreat or be kicked to hell, which was sometimes the case. On one such occasion in 79, Troganite was punched in the face at the Civic Hall by a large mob of local skins who bashed a few Trooper and chased them into town. One phone call was made to the Trooper telephone box across the road, and three vans and two car loads of Trooper now properly landed in Solihull and ended up breaking people's jaws and stabbing a number of local skins who were now being chased all over town.

From an excursion to Benidorm in 1980, one of the Chelmsley lads brought back an array of Spanish stiletto blades, and gave them out to members of the Trooper mob.

There was snow on the ground and ice everywhere, but never the less the Trooper and The Friendly ended up having a mock knife fight on the shopping centre with one of the lads ending up stabbing a friend because he slipped on the ice, nearly resulting in one them losing his life.

The Endeavour mob was another well-known gang based in Chelmsley Wood who were slightly younger than the lads at the Trooper. They would congregate further up the road at the top of Berwick's Lane Park messing around and generally doing what teenagers do. They consisted of a number of male and female characters who were notorious for one reason or another, and this is where I used to hang out. Pencil, Bona, Big Louis, Little Louis, Baxter, Doss, Jamie Elliot, Hunki, Astro, Tony Burns, Tippa, K. Rice, Frankham, Brotherson and Keegan. The Lennon's and a gang of skinhead girls who used to drink and swear a lot would mess around on the park and wrap the swings by jumping off them after swinging as high as possible, then jumping off when the swing was just above their head and then running underneath causing the swing to circle around the bar until it's completely wrapped. Some of the members of The Endeavour also had a punk band called Ariel Pollution. I don't think they played any gigs anywhere except in Deano's garage, but it was something they all enjoyed being a part of at the time.

Mad Rob would jump off the top of the high rise slide, and then hang off the top of a block of flats for a small firework / A banger. Some local girls would also have sex on the football pitch in broad daylight with the Endeavour lot, and we would just sit about on the swings or doze about on the mushroom watching. If you were lucky, mad Rob would sometime do a mad dance if you sang "Cockles & Mussels" to him, but he was never the full ticket.

(Zion Youth) was the earliest Chelmsley Wood sound back in 76–81 run by Carl Baxter, Howard, Morris Berry and Kevin Hewitt. All these guys were good community people who would entertain the locals with the Jamaican dancehall vibe that was important to the identity of the young black youth. (Killerwatt) was another sound around 78–81 consisting of Rob Berry, Byron Dobson, Paul Edman and Steven George. (Manesis) was a next early sound system on Chelmsley Wood involving, Charles May, Glenford Williams and Handle. Glenford also had another sound, which was called (Dubs).

Alan Buckley was the man to watch at Birmingham City, getting eight goals in the 78–79 season. Later in the 80s, Chelmsley developed Gibbs / Onyx sound; Joseph sound system from Arran way and King Astra, around the mid 80's. There were also a number of white people on Chelmsley who had embraced the black culture to such an extent that they would speak patwah all day. Eddie Partridge, John The Moment i.e. Ten strings, Mickey Minnahan i.e. Fish. As a young lad standing up the Trooper, we would have many of these characters coming up and giving us their philosophy on life, which was very entertaining. One guy called Braidy used to wear very short trousers with the lining of the back pocket hanging out, and we as youths would ask him why his trousers looked that way. His response was, "You see me now?" "You see a Rastaman wears his chowdiz till dem fall off im backside." Then he would strut off into the Trooper for a drink. Chelmsley Wood itself had a smaller black community than areas such as Handsworth, Small Heath and Winson Green, but what it had that made it different to those other areas was a strong community spirit through black and white people. When you push people who are categorised as the lower socio-economic group, and try to brand them all as troublemakers, you are asking for a whole heap of what you were looking for. There was no difference between black

DAVID C GEORGE

and white as far as we were concerned on Chelmsley Wood and when it came to enjoying ourselves and sticking together, that is exactly what we did.

Troganite was one of the first black skinheads in Birmingham at the time, which I thought was a bit weird, but he had always supported Birmingham, and used to come and tell me about the mad fights he used to be involved in with rival supporters home and away, which left me puzzled until years later. He was very much into the jazz funk scene in Birmingham at the Lacano and would attend nights out with groups of guys from the local area.

The Trooper pub was a den of iniquity but loads of fun. It was the only place I knew where you had dog baiting in the bar and seventy year old ladies having a straightener outside the boozer, with the rest of their coffin dodger friends telling young crooks to piss off cuz they don't wish to purchase a fridge. Some of the real tough people who drank in the Trooper were ex Military or Navy and good solid community people, but you also had your drunkards and your lunatics who made up a large percentage of the congregation. Imagine the Manchester drama Shameless, and times it by ten, then you will have more of a real feel for this environment we lived in. If you are from a place like Chelmsely Wood where 90% of the police were racist and the surrounding areas hate your guts, it's easy to become immune to the crazy shit that happened up there. Now don't get me wrong, there were many other tough people bowling round the Wood in the seventies and eighties who were very much into martial arts or self defence and they had respect from the HTBB even though they never went down the football at all, apart from big Tony G. My hat is well and truly tipped to Frank – Monk – Rob Hunt – Mark Astell – Eugene Williams – Big Lurch – Tony Gardener RIP – R. Palmer – Jimmy Humphries – L. Morgan – Howard – Harris – Martin Clarke – Simone Henry – Karen Barry – Serena Cashmore – Sue George.

The list of heads goes on and on and they are all remembered by me for many different reasons, but for mostly making Chelmsley Wood a lot more interesting than it would have been if they were not here, I thank you all. Apologies if you are not mentioned as the list keeps on evolving.

APEX TO ZULU A2Z!

Trooper skin girls 1977 – 78 Etta, Miff, Usher.
F. Soady, Spike, Fish, K. Braid, John The Moment, A. Keagan, Big Brass, Little
Brass, Handle, O'Connell Bros, B. Nunes, G. Nunes, Fleagal, Fozz, JB, Squirl,
R.Earl, C. Williams, Gl. Williams, D. Palmer, Bobby Groves, K. Prentice, Bo-Bo,
Footie, J. Cooke, Gaz McQuaide, Toads, M. Cotts, Booya, Brownie, J. Fisher, John
McCoy, Jenx, Jaffa, Snook, Willie, The Pendleys, The Smiths, Pickering,
Franklin Thompson, The Barnes, Creswell.
Drayton, The Hewitt's, Ronnie Shoe Dem, The Golding Bros, The Baxter family,
The O'Burns Bros, The O'Gormans, Mickey Reid, Sunbeam, Worzell, The Halls,
The Glave family, G. White, Carl Myatt, Wilf RIP, The General, Marlon, Farley,
Rob Henry, Junior Roberts. The Trooper Nippa Posse – TNP. The Beckfords,
Steven Thomas, Keith Thomas, Toads, Nesbit, Danny Henry, Tippa RIP,
SandyRIP, The Timullty's, Dennis Lee, Robert Teasdale, Chris Teasdale,
Steve Hodgkin's, Mark Ellerman, David Ellerman, Bez, Mullins, The Baxter's,
The Browns, Simon Scott, The Elphics, David Tredwell, The Cartmells, Eggo,
Lesley Malone, David Brown, Noel Brown, Lloyd Barret, Paxo, The Rooke Bros,
Doormouse,
The Douglas Bros, The Sam Bros, The Carter Bros, The Carberry's, The Mullally
Bros, C. Farrell, The Quantrill Bros, The Thomas Bros, Irv, Bones, Cool Thomas,
Wogga Thomas, The Bruvs, Big Glyn, Shay – Glen, Sherlock Bros, Anthony

DAVID C GEORGE

Barry, Dawson Bros, Stan, Deano, Steven – Lyndon – Susan – Georges, Killer
Killeen, Kay Roberts, Louise Ford, Lyn Soady, Sacha Keagan, S. Faulkner, Denise
Thwaites, Amanda Wood, Carol Waugh, Janet Smith, The Heven Family, Paul
Henry, Dean Allsop, Fabian, Joey Courtney, Benson, Stuart Maynard.

Chelmsley Wood was by no way the only residential area in Birmingham that had gangs of youths that stuck together and moved as a unit. The rest of Birmingham and further a field also had and still have gangs of individuals who could put the cat out. In no particular order, they are: The rest of Birmingham and further a field also had and still have gangs of individuals who could put the cat out. In no particular order, they are. Lea Hall – Acocks Green – Yardley – Bordesley Green – Small Heath – Ward End – Shard End – Kings Norton – Billesley – Highgate – Basall Heath – Cotteridge – Castle Bromwich – Erdington – Northfield – Handsworth – Longbridge – Kingheath – Nechells – Newtown – Yardley Wood – Stirchley – Sheldon – Alum Rock – Bromford – Westheath – Warstock – Maypole – Redditch – Milton Keynes – Meadway – Rubery – Ladywood – Quinton – Kingstanding – Great Bar – Aston – Perry Bar – Castle Vale – Witton – Sutton Coldfield – Leamington Spa – Warwick – Halesowen.

A sizable amount of these areas had rivalries between each other on the town or at the football, and would regularly fight each other at music concerts when well-known skinhead or punk groups played a live gig in the city.

The first musical influence in my life came from my family. Being of Afro Caribbean descent, and having three older brothers, the diversity of tunes we listened to was vast. From 'The Jackson Five' to 'Sham 69' and 'Adam And The Ants' to 'Studio One', I grew up on a musical diet that took its influences from far and wide.

In 1977, when I was ten 'Anarchy in the UK' by The Sex Pistols taught me that if you don't like the way things are, then stand up and make a statement that creates a reaction, this was a volatile view to have living on a council estate such as ours, but sometimes it felt as though it was the only way to get peoples attention. John Lydon was right when he said, Never Mind The Bollocks, be who you want to be, and believe in what you believe.

'The Specials' took to the stage in the early eighties, and made a massive impact in British pop culture and forced my friends and me into stay press trousers and to jump up and down at school discos.

Angelic Upstarts, Cockney Rejects, Sham 69 the initiators of Oi!, Sioux And The Banshees, UK Subs, Blitz, Cocksparrer and Last Resort were all a part of this scene and drew a strong reaction from youths on a social and political level.

The Introduction Of The Sauce Force

In 1977 a band of five Birmingham City supporters used to stand at the front of the Tilton at St Andrews watching the match and making up random songs about anything they could think of. Songs were churned out on a regular basis on subjects revolving around food or household toiletries. From making up songs about bacon, fish, beans, salmon, eggs, cheese or Vosene shampoo, these guys kept the whole of the Tilton entertained with their surreal humour and noisy chants. The Sauce Force were a group of young aspiring Mods, who followed Birmingham City with passion and pride. When Wire, who was a member of The Sauce Force, went to an Arsenal game and ended up in Camden in a pub called The Bridge, he seen a huge number of Vespa scooters and Lambrettas all parked in a row outside the pub stretching way, round the corner.

A young band called "Secret Affair" was playing live in the pub, and from seeing this as a young school kid he realised this was the scene for him. The Sauce Force has stood for Birmingham many times and is classed the same as any other bluenose who has represented home or away. They should never be forgotten as they are still around today with the warm Brummy wit and humour that has survived through many years of watching Birmingham City play. (Keep Right On)

The Angelic Upstarts were the most popular of the Oi! Skinhead bands Birmingham fans used to listen to. Forming in 1977 in South Shields they burst onto the scene with tracks called The Murder of Liddle Towers in 1978 and I'm An Upstart and Teenage Warning both in 1979, all tracks with a stronger more so than the pop music of the day. The bands full on delivery combined with their denunciation of racism, was particularly admirable considering at the time a number of other skinhead outfits were in love with the much darker right wing elements.

It was well documented at the time that Birmingham skinheads would attend these gigs and kick the crap out of each other and complete strangers while pogoing on the dance floor. Chelmsley Wood and Acocks Green were the only two larger well known mobs that had a number of blacks in their ranks, and for this reason they stood out to most other skinhead gangs. In the centre of Acocks Green, there were a number of public houses that lived the dream, including; The New Inns – The Dolphin – The Red Lion and The Gospel which was full of local hustlers and blaggers on tap. With numbers of around 150 people each, for a good home game, Acocks Green and The Trooper would fight each other at venues in and around Birmingham on a regular basis, including Solihull Civic Hall. The difference was that both The Trooper mob and Acocks Green were not racist, even though they took the style of the skinhead; they hated most of the other skinhead gangs at the time because they simply were not from the Green or the Wood.

On one occasion in 1982 a local Acocks Green football team called Western Wanderers were playing a cup final over in Earlswood against Wake Green.

Before the match a large contingent of local Acocks Green lads were a little worse for drink when they turned up in two coaches and a convoy of cars. As soon as the lads get off the coach, the Wake Green lad's dressing room was robbed. They then robbed the bar and the canteen. While the game was taking place, the Acocks Green supporters were throwing chocolate bars at the Wake Green players and the referee. The linesmen were assaulted and tripped up every time they ran down the wing. Clumps of mud were thrown at Wake Green players who were near any of the touchlines. The referee threatened on several occasions to abandon the match, due to a number of the opposition's players being punched or nutted while going in for a tackle. It was complete chaos, as the alcohol had run out in the bar, and more was sent for from the Shakespeare on the Stratford Road.

When the lads arrived back in Earlswood with barrels of cider, the police were there and refused them entrance. The lads set up a stall outside on the country lane and anybody who wanted to have a drink had to go and get a swill just out of site of the police. Nobody even remembers what the final score was because it was completely irrelevant.

Northfield, Quinton, Stirchley and Spkarkhill all had good crews, but nobody ruled anything at the time and it was just dog eat dog. While standing in the Tilton or the Kop end of the ground at St Andrews, each area of Birmingham would try to outsing each other by screaming as loud as they could about where they were from, and Chelmsley Wood and Acocks Green mobs were so big, they would usually be louder than the rest.

On one occasion at the Cedar club in Birmingham, the Cockney Rejects played a gig and during the gig, and were pelted with chairs and bottles from the audience. At the time, the security for the Cockney Rejects were known to be West Ham supporters which made this the ideal opportunity to cause mayhem. At the front of the crowd, West Ham security used to stand and trade blows with the crowd and would never need much encouragement to bang it right off, as they were the young ICF.

Other clubs that were the in places to go in Birmingham in the late seventies were. Romeo & Juliet's, Millionaires, The Rum Runner and Mayfair. The new romantics appeared in the late 70's early 80's as a continuation of punk style, but more dressy and showy.

The football trendy captured the hairstyle of the new romantic, and took it into a completely different direction. Young English lads across the country were now dressing like professional golfers with new romantic hairstyles and working class attitudes to match the clothing.

Preston NE Vs Birmingham City 1979 League Cup
Mr Morgan

We hired an LDV Luton van with no seats with 22 of the then young Trooper in the back and off we went. It was an 8.00pm kick off, so we went into Blackpool for a drink before we went up to Preston.

DAVID C GEORGE

Cona, Big Cookie, J. Morgan, Pip, Dungie, Smith, Crafty, Bobby F, Spike, ECT. We've had a right good day in Blackpool hitting the pubs and getting the ale down our necks. The lads have gone down onto the beach, stood in a huge line and pulled a moony. We set off up to Preston and Frankie Wood kept me company cuz they were all kids really. Now I look back it was fucking crazy. The Trooper lot all went to the game, and we went into a local pub in Preston instead. We've come out just before the end of the game and were going towards the car park, and a few guys are now chasing about 13 Trooper up the main road on trials bikes. The guys have done a left into the car park and so did the guys on the bikes. This was the last you seen of the guys from Preston as they were severely dealt with. The bikes were thrown over a wall, and the Trooper had to get back into the van. The club that these guys come out of was smashed to fuck and so were the idiots who tried to chase them on the bikes.

APEX TO ZULU A2Z!

Summertime heat outside the Roundhouse – 1991

Chelmsley friends – 1986

DAVID C GEORGE

Chelmsley lads and Meadway – 1986

Trooper Skins en route to Preston 1978 League Cup

APEX TO ZULU A2Z!

Left: Chelmsley lads in Glasgow – 1978
Right: Chelmsley Wood Skins – 1980"

CHAPTER 1

From Bold Head To Wedge Head

IN 1979 SKINHEADS AND ROUGHNECKS were the mobs to fear down the football, Birmingham City's mobs were mainly skinheads and window lickers that could fight, but had no real organisation with regards to large mob-to-mob fighting. It was as simple as; if you see any away fans, kick their heads in. If you were black and following Birmingham City at this time, it was strange to hear all the monkey sounds coming from local fans and racist abuse hurled at any black players. Even though Birmingham had a sizable amount of black fans, the racist chants never stopped especially from the Kop end of the ground where a large skinhead group gathered to watch the match on a regular basis. Lenny Henry, a Cradley Heath born comedian had recently started a new career performing on a local children's cult TV program in Birmingham called, Tiswas. At the time, his job was in the balance after the first series, and the then producer Chris Tarrant asked him, to come up with some new comedy characters or he would be out of the door. I'm sure Lenny was not aware of the amount of stress and violence his Rastafarian look-alike character Benjamin had brought into the playgrounds and schools across the whole country. This character talked with a stupid high-pitched voice, and ate sandwiches of bread and condensed milk. His catchphrase was, OOOOOOOOOOOOKAAAAAAAY! Which made thousands upon thousands of black children lives at school a misery.

APEX TO ZULU A2Z!

This is what Lenny Henry done for us, by simply thinking of the money and the fame and not about the struggle.

I can remember standing back to back in the playground at Alcott Hall primary school in the late 70's with my brother Gary, taking on all comers while holding a compass in each hand. Kids can be very cruel when you're young and it is best to wake up to it as soon a you can, especially when another new TV show was about to start which was very popular at the time called Roots. With one of the main protagonists called, Chicken George, you can guess the rest. The George's stood up early, including, another George family on the Wood that of Steven, Lyndon and Susan, and like so many other likeminded black people from all over the country, we looked after each other. By any means necessary.

The Irish and black connection in the Apex, Zulu Warriors and also the Junior Business Boys was very strong mainly due to both of these groups of minorities being oppressed by the social and political situations in our country at the time i.e. pub bombings and school education system. The education system was not flexible enough to cope with the differences that particular ethnic minorities brought to the table; therefore a lot of minorities were set up to fail academically. With this, both black and Irish felt a true camaraderie with people from the same social economic background and status. The area surrounding St Andrews has a very large Catholic and black community who live hand in hand with many other working class minorities. Also with great multiracial bands like the Specials, The Beat and The Selector & UB40, dominating the charts at the time, it made the coming together of multi-ethnic British youths more accessible to a much wider audience.

The first black people to be noticed at St Andrews were back in the early seventies when it was very popular to be racist and dress like a skinhead.

This was the most turbulent time to be supporting Birmingham City as a black fan, because you were one face in a sea of bold heads and flying jackets. Morphs mother at the time couldn't understand why her son enjoyed going to St Andrews every week, and she would say to him, "I don't know why yu warn fi gu dung di football fi gu get beat up by di white skinhead dem?" Junior, Gibbo and Jayo were three black faces that represented very early at St Andrews, and at first, must have taken a hell of a ribbing in the beginning.

Most of these people were from areas that were predominantly white and would because of this, be called particular names by other black people from areas with larger black communities. If you came from areas such as Warstock, Kings Heath, Chelmsley Wood, Lea Hall, Sheldon and Yardley, you would be classed as a bounty or a cocoanut, meaning that you are dark on the outside, but white on the inside, just like the chocolate bar. This name makes me laugh, because if any of the black people who actually believe this to be true, thought about what they were saying, then they should speak to their parents with about why they started a family in this country and stayed! My parents didn't really want me talking patwah all day and kissing my teeth, because they wanted us to get on in life and experience different cultures and beliefs without having a ghettoised view of the world. How many people do you know in Britain who speak with a broad Caribbean accent, and have a high-powered job? Anyway, I was born in Marston fucking Green, not Dunn's River.

The cross-fertilisation of cultures and musical styles such as reggae ska, punk-rock and pop turned the heads of many when the Two Tone label started to churn out music that instantly touched the young British generations hearts. In a way, you could say that the Two Tone label, and also UB40 DEP International was very similar to the Zulu Warriors way of thinking, because regardless of what society thought about their exploits, they knew they had a good thing going, and it was a mindset that enriched the creativity of people in Birmingham. It was all very exciting at the time. It was as though there was another way of thinking and another way to progress in life, rather than listening to Thatcher's view of Britain on how we should feel about other people who we didn't even really know. Black and white people were not supposed to get along according to the Governments view, but if anybody is to follow blindly the views of others, even though they have no real evidence to support the claims that black people and minorities in general were no good, this can only cause unnecessary harm. The West Midlands Police force were very worried about this situation also, because black and white working class people who enjoyed the same music and supported Birmingham City football team gradually started to connect on a level never seen before.

At the time, a number of black people had died in custody at the hands of the British police force after all night blues parties, and to most black people knowing how the system works against a man of colour when in court, made them very cautious of any meetings. We knew as fans that if you move in numbers even just to walk into town after the game, you had a chance of getting into town in one piece. But if you walked into town in small numbers, you have got more chance of an SPG van pulling up beside you and of course being beaten up, then nicked. At the age of eleven I remember walking into Birmingham City centre after the match and having a van full of police kerb crawling at the side of the road, with the back doors wide open, and all the police officers would be snarling while pulling on their leather gloves. It was very strange to see grown family men looking at the floor making sure they never made eye contact with the Police in the vans. You could say it is similar to what happens on the plains of Africa, when a pride of lions are looking for something to eat, they will normally go for the easy prey in a herd to feed on because realistically, who wants the job to be difficult?

I went to a comprehensive school in Chelmsley Wood called Whitesmore, but I renamed it More Whites. There was a lot of racialism in our school when I first arrived in 1979, but due to the mentality of most of the black and white people that attended the school, it was dealt with by the best method possible. Which was, finding out who they are, flush them out, and cave their fucking heads in. The only famous person to come out of Whitesmore comprehensive was Miles Hunt who was the lead singer of the cult Indie band, Wonder Stuff and a fashionable punk at the time, but racialism was still about but not as prolific as some people would wish it to be.

For instance, if you were black in the seventies and couldn't handle yourself, and you showed any sign of weakness, you might as well have a put, "Stamp on my testicles" sign around your head and curled up in a ball to cry yourself to sleep. You had to stand up and be counted at an early age or it would be curtains for you and your way of thinking and living. I'm not sure if racism was as bad for the Irish population at the time, due to them not having an all over tan, which makes a large difference in your treatment as a human being, but I'm sure they did go through there own bad experiences of being slightly different to the majority.

The year is 1974 and the pop charts were sending us allsorts of mixed messages. Barry White said he couldn't get enough of your love babe. The Rolling Stones said its only Rock and Roll, Bo Donaldson was telling Billy not to be a hero and Carl Douglas was Kung Fu Fighting.

Around the time of the Birmingham pub bombings at The Tavern In The Town, a basement pub on New Street, and the Mulberry Bush, at the foot of the Rotunda on 21st November 1974. I remember my mother telling me that after this barbaric act, nobody in Birmingham's Accident Hospital, where my mother used to work as a ward sister, really talked to Irish people for a long time, because the pain of what had occurred was hard for many to deal with. It was difficult for descent Irish people to carry on about their lives normally and many were shunned and beaten up on numerous occasions. The so-called Birmingham six were found guilty in August 1975 of carrying out the bombings and were sentenced to life imprisonment.

It was also a common occurrence for Irish parents to tell their children not to mention the fact that they were of Irish decent when outdoors for obvious reasons.

Hundreds of Irish family men around this time had THE KNOCK! At 6:00am, and were systematically dragged out of their houses for questioning. As we know now, stitching up people for major and minor crimes in Birmingham was very popular, and still is today. This was truly a sad time for people from every race, creed and colour in Birmingham.

Miscarriages of justice for Irish and black people were a regular occurrence in the UK and the Government and the police would always congratulate themselves for such sterling work on TV and in the local press. In 1991, after 17 years of wrongful imprisonment, the Birmingham six were freed on the 14th March. These kind of circumstances are reasons why good working class youths can get caught up in the, them and us thing with the Police very easily. It can make you very bitter to think that the people who pull the strings of the country with regards to law and order and also politics, are only giving the masses what information they think you should hear, in order for you to act a certain way. If the government wants you to be paranoid, then you are, if they want you to think its them and not us, then most of us do. It also makes me think the government do not really see you or treat you as a regular human being. More of a sub – human, because you do not see or hear what they know, and never will. Institutional racism was and still is practised in this country on a day-to-day basis, but only comes to the forefront when major blunders take place. Guilford Four – Birmingham Six – Brixton riots – Handsworth riots – Toxteth riots – St Pauls riots – Broadwater Farm riots – Notting Hill (Teddy Boy Nigger bashing) – Stephen Lawrence inquiry.

Bammo; The Night of the Bombing 1974

I was living IN SALTLY, which is situated about a mile ½ into the centre, so it would take about fifteen minutes to get in town. On this particular night I would have been roughly about twelve years old, so bedtime for me 9.00pm. This didn't mean that I would go straight to sleep.

I was reading my comics in bed, I don't think I was in bed for ten minutes when I heard what at the time reminded me of a huge firework and you've got to remember it was in November 1974. To here fireworks going off at this time of the year was a regular occurrence, but at that time of night and being that loud, it got me out of bed. My mom was down stairs and I shouted, "Mom, what's that, what was that noise?" She replied, "I know son, I heard it." I went to the front bedroom window and all I could see from my view of the centre was a flash of light over the centre of Birmingham. I knew something was wrong but I didn't have a clue what had taken place. I ran downstairs into the living room, and we had a balcony you could get onto. All our neighbours were out looking at the sky over the city of Birmingham knowing something was wrong, and then around twenty-five minutes later, a newsflash came on TV explaining the situation. Double bomb explosion, in city centre one after another. That gap between the bombs exploding was about ten to fifteen minutes. Unknown to us, we had a neighbour who was killed in the Mulberry Bush explosion, 21 years old girl.

Even when you were sitting there as a young lad seeing all that was going on in the centre of Birmingham, it didn't seem real because it was the city we lived in. Things like this happen in countries hundreds of miles from us and then all of a sudden it's on your own doorstep. That was truly a surreal frightening experience that will never be forgotten by Birmingham people who suffered.

My mom at the time used to enjoy her nightlife, i.e. pubs & clubs ECT, but this changed Birmingham night life for a considerable amount of time, as a lot of Birmingham people didn't want to take the risk of going for a meal or a drink, and dying for it.

In 1978 when the trauma of the bombings had died down, some of the young black, Irish and English football population united, and it became time for the new football supporters to stand up and be counted. The racists at Birmingham City's ground and some of the skinheads were going to get a wake up call very soon, and a new era would begin. The racist Bulldog magazine was freely available at the ground and this was an issue that needed to be dealt with. This was implemented by gangs of black Irish and English youths rushing into the Kop end of the stand, and smacking the crap out of anyone who wanted to know. This happened on a regular basis throughout seasons in the late seventies until gradually, people who read the racist bulldog magazine, or would freely shout racist abuse at the football ground, thought about their actions due to there now being consequences to their right wing views in a multi racial city. The Bulldog magazine, one of Birmingham's popular reads at the time, was pushed further underground and out of the Tilton and the Kop. There was a feeling in Birmingham City that things were going to change and a number of blacks Irish and English fans who used to venture down the football teamed up together due to being disillusioned with the situation, but also it must be said they liked to provoke and have a fight or tear up as well. After leaving the game, some black fans even experienced having balls of spit covering the backs of their jackets and heads regularly. The mood was one of, "We've had enough of this crap and we are going to sing our own song." Acocks Green and Chelmsley Wood were two of the biggest and handiest mobs down the football at the time, and used to regularly have running battles in the Kop end of the ground.

Both Chelmsley and Acocks Green with smaller crews from all over Birmingham used to kick the crap out of each other and laugh about the events afterwards. After realising they all supported the same football team and through meeting each other at many court cases in Birmingham, Chelmsley Wood and Acocks Green came to the conclusion that they had a lot in common, such as drinking fighting and shagging women, so they started to travel to away matches together.

Fighting for working class people is a part of life that is learned from an early age attending infant and junior schools. You are encouraged to fight at school for many reasons, but the main one is that this society breed's violence and competitiveness from the day you are born. It is in the nature of most working class people to defend themselves and friends due to instinct and social environment. Whereas the majority of middle class people are educated to obey the law no matter what, and report somebody for assaulting themselves. Working class people are more likely to react with physical violence to a dodgy situation instantly.

If you are standing with a group of friends you've grown up with, and a mob of strangers come at you shouting the odds, then people who have a bond through the team they support, and the area they're from, will have a hardcore section of people who don't want to run and scatter, but they wish to make a stand by encouraging less game people to think about the situation they find themselves in more clearly. Even though the police would expect you to run away and phone 999, the reality is that you have to make one of two choices. Do you run away and get chased up a street and risk the chance of being kicked unconscious on your own? Or do you stand with your good friends and keep it tight and hold the fort? This is what people in the media call a firm, but to me this is called standing up for yourself and doing what you feel is right at the time. After years of being with your friends at the football and like minded other people from all over the city, the crew of people you hang around with turns into the people who don't like running. If you run when a situation gets lively and everyone else stands, there is no way you will be accepted into this group of people again, plus you have also got a very good chance of being chinned every time you're seen at a game by your own supporters.

The word hooligan from a working class perspective is not used very often by the general public, except those who read too many newspapers and don't get out much. People who are involved in supporting their local team and are not prone to running from rival supporters are called the lads, and are equally as important as any other person within the community. Similar to your friendly neighbourhood pirate from way back in history, a lad is the person who is in the know and usually has an ear to the ground with regards to what happens in the local area.

Fashionable clothing down the football in 79 was changing and evolving from your Harrington or American flying jackets that you could get hold of from Oswald Bailey in the Bullring, and checked shirt with Doctor Martin boots, Brogues, Monkey boots or Gibson's shoes and Levi's, to introductions of style that would make your average skinhead piss himself laughing, but at the time there was only a handful of people in Birmingham City who were switched on to this new fashion movement. A brand new style of music from a group called the Sugarhill Gang were to give youths growing up at this time of their lives, a huge choice in great music.

From The Clash to Pop Muzik by M to Ring my bell by Anita Ward. Music was evolving and metamorphasising all the time. Just like the fashion of its time was also moving into new territories and undiscovered areas of terrace cool.

Teams such as Liverpool – Everton – West Ham and Tottenham and Aston Villa were wearing your Slazenger V-necks, Second Image cords, Sergio Tachini, Ellesse with a pair of Levi jeans or bleached Lois, and on their feet, a pair of Kios or suede adidas specials – SL76's. Ski – jumpers and Adidas Samba were popular in Birmingham, as well as Patrick cagoules, Pierre Sangan roll necks and Le Coq Sportif cycle tops, with leg warmers.

But it must be said right now that Villa were dressing in Slazenger and dropping the wedge haircut before Birmingham City, and had a firm at the time called the C- crew who had quite a sizable amount of hot dressers who were very good thieves on the town and up and down the country and abroad. With the success of Aston Villa winning the European cup and league, the numbers of people prepared to fight for the course very much outweighed their local rivals Birmingham City. Football fashion was now becoming more important than at anytime in the last decade to young working class youths, and over the next two decades would invent and reinvent itself time and time again as new styles evolve and become part of the football terrace catwalk. In 1981 and 1982 a number of lads from Lea Hall who were Birmingham City supporters were known to travel with Aston Villa fans on their European ventures with fake tickets and shoplift from the fashionable boutiques, then travel back with the Villa supporters. After this little escapade, they had the arduous task of working out which garments to sell and which to keep. Anything else was either sold or ordered before they went abroad for other people. Lea Hall were wearing Fila BJs and Diamond Pringles,

Farahs and Lyle & Scott in 81. Powell & the Gayle brothers had the capability of travelling abroad on a regular basis, and were the first known people in Birmingham to drop Giorgio Armani. The connections in Liverpool and across the UK enabled them to travel to Germany and across Europe and bring back some marvellous tracksuits and the most comfortable and magnificent Adidas shoes that were very difficult to get hold of at the time. This new style of dress was about to make a huge entrance on the youth culture scene and would primarily be linked to other like-minded individuals who were keen on getting in touch with this brand new fashion phenomenon. The football trendy had well and truly arrived and with vengeance. Some of the pioneers of this scene in Birmingham who were very good thieves, could obviously see there was a lot of money to be made from these sort of shenanigans, and exploited the lack of clothing in Brum to the fullest. The rivalry in Birmingham at the time was not really there in the early days, as Villa lads and also Townies and Birmingham City chaps would all earn without any trouble between groups. With many different shopping firms operating from many areas of the city, this was the best time to earn on the town; many of the shops didn't have security systems that are around today. From Handsworth to

DAVID C GEORGE

Kingstanding, Bordesley Green to Castle Vale, Moseley to Kings Norton. Earning was a lucrative trade at the time and for some people it still is.

The first known contempary trendies or dressers to be noticed at Birmingham City's ground were, Nicky Falleta and Martin Canning, both from Chelmsley Wood and also Powell from Warstock, and Gayle, who was a Villa lad off the town around 1979. Both Nicky and Martin were sporting American baseball tops with the perforations in, Kios strap-over boots, you could buy from a small Country and Western shop in Birmingham called The Westerner, at the top of the ramp near Austin Reed. There was another shop in Birmingham at the time called Browns which sold exclusive garments for a while, but didn't like the fact that people now started to put their windows through, and they moved after a few years of hell. Second image cords or jeans, Pepe and Hardcore were all popular makes of jeans at the time, but this particular style of dress could easily have got you beaten up, as most of the fans at Birmingham City's ground were not associated with this style of dress, unless they were confronted by Liverpool, Manchester United or Everton fans.

> **The Apex Terrace Song**
> There once was some lads called the Apex
> Catholics Protestant Black & White
> They followed Birmingham City
> And they loved to sing and to fight
> If you ever go to St Andrews
> And you manage to get to the ground
> Take a look at the seats on your right right right
> And you'll hear this mighty sound
> Oh The Apex lads have been dreaming
> They've been dreaming for so so long
> They've been dreaming of going to Wembley
> And The Apex lads are never wrong.
> Apex – clap clap clap The Apex – clap clap clap The Apex – clap clap clap

APEX TO ZULU A2Z!

Before the name Zulu Warriors was used, Birmingham City's firm was called the Apex. It came from one of the advertising boards around the ground in 81. It was the name of a local building company and its meaning, is where the two half's of a slanted roof of a building join. The top, the peak. Also, it was the name of the cheap away day returns to Dublin from Birmingham Airport, so I would say the name Apex was a combination of the two influences, at the time. The train influenced the ICF, and the plane influenced us. The Apex themselves were a band of blues fans who had fought and won but also suffered a good few kicking's as youths growing up and travelling away with Birmingham City in the late 70,s but were now coming to the age where they were more accustomed to dealing with any altercations that might arise. The Apex themselves numbered around fifty and consisted of a combination of Irish, black and English fans well known in their respected areas of Birmingham for underground networking or being able to look after themselves. With skins and Rude Boys from around Birmingham City, plus a sprinkling of people who were half into the new style of trendy clothing. Combined with the best attire worn by the skins at the time. These people were the pioneers of this movement, and were responsible for the beginning of the biggest change in football terrace politics ever seen. The black and white firm. Ultimately the Apex would evolve into an even bigger and more dangerous firm called the Zulu Warriors, but 1979 to 1982 were difficult times for Birmingham City's gangs because they were split and in a transitional period with regards to direction. On one hand, you had the very hardcore skins that had ruled the turf from Oasis cafe to Manzola Gardens and New Street to Moore Street station for a considerable amount of time in Birmingham City. Also, you had the Rude boys who had a big crew on the town from 81 but instead, evolved through the alldayer scene and then onto the football. Also you had the trendy or the dresser, who enjoyed the finer fabrics and the cut of the cloth more so than the skin. Birmingham City's crews were in disarray. It must be said a lot of them still needed help with the clothing situation though, as Birmingham City Football club had never won any silver wear in Europe or domestically at all, so never really got the opportunity to pillage the foreign shops in Belgium and France, Germany and Italy in huge numbers. This was

DAVID C GEORGE

left to the successful teams at the time such as Aberdeen, Tottenham, Liverpool and Villa, so Birmingham City fans improvised and got hold of clothing by any means necessary. For instance the American flying jacket, which was worn by skinheads across the country, was so well loved that it carried on being an in- form of clobber to be wearing because it looked the business. It is very similar to the Stone Island label that become popular in 1987. If you wore Massimo Osti in 87, you were a thug, full stop. No hiding from the fact that it used to be the in label in the 80s. Just as the flying jacket in the late 70s early 80s also had the same effect when placed on your back. Fred Perry was another garment that seemed to stand the test of time even up to 2005. In the early eighties Fred Perry did take a significant drop in interest mainly due to the huge number of new polo T shirts that were available across the UK.

On Canning We Assembled
First visit to a face from the past,
The images I had conjured up in my mind,
Of this man couldn't be further from the truth,
I was guilty of pigeon holing and presuming,
A monster I thought near section,
Under the pre positioned spotlight,
In his self built show-home kitchen,
There was a relaxed and content individual,
Waxing lyrical with affection of tales of old.

Not about a struggle or a way out,
In the darkness of a new world order,
A sociology case study of ethnic integration,
Amongst urban degeneration,
'You Whaaaa!!??'
You Ejjit it was sport,
Dressing up showing off,
Telling stories holding court.

The age-old mythology,

APEX TO ZULU A2Z!

Of firms group hugging in Biology,
Influenced on the decadence of the periods ether
Wearing Kios' and CP,
Instead of on French blues in Brothel creepers,
It was brought to my attention,
When he happened to mention,
That he was nil by mouth,
When it came to that pre occupation.

Indeed he had a certain misdemeanor,
To cool for school but still home for dinner,
Bathed his daughter gave his wife a rest,
Played with his offspring,
Loved and caressed,
Parried her moods,
Massaged her shadows,
Stayed silent in quiet rooms,
Born to lead not follow.

Him why?
Another man another time,
Insecure frame of mind,
Married the first thing that showed an interest,
In his misinterpreted subconscious weakness,
The things before thirty on his to do list,
Thirteen years aiming,
Seventeen years missed.

A kick in the shins or a poke in the eye,
A Bailiff to dodge or a lie to deny,
Reach for the prescription get pissed,
Hiding denying a cancerous cyst,
Do you spare a thought?
Ring a variety club bus?
Six billion ants with a road to cross!

DAVID C GEORGE

Nothing further from the truth here sir,
A loving family leads to a loving family,
Guidance and trust,
Through experiences shared and honesty,
You receive praise you get cussed,
You get knocked down you get up,
You're never late always well dressed,
As a result in the end you tend to land butter side up.

Now when my man started there was no stopping,
Dropping names now dearly departed,
To the away day juniors,
Who arrived early for a spot of shopping,
Thought nothing of dropping on the spot,
A geezer twice their size on his manor,
In the precinct where his missus shopped,
Can you imagine the humiliation?
Of being subjected to the interrogation,
Of the second cities away day trippers,
The dapper 'Zulu Nation'.

Barbour's and brollie's,
And that was the fuckin ladies,
You never heard of them don't believe me?
Stands to reason really,
Away day fans arriving home early,
Beaten up taxed or Pringle ripped in bits,
Taking to the grave,
They got slapped,
She had tits!

In their day their acid tongues scarred,
Whether you were from the estate a townie,
Screaming high-rise or back a yard,
Farah's high heels cashmere scarves,
Jewels before Missy from the bruk shop stars,

APEX TO ZULU A2Z!

The early cognoscenti,
In your jeans at Gino's,
You came so far,
Second image,
Slazenger!
No matter Falletta dressed so sharp,
White power blazing on his arm,

Then came a casual waiting in the dark,
An out of it Chambers from Meriden park,
Parading Armani Knitwear,
Like he was Richard Gere,
Not in Milan or Hollywood,
An 82 Trooper sharp and booted,
An original Chelmsley hood,
A natural born engineer,
Wore the right gear,
With a two season ahead of the pack,
Grinning from ear to ear,
Innovating time and place,
Correct! Ace of face.

Decades past now all the boys done good,
Achieved the accolades that their teachers never said they would,
Mindless and wild,
Satan on side,
You're a mug if you fell for that,
Listen to your self,
"It's just a ride!"
The fiction depicts a risk,
The truth,
Gentlemen,
Fact!

Kingy..!

DAVID C GEORGE

Sales assistants in shops such as Press Burgers and Robin Hood in Birmingham, must have been wandering what the hell was going on when their shop windows were being put through on a regular basis to get hold of such quality garments as Lyle & Scott, Pringles, Grand Slam, Pierre Cardin, Slazenger, Chemise Lacoste and Pierre Sangan roll necks also Gabicci. Press Burger's was the place for anyone who was switched on and appreciated tailor made clothes to fit. This was one of the places to go in Birmingham in the late 70s. George Saunders, was another tailor based in Birmingham who had serious skills when it came to cutting and matching material for hand made suites which he was well known for in Birmingham for many years through the 50s, 60s, 70s and 80s. He was a proud man who paid great care and attention to his work, which is why his business is still up and running now in the hands of his son. Mods from all over Birmingham would use Press Burgers for quality shirts and suits, as this was the number one place to go for quality tailored clothing. It would be wrong for me to say that the entire Apex was switched on to the new fashion and style, because there are a number of Birmingham people who have never been interested in the fashion side of things at all and their only aim was to crack some skulls. It is true a lot of these people involved in the dressing, were sheep with regards to style and it was only a handful who had the vision to try something brand new. The years of 81–82 saw Birmingham stores such as Rackhams, and Beaties of Solihull having a larger selection of garments to choose from. As the years rolled by, even more brands were accessible to people on the town and also to the football fans. 83–84, Cockney B, and Boady, were two Blues fans who had style on the town from head to foot. Snake skin belts and Cockney B wore crocodile shoes with slick silk shirts and tailored slacks were a head turner back in the day. Boady was dropping allsorts of garments such as Giorgio Armani and Chemise Lacoste like an A-list celebrity. The birth of the professional shoplifter had now hit epic proportions, and it was about 1982 that Birmingham's dressers really came to the forefront. Brummies started dropping the double-breasted Burberry macks with navy blue kickers and Farah action slacks. Adidas gazelle were also very popular, also Fila, Ellesse, Sergio Tachini, Lutha, Skila, Head, HCC, Nevica, Nino

APEX TO ZULU A2Z!

Cerutti. As a youth on Chelmsley Wood we had a handful of people who were ahead of the times with regards to fashion such as Canning, Chambers, Macco, T. Evans, T. Barnes, M. Evans, E. Crawford, N. Falletta, R. Davies, C Rankin, C Wilson, A. Shaw, Cockney Al, C. Moore, R. Drayton, McCormick, R. Jenkins, Pipkin, and Bobby F.

Chames was dropping Adidas Trim Trabb, Levi 501s Cerutti shirts and Giorgio Armani jumpers and jackets when most people on the Wood were wearing stretch jeans and T-shirts with the sleeves cut off. Another guy called Macco, a well-known Villa supporter was equally on the ball, and would make most people envious about what they had on. It wasn't always like this though, because I remember Chambers being a Rude Boy and wearing a Two-Tone suit and loafers a few years earlier, and having a fight with a skinhead on the town at the Top Rank club. The skinhead was called Duffy, and years later; Duffy would become one of Chames friends due to them knowing the same network of people, and supporting the same team.

Chames always wanted to stand out with regards to style and was one of the first people to introduce new names and labels to numerous dressers in and around Birmingham City. When we first clocked eyes on Chames over the shopping centre on Chelmsley, we all laughed at him because he looked so different to what we had on. His jeans were parallel and slightly loose, his shirt was buttoned up to the top and stripped, and his jumper had strips of different colour leather. We just fell about laughing at him, then he called me to one side and said, "I'll give you two years and you will all be wearing it." To be honest, I thought he had completely lost the plot, but how wrong was I, and how right was he. In 1981, Chames was in a sports shop in Birmingham at the top of the escalators from New Street station having a mooch, when he was confronted by a London firm of dressers. This was Tottenham's Yids, and they were very interested in Chames as his designer clothing made him stand out to anyone who was serious about dressing. He had on a Fila BJ and a pair of burgundy Lois cords and adidas gazelle. A guy called Nicholas from Camden asked where they could get hold of some clobber in Birmingham, and Chames told them that there was a shop up the road called Rodney Webb. The Tottenham lads asked Chames if he could show them where the shop was, and he declined because he wasn't insane. The Tottenham lads left the shop and went down to Rodney Webb and robbed the shop, then came back up to New Street and bumped into Chames yet again, but this time, they had a bit of respect for him because of his character and the way that he put together his threads. Nicholas – Nickname E.T and Izzy asked Chames if he fancied going to the game with them as they were off to Aston Villas ground, and being interested in these Londoners style and how they operated, he accepted.

This was the first time Chames had seen a proper mob of Tottenham and they were all dresssed from head to foot in mint clobber and numbered around a hundred. A well-known Villa lad called Brittle came at a section of Yids, pulled a blade on E.T and Chames frowning and beckoning them over with one hand while holding a blade in the other. This was the first time Chames had seen a London lad do nothing and something, but still make himself not look like an idiot. The front was popular in the south, but not heard of in Birmingham really. Brummies at the time would either fight, or run but most didn't know how to front it out with rival fans. The idea of fronting someone with a blade in their hand and walking with them parallel in the road with shoulders back and your arms going like a window wiper, and edging closer to the police so you don't get slashed up in broad daylight is a skill that London lads brought to Birmingham. At first we didn't know what to make of it until we worked it out. The front can be used in many different ways and in this case, it was used to confuse and delay the reactions of the C- Crewmember to get the attention of the police. London was definitely the capital when it came to clothes, as fashion changed so quickly down south that particular garments could be in for just a few months, and then relegated to school kids. When shopping in London, Chames would find some really tidy bits of clobber, and would be advised by the London lot what was hot and what was not. London had boutiques all over the place on standard high streets where you could buy your sugar and your cornflakes, which was a far cry from our meagre handful of shops in Birmingham at the time. Next Door & Nichols were the shops that were on the money in Birmingham. With so many firms in the capital, the competition was fierce for new style and being one step ahead of the crowd. These were great days to be a dresser or your contemporary mod, as mod is just an abbreviation for modern.

A classic casual item so popular in the early eighties was the beige or navy Burberry golfing jacket. The reason this garment was so fashionable was the cut of the jacket itself, and also because it was quite a subtle garment compared to some of the brighter cashmere jumpers and skiwear available around the same time.

The Burberry golfing jacket was one of the most fashionable and versatile jackets to ever be introduced on the football terrace catwalk, because you could not really go wrong wearing it with anything. It still looked the business, and that was very important to the majority of Blues fans, as well as doing the business. Birmingham City were by no stretch of the imagination one of the first dressers in the country, but what they did have was style and the ability to plagiarise and re-mould the best from other firms style, whether from the north or south, to make it their own.

CHAPTER 2

The Apex & The Townies

1981–1982 **MARGARET THATCHER** and the Conservative Party were taking Britain to the highest unemployment the country had seen in decades. I can remember in the early eighties when we were always being sent home from school half day, because the teachers used to be going on strike nearly every week. At the time, we all thought it was quality to go home at 1.00pm, but when you look back, we missed out on tons of education. I used to have nightmares about Thatcher, where she was in 10 Downing Street, and for some reason in this mare, I was outside her house in the back garden, when I heard a crunching sound. I tiptoed to a window to a peep through, and she was sitting on her settee with a queue of babies in prams crying. She was pulling the prams towards her one by one, and picking up the babies, and then biting the face off the children, then tipping them up in the air like a pint of beer, drinking the liquid contents from the body until they were empty. She would then throw the corpses against the wall burp, then laugh like a banshee from a Hammer House Horror movie. The floor was covered in baby corpses and blood. I never slept well in those days. When you see someone who rules the country with that much power, who is so smug, and has no real empathy towards the majority of the country, it is scary to think of a future of unemployment, stress and frustration for working class people all over the UK. This woman did not care about the working classes at all and saw the majority of the country as drones in a huge bee hive who keep the machine working. Comprehensive school cannon fodder is what the government think of the inner city working classes. You are the first to die in a war, and they will always try to make you feel guilty for not going to kill strangers on the other side of the world for them. We have enough problems fighting people who only live a couple of miles up the fucking road, so why the hell would anybody in their right mind want to fight for a government that lies to you and then smiles in your face?

The miners were on strike, fighting for justice and all there was for working class people who had just left school was Youth Training Schemes for £25 a week. The working class youths of Britain did not have a pot to piss in, and were looking for excitement, for something to light their fire. The Police were in the charts with Every Little Thing She Does Is Magic, but I'm sure they couldn't have been referring to the Iron Lady. Later the same year, The Police released Don't Stand So Close To Me, which I hope was referring to her. Olivia Newton John was asking us to get Physical, and the Birmingham mobs gladly obliged.

Birmingham fans were frequenting a cafeteria called Gino's, situated, in the Bull Ring shopping centre. This is where skinheads, roughnecks and trendies from around Birmingham used to congregate before going for a drink in town, or just to have a bit of a chat with other lads from different areas before and after football matches. It was also a place to buy quality-stolen garments or gadgets from on the town. There were also other groups of individuals from on the town who hung around on the ramp and near the fountain. They were known as townies and most of them were also Birmingham City supporters. Some of the names of the crews in town who became part of the Zulu family were, The Tiger Posse, The Nigger Squad, The Convicts, The Rat Pack, Bitter Creek, and The Junior Convicts. These people were well into enjoying life on the town and exploiting every opportunity to make money. Taxing and robbing was popular at the time and these crews used to scare the living daylights out of away supporters who were naive enough to not know that when you come out of New Street station, do not go up the escalators unless you like the idea of being beaten up and mugged.

Townies were a large group of individuals that came from many other areas of Birmingham such as Edgbaston, Lea Bank, Ladywood, Handsworth, West Brom, Winson Green, Hockley, Basall Heath, Highgate and Bartley Green. The ramp outside McDonalds consisted of a number of Rasta's and black and white youths who treated that part of town as their turf, and it was. Fashion changes had influenced the Birmingham firm to the point that in 1982, the skinhead fashion had almost been abolished and replaced by the football trendy. In the early 80s there were a few confrontations between the skins and Rasta's, Rude Boys, Mods and townies in Birmingham, at numerous venues across Birmingham including, The Barrel Organ pub but this seemed to vanish when fashion and music influences overwhelmed our city. Some of the townies didn't get on with the Birmingham City lot in the early days, as there was a lot of mistrust and snide comments passed about town. Some of the Apex were not keen on being involved with the black lads on the town, and this led to the Townies and The Apex sometimes ending up rowing each other. Some of the Apex were racist at the time, as it was fashionable to think and act this way. If a skinhead was wearing black, or oxblood Dock Martin boots, with laces that were either yellow or red, this gave out a meaning to most people that knew this. The yellow laces meant that you supported the National Front, and the red meant you hated Pakistanis.

Black and white faces from the football started to attend the Powerhouse nightclub all-dayers in Birmingham's Chinatown in 1983. The Powerhouse used to be known as the number one place for roller disco before it changed its name, it was known as The Lacano.

The late seventies and early eighties saw the alldayer scene mainly concentrated in Wigan, Manchester and London. Both The Pier and Legend would be the in places for people who were into dance challenges and listening to black soul music from around the world that made your body move.

Ralph Randall was the first resident DJ at The Powerhouse and had a reputation for taking the crowd on a musical journey through Jazz, Soul, Disco, Funk, and Electro Funk. IMD and Scooby Swift, who went on to win the world Techniques DJ championship, were also doing damage on the DJ scene at The Powerhouse and across the UK, which made evenings out in Birmingham very entertaining.

APEX TO ZULU A2Z!

Jazz-fusion dancers were kings before the break-dancers took over, and would show off their skills on the dance floor spinning and using floor work combined with parts of furniture in their routines.

Tracks such as "Dance With Me" by Bobby Mcferrin and "The Samba" by Jeff Lorber Fusion were real floor fillers and classics of their time and still are to this day.

Great music and good times with girls from all over the country was the name of the game, and the townies revelled in this scene. At the time, a lot of the townies were wearing Adidas track suites with Puma trainers, which were standard in most sports shops in town. Jazz dancers wore spats, which were patent leather shoes designed for slick footwork when challenging someone on the dance floor. Dance crews from Birmingham at the time who were always in the thick of the action were called, The Pirates, Street Force, Bboys, Supreme Rockers and a one-man army called Flex. Not forgetting the legendary Bulldog from Aston who was one of the finest jazz-fusion dancers in the country and well respected for his slick moves on the dance floor. Leroy Baptist from Moseley, Russian from Handsworth, Desmond Taylor from Chelmsley Wood, Barks, Zarkoff, Brezneff and Lizard, were all excellent dancers at the time and were known for tearing up the dance floor at the Powerhouse and up and down the country throughout the early eighties. Crews from across the UK had names such as Smack 19 from Sheffield. At the same time, a guy known to be connected with the Apex called Morph introduced the townies to Fila Borg, Nike Wimbledon and Farah slacks. Most of the townies dressed well already, but Morph was to drop style on them that turned heads like a Barn Owl. Alldayers were an important part of youth cultures evolution in Birmingham, as it was a time to enjoy yourself and meet people from all over the country. The main rivalries on the scene were from the three main cities London – Birmingham – Manchester. All of these had groups of individuals that were similar to themselves, but as you know with some teenagers, if you put to much testosterone in one room, sometimes the consequences can be lively. On one occasion after a fight at a Manchester alldayer between Birmingham lads and the local manks, the Brummies had to fight their way out of a club up the stairs with doormen being called from many other areas of Manchester to come and turn over the Birmingham lot. Birmingham had to fight all the way up the stairs with doormen on either side tooled up or smashing people across the head and face with bats. Outside was no better, with two lines of doormen on each side hitting anyone who came out of the club all the way to the coaches outside. The windows were smashed in and to be honest, the whole town looked as though they had turned out to have a go on this evening Not just rivals on the dance floor, the lads from the three cities were into proving that they were number 1 in everything. Good dancers can usually make good fighters, and this was the case. A lot of routines that people used on the dance floor were similar to routines and Karta's from martial arts. People who could pick up dance moves pretty quickly could also pick up martial arts tequniques with the same ease. From dressing to pulling and fighting, the competition was fierce on the alldayer scene with regards to who was top. When leaving alldayers, groups of individuals used to smash shops to make some money in Birmingham city. The main shops that were targeted were ones where you could make a decent amount of money. ie – Watches of Switzerland –World of Sport – Snow & Rock or Laskeys Hi Fi store in the centre. If it happened on a Sunday night after 12.30am, nine times out of ten, it would be the alldayer crew having an earner.

And Everybody was Blues.
Invited along for the ride for a change passenger side,
Next to the madman on a mission to put things right,
We met with every cultures creations,
That you could ever imagine to meet,
And they were all Blues!

I've met the players and the hustlers,
The grave robbers and armed blaggers,
The low life the liars the social pariahs,
The young predators pending and the war-torn heroes wise,
And they were all Blues!

From the undignified to the done up to the nines,

APEX TO ZULU A2Z!

The privileged impresarios the high fliers,
The landowners the gentry,
Met with rock stars and got interplanetary,
And they were all Blues!
Talked with gangsters and bullies,
Interviewed the tattooed,
The BNP The Apex The Dutty,
The Burger Boy The Flower Crew,
And they were all Blues!

We Sikh Hindu's Jewish Catholic and Muslims,
Atheist Agnostic a lot of them lost it and C of E Christians,
The indigenous Pagans Masons Saracens and Crusaders,
Roundheads Cavaliers Rastafarians and Al Qiada,
Some were intriguing some were see through,
But they were all Blues!

Upper lower middle class,
From working men's social legends,
To gents on the green passing time at their leisure,
Or in the green at her majesties pleasure,
Yet they were all Blues!

What does a man take comfort in when he closes his eyes,
This is surely universal which all Mother Nature's men seek,
Blues!
Tries to find a peaceful place from the things in this life sent to occupy,
Finds strength in his beliefs to get through the week,
Blues!
The day after pay day when every ones happy to satter,
Weekend starts whistle blows we stand shoulder to shoulder,
Blues!
Content in knowing when the fat lady sings,
Its just a game its all over goodbye.
Are we all Blues?

DAVID C GEORGE

Testify!
Kingy.

Popular Alldayer Venues Across the UK late 70's – 80's

Birmingham	The Powerhouse / The Hummingbird
Derby	Pink Cocoanut
London	Hammersmith Palais
Manchester	Legend
Wigan	The Pier
Nottingham	Rock City
Preston	Clouds
Glasgow	Panama Jacks
Bristol	?
Aire	Bobby Joes
Doncaster	Seventh Heaven

The townies at the time never really clocked the new fashion movement to the fullest until people like Powell, Gayle and Morph, were to show interested individuals who frequented the alldayers, that such garments were transferable from football to alldayers without changing a thing. From this, townies saw a market for business here that was insatiable. Thieving of garments from around shops in Birmingham and the rest of the Midlands was at an all time high. Even people, who were not connected to football in the slightest, started to dress like casual hooligans. This also brought problems for people not affiliated to any particular firm or gang who enjoyed dressing up like hooligans. If you look at it this way, if this was the nineteen twenties and you dressed like Al-Capone, people would mistaken you for a gangster. The consequences could be detrimental to your health. Therefore, if you were not a gangster, why the hell dress like one?

Taxing/draipsing of other peoples garments was now also at an all time high, and people who walked through the Bull Ring and around town who didn't know a soul, would likely to be beaten up and jackets, coats, accessories such as trainers, scarves, hats, and jewellery of all kinds would be forcibly removed from their person. No matter if you were

APEX TO ZULU A2Z!

from Birmingham or if you were an away supporter, you could end up in a whole heap of trouble if you bumped into the lads off the town.

Brummies were by now beginning to innovate as well as imitate, and it was around this time when Lea jeans where worn with splits at the side that settled on a pair of Forrest Hills like a glove. Removing the badge from the waistband and then replacing it at the bottom-front of your jeans was a brand new Brummie hook that came from the jazz-fusion dancers from the Handsworth alldayer scene who took it from the London dancers.

As well as the Gino's cafeteria, Birmingham City fans also held the fort at a number of public houses, all in spitting distance of New Street Station. The Crown on Station Street – Sam Weller's on Hill Street – The Grapes on Hill Street – Boogies Brassiere on John Bright Street and The Knightrider. The Kaleidoscope & Edwards No 8 nightclubs very popular with blues at the time, were also on Hill Street.

The Knightrider was situated below the ramp near McDonalds and half way down the row of shops underneath Numero Uno and Next Door designer stores. This pub in the early eighties was the buyers and sellers pub, and would be full of the young movers and shakers on town selling everything from a Diamond Pringle to a television or a gold chain. The Apex would drink in the Knightrider and also The Crown and would easily get word of any rival factions entering the City by train. A number of the old guard at the Knightrider especially Mooney, used to take the piss out of the new trendies standing outside the pub, and would mock them saying, "What the fuck are you dressing like a bunch of Scouse cunts for?" At the time, there were a good few dressers following Birmingham, but the best at the time were Aston Villas C-Crew. The majority of wedge heads in Birmingham at the time followed the C-Crew, who also had most of the best dressers in Brum, and Birmingham's Apex had some catching up to do. A lot of Birmingham's firm at the time hated the wedge heads of Villa, and would walk round to local night club queues, and chin anyone who had a new romantic haircut with a V-neck sweater on.

If you left New Street station through the barriers and walked up the escalators and down the ramp, you would be clocked by every townie around the vicinity. If you left and did a sneaky out of the back of platform twelve, you would also be clocked, as The Crown pub is on that street. In those days, there were eyes all over the City that could clock a rival firm by the way they dressed. Even if you were to walk out of the glass doors and try to find a pub, the guys on the flower stalls on New Street and across the city were also Blues fans, and would inform the Apex when dressers from out of town where drinking in a pub.

The transformation of fashion in Birmingham's firm and throughout the City was now beginning to bring the town dwellers and the football fans together. Rasta's started to take more time in their appearance, and names like Gabicci and Farah became high priority on their shopping lists.

Young men started to drop the casual look in order to get into nightclubs such as Edwards No 8 and The Kaleidoscope. Teenagers would normally wear Gabicci because it gave the illusion that this young gentleman is older than he really is, and he also takes pride in his appearance.

In early 83, the Birmingham City Apex travelled to Manchester City, and because of Birmingham's large black following of fans, Manchester City taunted the blues fans throughout the game, shouting Zulu and random made up African names.

While a few Manchester City fans where jumping around in the stands doing their best impersonations of the sounds of monkeys, Birmingham City supporters were sticking their two fingers up at the home end and laughing at them. Round the same time, one Blues fan was singing an old Rugby song, Get`em down, You Zulu Warriors, but had modified the words a bit to suit the occasion. Half way through the game though, something had changed. The consensus was that the name Zulu, wasn't bad at all and the Birmingham fans had a change of heart, and flipped reversed it by singing Zulu in unison back to the Manchester City's home end. Around the same time or even slightly earlier than Birmingham's firm, the town crew were using the name Zulu at the alldayers up and down the country. Afrika Bambaataa and The Soul Sonic Force had a track that used to tear up the dance floor called Planet Rock, which was an underground hit in 1982. Bambaataa, ex gang member from the Bronx NY, had created a collective of artists called The Zulu Nation who were into being creative and helping out within their own local communities and producing the some of the first block parties in the US after cool D.J. Herk.

At the Powerhouse alldayers in Birmingham, the atmosphere was incredible. The local DJs used to shout on the microphone to the entire crowd. Zulu, and depending on what part of the country you came from, you would shout out the region your team represented. Example; Zulu, Nottingham, Zulu, Leicester, Zulu, Bristol, Zulu, Manchester. Undoubtedly the biggest roar came from the Birmingham crowd who revelled in the notoriety of having the biggest and loudest group on the alldayer scene.

After the game, the Birmingham fans were put on four coaches and escorted into Manchester City centre. The police escort was only at the front of the coaches, so this meant the back two coaches could try to get off and walk into Manchester to find Man City's firm. The way this was achieved was by somebody on the third coach speaking to the driver and telling him to pull over because the coach was on fire.

As the third coach pulled over, the fourth coach did exactly the same and around 150 Blues fans marched off the coaches and into Manchester City centre. The other two coaches carried on up the road and the Manchester constabulary didn't even notice that two coach load of fans had gone walkabout. Birmingham City fans now had marched into Manchester's bus depot and waited for Man City to come into town. As Manchester City walked up towards the bus depot in the square, Birmingham City fans came running out of the depot at Manchester City, and one of the Birmingham fans shouted at the top of his voice. "ZULU!" And then everybody shouted "ZULUUUUUUUUULU" as they ran towards Man City who were bashed in their own shopping centre. This was the first time Birmingham City fans had used the battle cry of Zulu towards an enemy, and this was just the beginning of the many times throughout the eighties and nineties that it would be used.

From reading the many silly bits of information that has been slapped onto the Internet regarding The Zulu Warriors and also The Junior Business Boys, I would just like to clear this up for all you who have taken the time to buy this publication. The majority of Zulu

DAVID C GEORGE

Warriors and juniors were and are white and always have been. Many people for absolutely years have thought that Blues` firm is a bunch of black lads wearing expensive clothes, and that's it. You couldn't be further from the truth, as there are a number of well-respected Asian lads as well as black and Irish within the family.

APEX TO ZULU A2Z!

Blues outside The Crown just before they are set to travel – 1985

Zulu's in Boogies – 1984

DAVID C GEORGE

Early Burberry Hi-Fi sound

Travelling away – 1984/85

APEX TO ZULU A2Z!

Music was always important to Blues

Bottom right: Kingy teaching Darren how to sing

Us on the pitch with flag in the middle
(after playoff victory

DAVID C GEORGE

Morph – 1985

CHAPTER 3

The Wimbledon Tennis addiction 80

THANK GOD FOR THE SCOUSERS who were the first people who had an eye for quality before Scotland and London. I shudder to think what we would be wearing if they didn't introduce to all of us the tennis and ski gear in 78–79. Liverpool was not the only place in the country at the time that had thousands of youths skint, and without a pot to piss in. The idea of stealing clothes from European shops abroad was a stroke of genius, and was also in keeping with the celebrities' fashion status of its time.

If you wanted to find out what was hot with regards to tennis sports wear back in the early 80s, millions of youths found themselves having a strong interest in tennis fashion. This is where you could see a huge number of different styles of tracksuits and T–shirts available in every designer name you could think of. Certain people were sponsored by different brands, and if you were addicted to this new movement, then you could tell what brand the tennis player was sponsored by, just by his name.

Jimmy Connors ~ Nino Cerutti 1881
John McEnroe ~ Sergio Tacchini
Bjorn Borg ~ Fila + Diadora
Guillermo Vilas ~ Ellesse + Puma
Henri Leconte ~ Chemise Lacoste–Izod Lacoste blue crocodile.

All these professional players were sponsored by the branded companies, which meant the size of the labels and motifs on the T-shirts and tracksuits were bigger than average. This made these garments more of a must have item with regards to fashion at the time. Weeks before Wimbledon took place, there would always be smaller tennis tournaments around the country for tennis players to warm up, and one of those is held in Edgbaston, Birmingham. This was the ideal opportunity for switched on thieves to dress up as tennis players, and walk into the changing rooms and steal the players T-shirts and tracksuits. Thieves would even wear designer shorts and T-shirts and carry a tennis racquet with case to fit in with the crowd. Even if you wanted to have a chat about tennis with a fan, the thieves were clued up enough to have a reasonable conversation about a number of players, due to them being addicted to the clothing and the brands.

Just Met a Morphs Thesis

I remember one time springs to mind, to recall the events isn't hard,
Sticking out in the crowd wasn't my chosen way I'm quite the humble soul if the truth were said,
I'm the type of guy who at the time was tripping to the sounds it's all in the walk man, which resonates in your head,
My mother saw straight through the theatre,
What do you want to hang around in gangs and taunt them that'll beat ya?

We as young soul rebels in times of social unrest,
Were the masters to the apprentices', who invited the ignorant to come test?
The one time that springs to mind which illustrates this,
Was a usual Sat post match when we found ourselves in the company of Zulu's?
Walking shoulder to shoulder with fellow pugilists,
Approaching the fire station that had historically served Aston,
We sauntered on won side of the street,
When the vile on site intimidating crossed no mans land,
Even being used to the game, not a hanger on,

APEX TO ZULU A2Z!

We flapped we thought curtains,
Mum you were right,

Respecting protocol the ranking officer of the opposing regiment
Conferred with the duty sergeant of our brigade,
Finalized the rules of engagement,
Thus the location of the battleground was decided
The mobile-phone-less messengers were dispensed,
Within an hour the firm had landed,
Anthropologically we are a species who can use tools,
But when an unexamined mind is explored there's no room for fools,
Time to think as one and not let the weakest link lose their cool.

We were aware the arsenal were in town to play with the claret and blue,
After collectively subconsciously leaving early,
Remember no mobile phones,
The warriors came out to play and assembled,
And before you get carried away it wasn't a scene from Brave Heart,
It was far darker,
To the bushes by the subways we were dispatched,
Hide your colors don't holler 'Zuluuuu!'
A plan was hatched,
The element of surprise wasn't wasted.

The passage of rights to the now newly initiated,
Buzzing rushing from what they'd just tasted,
Trying to internalize,
At overdrive,
Then the main event arrived,
Two hundred of em,
'Claret and Blue'
Sorry that's Brummy casual for' haven't a clue'
Strolling with nonchalance,
Lambs to the slaughter,
And do you know I clocked that they knew,

DAVID C GEORGE

Standing up for a cause like it was meant to be,
In the wake of an epiphany becoming aware of telepathy,
Justified by the look in the eye,
By everyone that was there!

Then on the B of the Bang,
From this band of brothers,
I witnessed a force that was not of this world,
Or for that fact at the time I thought,
Like any other.

'BANG BANG BANG CHASE THEM CRAZY BALL HEADS OUT OF TOWN'
'IVE BEEN A FOOL I HATE MYSELF IVE LET MY LOVED ONES DOWN'
'FUCKIN JOHNNY FUCKIN FORIEGNERS EVEN IF YOU WERE BORN HERE AND LIVE IN THE SAME STREET AS ME'
'DON'T CALL ME A RASCIST I HATE EVERYBODY'
'LOVE A GOOD RUCK ME'
And on and on you with me?

Then the siren sounds the dog's bark,
The chaos fragments the crowd disperses,
Isolated incidents going to far,
Blue lights flood the streets,
Batons raining down on anyone well dressed,
Lashing out panicking indiscreet,
Making the most baby of faces a mess,
A who dey are they tried to segregate,
'Easy officer I'm a Brummy mate!'
Funny to see they couldn't separate.

We chose to hide then land like thunder,
The villa the police were left to wonder,
Where was this firm from?
Bar Saint Martins beneath the Rotunda,

APEX TO ZULU A2Z!

They drink and unite and are game for a fight,
Stand shoulder-to-shoulder all day and night.

Decades now past,
All good things don't last,
We moved on grew up some got nicked,
Some even got married,
Got youth of their own,
Settled down provided a home.

Not me individually I surf now,
Still need the release of the impulses man feels,
It left its mark them days,
'A geezer needs excitement,
Otherwise he stays inside violence,
Simple common sense'
The streets said.

The times have changed but there is no question,
The impact them times made on a nation,
Will in the future have an impact,
Will go down in history,
When the instigators are remembered,
Hopefully appreciated for the things they did.

You youngsters should extend manners to your elders,
You elders Generals should satter the fires in the younger generations,
They are the futures great hope and will lift the Zulu nation,
To the next level,
And that don't necessarily mean using violence,
Maybe intelligence education and passive resistance,
Postponing pending trouble with diplomatic eloquence,
Yet never letting the oppressors forget what can happen if they come test!

Peace – Kingy..!

DAVID C GEORGE

The Golf & Rock climbing – Skiing addiction

Expensive fashionable clothing was linked to successful people of their time when they were at the peak of their celebrity pedestal. People such as Seve Balesteros who wore Slazenger V necks and Farah action slacks, and Ronnie Corbett who had an amazing array of Lyle & Scott and diamond Pringle cashmere sweaters that many lads would comment on back in 82. The rock-climbing link was mainly through the vast number of quality boots and waterproof jackets that could be found in an outdoor pursuits store. I'm not sure when Dock-steps were first worn at the football, but they were definitely the earliest form of designer walking boot/shoe worn down the game around 1982. In the early eighties, if the weather was mild and it started to rain, you would usually pull out a cagoule that could fold away and strap it to your waist. Patrick and Adidas were the best brands at the time. If it was winter, the Ski coats were king. Fila bubble, Lacoste, Helly Hansen, Ellesse bubble, Nevica, Lutha, Henry Charles Collsent, Head, Berghaus and Sergio Tacchini were the most popular brands. At the time in Brum, you could never go wrong with a Fila, HCC or Ellesse ski coat as all three were the cream of the crop.

A Short History of Adidas

Adidas started in 1924 in Germany with two brothers named Adolf and Rudolf Dassler. In 1949, Adidas became a registered company, named after its founder: "Adi" from Adolf and "Das" from Dassler. They have made some great shoes over the years and eventually ended up getting their shoes in the Olympics. The pair made a lot of shoes together until 1948 when Rudolf left Adidas to form his own shoe company; Puma.

The Adidas trademark is the three stripes registered in 1948 which means mid foot stability. The trefoil' logo was introduced much later in 1972. The three leaves symbolised the Olympic Spirit, linking the three continental plates. This can be found on the old model shoes and clothing – for example, Superstars, Stan Smiths, A-15 warm-Up tracksuits and the classic T-shirt.

Over the last 50 years, Adidas has made a lot more shoes and has moved into mainstream sports and street cool.

APEX TO ZULU A2Z!

Brief Nike History
The Swoosh logo is a graphic design created by Caroline Davidson in 1971. It represents the wing of the Greek Goddess Nike. Caroline Davidson was a student in advertising at Portland State University. She met Phil Knight while he was teaching accounting classes and started doing freelance work for his company. Phil Knight asked Caroline to design a logo that could be placed on the side of a shoe. She handed him the SWOOSH, he handed her $35. In spring 1972, the first shoe with the NIKE SWOOSH was introduced... The rest is history.

Both Nike and Adidas sports shoes have been responsible for assisting the casual in looking as cool as he/she has for over two decades and I salute them both. For me, Adidas easily edges Nike out of the way when it comes to the list of quality sports shoes produced, but youngsters in the early 80s were hooked on these new sports shoes that were taking us to new areas of street fashion.

New Balance
The story of New BALANCE begins at the dawn of the 20th century in Massachusetts when William J Riley, a 33-year-old English doctor, found himself helping people with problem feet by making arch prescription footwear to improve shoe fit. In 1934, Dr Riley went into partnership with his leading shoe and was highly successful selling arch supports to policemen who were on their feet all day. In 1954, Arthur Hall sold the business to his daughter and in 1961 manufactured the Trackster, soon to become the shoe of choice for college YMCA fitness directors.

Together, both Anne and Jim Davies now lead New Balance with Fidelity with one of the world leading manufacturers of high performance footwear.

Puma
The history of Puma is a journey through the greatest achievements of the last fifty years. Puma has accompanied Pele through World Cup finals, Boris Becker to the grass court championship at Wimbledon and Linford Christie to an Olympic gold. It is a history of the constant search for improved performance through technological innovation and symbolic sports performers. Rudolf Dassler founded Puma in 1948

in Herzogenaurach, Germany. Direct business competition from his brother Adolf created the environment that was to change the modern sports trade for decades.

Fred Perry

Fred Perry was born in Stockport, Cheshire on May 18th 1909. He became three times Wimbledon champion and was considered by some to have been one of the greatest male players of the game. The Fred Perry brand has been popular for many years. It is best known for the laurel logo on the left breast of its polo style shirts. In the mid 1950s and through the early 1960s many considered the Fred Perry brand of male shirts to be the best available. The laurel logo on the shirt was stitched into fabric, for instance, rather than being merely ironed on, as with the crochet crocodile featured on competing early Lacoste apparel. Later the brand became popular with mods, skinheads, and other youth sub cultures.

Slazenger

Slazenger is a British sports equipment brand name sold in nearly all parts of the world involving a variety of sporting categories. Established in 1881, it can trace its roots to 1810 and today is one of the oldest surviving sporting brand names. Slazenger were one of the dominant (wooden) racquet manufacturers in the world of their time. Over the years they produced a wide variety of sports equipment, from tennis racquets to clothing from golf equipment to rifles. But it was a bold move into tennis ball manufacturing late in the 1800's that arguably saw their greatest business achievement. Their plant in Barnsley manufactured tennis balls and exported them around the world.

Le Coq Sportif

In Roman times, France was known as Gaul. The Latin word for a cockerel, "Gallus," also meant "a person who lives in Gaul." Over a period of time, this play on words meant the cockerel came to represent the Gauls.

World War 1 saw the meaning of the cockerel symbol change. It became a symbol of French courage and readiness to fight to the death in the face of war.

During the twentieth century, the Cockerel has become associated with French sport and the emblem for the country's teams, representing French pride, tenacity and courage. It is often featured on postage stamps as an icon of France.

Reebok

Reebok's United Kingdom-based ancestor company was founded for he best reasons possible: athletes wanted to run faster. So in the 1890s, Joseph William Foster made some of the first known running shoes with spikes. By 1895, he was in business making shoes by hand for top runners; and before long his fledgling company, JW. Foster and Sons developed an international clientele of distinguished athletes. The family-owned business proudly made the running shoes worn in the 1924 summer games by the athletes celebrated in the film "Chariots of Fire."

Lacoste History

In 1933 tennis great Rene Lacoste teamed up with Andre Gillier to start a new company, La Societe Chemise Lacoste, manufacturing shirts featuring the well-known alligator logo. This first became popular when Rene was given the nickname The Alligator by the American press in 1927.

The first shirts were all white and were first produced solely for Rene's use. They soon became very popular, however, and so began the craze which has lasted throughout the years.

Fila History

Few global sportswear brands can claim the rich Italian heritage that is part of Fila. With its roots dating back to 1911 as a textile manufacturer in Biella, Italy, Fila entered the world of sport in 1973. Today, the Italian design-led company is legendary in its own right and continues to inspire athletes the world over.

From Bjorn Borg and Boris Becker – the sporting icons of Fila's past to today's chosen heroes, Fila is edging its way to remain seen as an elite Italian sportswear company which is rich in design and tradition but also modern in its execution.

It was Fila who brought about the demise of the white shirt-only-tradition on the tennis courts, and introduced the first-ever range of colour-blocked tennis apparel.

DAVID C GEORGE

Sergio Tacchini
In 1966, Sergio Tacchini, a leading player of his day, started out to conquer the clothing market. His idea was original and innovative; the domination of white in tennis comes to an end, and one of the first coloured tennis wear makes its entry on court.

In the wake of this success, the new brand invades tennis around the globe on the clothing of the greatest champions; Jan Kodes, Jimmy Connors, Roscoe Tanner, Vitas Gerulatis and Ilie Nastase were just the first temimonials enchanted by Sergio Tacchini. In 1978, the legendary John McEnroe, the curly haired, eternal rebel, joined the stable, leaving his winning mark on the Sergio Tacchini brand.

Ellesse
On June 19th 1959, Leonrdo Servadio founded Ellesse – using the initials LS, to form the name of his new company.

Servadio had astrong fashion sense as his family was in the textile business. Expanding on his experience, throughout the 1960's he produced fashionable textiles and garments with innovative designs. Success hit fast. In 1967, Servadio moved his team into a 60,000 square metre state of the art facility in Perugia. The capital of Italy's Umbria region. In 1974, another design besides the revolutionary Jet Ski pants to break through for Ellesse came with the quilted ski jacket. Until then ski jackets were only worn on the slopes. But within a short time the Ellesse quilted jackets were seen not only on the slopes of St Moritz, Cortina d'Ampezzo and Val d'Isere, but also downtown in Milan, Paris and London. They were a status symbol of the late 70s and 80s.

Helly Hansen
Clothes company Helly Hansen has been a trendsetter for all weather outfits for over 100 years. The company produces over 500 product lines for women, men and children who work or like to spend time outdoors. A pioneering spirit, courage, innovation and the highest quality standards have turned a small enterprise into an International corporation, with Panalpina as its partner for logistics.

Daniel Hector
At the age of 18, Daniel Hector was selling his own designs to couturiers like Louis Feraud and Jaques Esterel. True success began when Brigitte

Bardot chose one of his designs for her role in La Parisienne. Four years later, he founded the Daniel Hector company. He then created ready-to-wear and brought fashion to the streets. In 1971, he was the first stylist to create collections for skiing and tennis. In 1972, Daniel Hector branched out into sports and founded the Paris Saint-Germain football club with his friends Charles Talar, from Notre Dame de Paris, and Jean-Paul Belmondo. The couturier also made himself known for inviting stars to an annual party during the French Open tennis tournament.

Lutha
Vihtori Luhtanen decided to start his own company in 1907. His wife designed and sewed whilst Vihtori was responsible for the sales. In early 1910s Vihtori Luhtanen employed two seamstresses and this was the first step towards creating his own sewing workshop. 1980s; Radical product development. Luhta sales continued to grow, both in Finland and across the Continent. Luhtas had found its niche in skiwear in the international markets. The production of its old lines was discontinued, although these were to be re-started later.

Lyle & Scott
Founded in 1874, Lyle & Scott have been manufacturing knitwear to the highest standards for 125 years. Today, the brand is known around the world for its exceptional quality and style.

Jaeger
In 1884 Dr Gustav JAEGER promoted the idea of scientific theories about the wearing of hygienic wool next to the skin. The health culture known as Dr Jaeger's Sanitary woollen system sought to encourage people to use wool fibres in all domestic textile uses from clothing to bedding. Jaeger sold his brand to an Englishman Lewis Tomalin. Jaeger shops selling quality men and women's clothes exist today in main towns in the UK.

Pringle
Pringle of Scotland was made a private limited company in 1922. In the 1930's they were the company to use wooden framed hand Dubed machines to knit intarisia – coloured threads being inlaid by hand to

produce elaborate designs. This enabled them to produce the argyle pattern onto sweaters, which has since become the trademark design of Pringle. By the mid 1930s Otto Weisz is hired as the Pringle designer. He creates the twinset and the fashion sweater is born. Two decades later and style setters such as Grace Kelly, Lauren Bacall and Brigitte Bardot were wearing Pringle. During the 1900s Pringle developed golf clothing for the Royal family and aristocracy. It was in 1951 that the P.G.A. asked Pringle to supply the official cashmere sweaters for the British Ryder Cup team for many years after.

Gabicci

GABICCI LIMITED WAS FORMED in 1973 by two entrepreneurial friends, Jack Sofier and Alex Pyser. Jack's wife Maureen suggested the name for the new company following a visit to the Italian seaside town of Gabicce Mare, and the brand was born. Operating offices and a basement warehouse in Maddox Street, London W1, the merchandise on offer was Italian knitwear, acetate/polyester for the spring season and wool with suede trim for the Autumn. Their designs were well received and over the next few years, business grew steadily. Towards the late seventies, together with the traditional Gabicci customer, the young and fashion conscious became interested and Gabicci became a major fashion brand. Those of you old enough to remember that far back will no doubt recall the trademark gold G.

Farah

After learning tailoring from his parents, Mansour Farah set off to New York to design clothing. In 1920, he and his wife relocated to El Paso, Texas, to set up his new business. The Farah's first shop was a 1,250 square foot hole in the wall with ten seamstresses on six sewing machines. Farah were also responsible for producing workwear for the Second World War. The Farah family helped put El Paso on the map in the apparel industry, but it is no longer known for this business anymore, though Farah will always be remembered for a large part of El Paso's history.

Thomas Burberry Story

Thomas Burberry started his business in Basingstoke in Hampshire in 1856. Burberry considered the problem of waterproofing from the agricultural point of view. Most of his customers were farmers and agricultural workers. They normally wore closely woven smocks of tightly packed gathered material with a double yoke that kept the wearer surprisingly dry. Burberry grasped that keeping out drizzling rain was dependent on a close weave and voluminous fashioning.

He began experiments on fabrics with a cotton mill owner. He produced long staple Egyptian cotton, proofed in the yarn before weaving. The resultant woven Gabardine twill cloth used no rubber.

In its original form the Burberry trench coat was part of the First World War airman's military uniform. Today it is a classic garment. Throughout the 1990s the House Of Burberry has employed various well-known international designers to update its image globally.

Aquascutum History

Aquascutum started as a tailoring firm called Box and Co., and established itself as Aquascutum in 1851 in London. The company invented a shower proof wool coat tailored with some style. The Prince of Wales, Edward VII was a trendsetter and soon had a range of informal sporting clothes made by Aquascutum.

In the First World War soldiers in the trenches wore ankle length Aquascutum coats that had military design features with epaulets and pockets. Aquascutum continued to make military coats between the wars and also supplied fashion rainwear. Naturally some of the military influence crept into the fashion designers and the trench coat became a fashion garment.

Daks History

The history of Daks Simpson began in 1894, when Simeon Simpson established a bespoke tailoring factory in Whitechapel in the City of London supplying top quality men's clothing shops. Simeon Simpson was especially interested the development of new and improved manufacturing tequniques, and at the time of his death in 1932, handed this approach onto his son, Alec Simpson.

In the early 1930's, Alec decided to introduce a good quality ready-to-wear tailoring range and in 1934, invented the "self supporting" waistband, for which the company held the world wide patent for many years. At the same time the brand name Daks was created, derived from the words Dad and Slacks. Under the Daks name, the company became the largest manufacturer of top quality menswear in Britain, selling throughout the world.

Barbour Coats

Since 1894 John Barbour & SONS made Barbour clothing in Newcastle, Northern England and the Scottish borders. Raised on a farm in Scotland John Barbour knew the kind of outdoor protection required to keep the elements at bay. After first opening a drapers shop he married and then developed his Barbour idea making oilskins and stormy weather outdoor garments.

Barbour jackets are very durable and seem to last forever. Like Thomas Burberry and other makers of good quality outdoor wear the firm uses high quality long staple Egyptian cotton, strong metal zips and brass studs with seams constructed to be waterproof. In the 1980s the Barbour was a feature of Sloan and Yuppie dressing and worn by Diana, Princess of Wales, and is still well liked by country lovers worldwide.

Belstaff

Back in 1924, Harry Grosberg and his father in law, Eli Belovitch, pooled their talents to produce, for the era, an unparalleled collection of waterproofs. Sturdily constructed and cleverly designed to combat the worst of the British weather, these prototypes of today soon caught the public's imagination. Based in Stoke On Trent, England, they made capes, leggings, rucksacks, haversacks as well as top quality waterproof clothing for men and women. 1980s, Belstaff dominated the motorcycle clothing industry; the brand branched out into other leisure persuits including fishing, shooting, equestrian, golf and industrial clothing.

1990s, Belstaff celebrated 75 years in the industry, making it the oldest clothing company in motorcycling, along with Harley Davidson.

Pierre Cardin

Born in 1922, near Venice, Italy, to French parents, he moved to Paris in 1945. There he studied architecture and worked with Paquin after the war. Work with Schiaparelli followed until he became head of Christian Dior's taileure atelier in 1947, but was denied work at Balenciaga. He founded his own fashion house in 1950 and began with haute couture in 1953. In the UK, Pierre Cardin was known for his quality slacks, tailored shirts and knitwear throughout the 1980s onwards.

Hugo Boss

Boss established his company in Metzingen, Germany, in 1923, only a few years after the end of World War 1, while most of the country was in a state of economic ruin. Before and during World War 2, the company both designed and manufactured uniforms and attire for the troops, officers and other governmental branches of Nazi Germany, including the SS. It is likely the factory used forced labour. After the war, Hugo Boss was labelled an opportunist of the Third Reich" and fined 80,000 marks. The company then languished in relative obscurity until the fifties. Hugo boss himself died in 1948. In 1993, 70 years after its founding, Hugo Boss launched it's first fragrance, and created a division which has since grown to be an important part of the company. In 1999 Boss Orange for men was launched described as sporty and casual separating itself from the trendy Hugo brand and its sophisticated Boss Black brand. Boss Green is a completely sporty brand selling items designed for sport or a sporty look.

Giorgio Armani

Born in 1934 into a humble family in Piacenza, a small town near Milan, Giorgio Armani went to the local public school and developed a love for theatre and cinema. After a short stint at the University of Milan medical school, in 1957, he took a job at the Milan department store La Rinascente. He worked briefly as an assistant photographer before accepting a promotion to its style office, where he bought and exhibited quality products from India, Japan, and the U.S., and. In so doing, helped introduce foreign cultures to the average Italian consumer. In 1964, without any formal training, Armani designed a line of menswear for Nino Cerutti. Encouraged by his partner Sergio Galeotti, Armani left Cerruti and in 1970 became a freelance fashion designer and consultant. Armani's penchant for using materials in unexpected contexts and combinations came to be known as the defining characteristic of his genius.

DAVID C GEORGE

Nino Cerutti –1881

Nino Cerutti was born in 1930, as the son of the founders. In 1950, he became head of the family woollen business. Drawing from his experience in producing excellent fabrics, Cerruti ventured into the production of clothing in the late 60s. His first men's collection was shown in 1967 and was considered a revelation in menswear at the time. Cerruti is well known for furnishing the movie industry. The most renowned film appearance of Cerruti designs can be found in the Hollywood blockbuster "Pretty Woman." Here, Richard Gere and Julia Roberts are both kitted out in Cerruti fashions.

Christian Dior

Christian Dior has been CALLED "The most recognised name in fashion. Born in Normandy, France, in 1905, this fashion and fragrance legend started off to study political science. By 1938 he had turned to dress design but because of his tour of duty in World War 2, he was not able to develop his design business until 1946. His first collection released in 1947 featured a "New Look" a richer look in contrast to the austerity of war styles which featured luxury rather than comfort. His creations helped re-establish formerly occupied France as the capital of world fashion.

Valentino

Fashion designer Garavani Valentino completed his fashion studies and apprenticeship in 1959 with Jean Desses and Guy Laroche; he then went on to open his first studio in Rome. Through his success in developing the House of Valentino in 1960, his reputation was secured with the enormous success of his "Collezione Bianca," the first clothes and accessories to have the magic "V" label designs the wedding dress worn by Jacqueline Kennedy for her marriage to Aristotle Onassis.

Gianni Versace

Fashion designer Gianni Versace was born in 1946 in Reggio Calabria, Italy; he became victim of a cold-blooded murder on the 16th July 1997. In the early days, his mother supported the family with her small tailor shop. There, Versace learned everything about making clothes and soon he designed apparel himself, which was sold in his mother's shop. Then, Versace acquired additional skills working in fabric procurement positions. He got his first chance to show his skills when designing a collection for Fiori Fiorentini, a Lucca, Italy based company in 1972. In 2005, Versace is still one of the most recognisable styles and brands in the fashion industry across the globe.

The more interesting shops to visit in Birmingham for fine clothing are Autograph on Ethel Street and A2. Also Uno off New Street and Bellushi's in Shirley Solihull. If your up in the north, then you cant go wrong with visiting Doncaster for a clothes store called Section 4 Menswear.

The Sound System Phase

In the summer of 83 in Birmingham a number of Blues lads put together a sound system called Burberry Hi Fi, which catered for a mix of different people who enjoyed good music. Lanks, Sharkey, Morph, Duffy and McBean were all involved in putting together good parties with a nice vibe. Sporting Burberry macks, golfing jackets, and hats and scarves all in Burberry made the lads stand out from the crowd, wearing clothes that were on the cutting edge of fashion at the time. The parties then moved to Farm Road in Sparkbrook where they had the opportunity to expand their promotional party idea to a bigger venue, which caught on very quickly and changed names and owners.

The Nationwide Tool Adventures
Courtney

In the early days, the Rubery lads had the monopoly on the fruit machines. Most of my home and away days at matches were funded by fruit machines. Back in the day, strimming was taken very seriously with some lads even buying a second-hand machine in order to make a tool that could trip the mechanism. When some of the other lads on the town would be interested in breaking a jewellers window, I was in the pub not baiting myself, getting money and drinks for absolutely free. Anyone who worked for Bell Fruits who owned most of the machines in the Midlands would testify the pubs in and around that part of Birmingham and Frankly service station on the M5 were clattered senseless in the early 80s. Sometimes we would only have enough money for the train fare to away games, the money to get into the game, and your drinks had to be earned. Soon this would spread to ferry trips to France and Holland where you would have the run of the amusement arcades on the ferries. One trip back and forth could earn you grands. This was definitely easy money at the time, because this type of crime was not taken very seriously. This would however change over the years with the introduction of mould crips.

The early eighties saw gambling on fruit machines high on the list of priorities for many people around Birmingham. A slim line brass tool was first used in the early days on fruit machines to clock up credits in the token slots. It was a peculiar shape that had a hook at the end, which was used to retrieve your coin from the slot after you had put your money in. Later, the brass tool turned into the plastic classic version, which was a lot more popular. The plastic classic came from the thin plastic wire used on Flymo lawnmowers across the country and was very easy to pick up. A team of people who travelled to away matches with Blues would use the tool on fruit machines in pubs and clubs throughout the whole weekend and sometimes not even going to the game at all. The game was always a good way to divert the attention from themselves and their activities and also to make some good money with the plastic classic.

Instead of using your own name while having a conversation in the pubs and clubs, everybody in the team was called Reg. Reg is a pseudonym for pal or friend, which is now being used by all sorts of characters stretched across Birmingham.

It would be easy for a team to earn £500- £600 in an afternoon and still have enough time to get drunk and sample the delights of whatever town they happened to be in. From Bournemouth to Plymouth, Barnsley to Stockport and some, these lads went on trips to most cities and coastal resorts in the country. Charming people with their Brummie banter, and ripping them off at the same time was how these chaps earned their living and it was Rubery, Northfield and Chelmsley Wood who definitely flew the flag with the plastic classic.

A map of Birmingham explaining the differences in the names of firms and the potency of their capabilities. The connection with the townies and how a large number of them became Zulus. The alldayer scene. Burberry Hi Fi.

CHAPTER 4

The History of Aston & Villa's C-Crew

AVFC Harcore Red Hand of Ulster.

IN THE DOOMSDAY BOOK of 1086, William the Conqueror made a list of what he owned. Aston had a church called St Peter & Paul, Aston juxta, which had a full time priest and a servant, a mill, 30 villagers, 18 ploughs with the land valued at 100 shillings and nearby Birmingham had a value of 20 shillings. Aston had a value five times that of Birmingham, but things were about to change for the prosperity of Birmingham city. The ancient parish of Aston was huge, stretching from Perry Common, Lozells, and Water Orton and over as far as Warwickshire.

Until only 200 years ago, Aston was more important than Birmingham due to the history relating to the Church and it's local people. But Aston people showed their true colours even way back then, by revolting against Parliament in the English Civil War and being besieged by 1,200 parliamentary supporters from nearby Birmingham who killed six of Sir Thomas Holte's soldiers who are now buried in the churchyard. At one stage a cannonball was shot at the balustrade on the main staircase in the hall, which has never been repaired to this day. Sir Thomas was not the nicest of gentry, having taken a meat cleaver to one unfortunate staff cook, killing him in the process. Aston itself was finally absorbed into Birmingham after a 100-year dispute years later, that ended in 1911. The Aston Villa football club was founded in 1874 by youths connected to the Aston Villa Wesleyan chapel. So you see that even from the very beginning of their conception, Aston people had ambitions well above sea level.

A number of well known Villa lads in the early eighties used to come from Northfield in Birmingham, and one Villa lad who was mixed race and the size of a body builder used to grab hold of Birmingham City lads' ears on bus journeys home, and yank them all over the place bullying them and taking the piss. When Mickey was chatting to another lad from Chelmsley Wood Trooper, he asked him if he had ever come across this guy before, and low and behold he had. Coo–coo was half the size of this Villa character, but what Coo–coo had that O'Say didn't, was a banger that was taught to him by one of the Grand Wizards of knuckle from Chelmsley, that of Monk. At the Digby in Northfield there has been a disagreement in the pub possibly over a girl, when O'Say has asked Coo-coo for a straighter outside the pub. Coo-coo has obliged and they both stepped outside to settle the score. As O'Say has come at Coo–coo, there was a loud crack, and all was peaceful in the world again. O'Say was lying on his back out cold with his mouth wide open, and Coo–coo went and finished his drink.

Black Danny Interview

Just before the end of 2005, Morph is sitting in his house chilling out when his mobile phone rings. To Morph's surprise, it is a person who nobody has really heard from in a long time Black Danny. Black Danny was one of the most notorious and game lads who has followed Aston Villa since he was a child. Morph and I arranged a meeting with Danny in The Britannia Hotel on New Street at 3.00pm 02/01/06. We sat in the Britannia Hotel bar joking and having a laugh, thinking that if he walks into the bar, will we actually recognise him, as it has been such a long time since our days of dancing in the main road with dropped eyebrows. As we are still laughing and joking, a tall 6ft 4 black guy, wearing a black baseball cap, glasses, a black cagoule, jeans and black shoes walks into the Britannia. Black Danny had arrived with a warm smile and was eager to tell his side of his early years regarding clashes against Birmingham City. I shake his hand, which smothers mine, and we sit down and start to chat. Even though, I have rushed Danny myself at the ripe age of 15 with a number of other Juniors on the ramp near New Street, I still have to give some respect to him, because this guy, on his day, was one of the gamest heads at Villa, along with Brittle. Danny really had to change his life and step off the football scene due to the influx of people who wanted to take him out. I show Danny a list of my questions, he smiles and says OK, and then we begin.

Q. How did you become a Villa Supporter?

A. I lived in Handsworth Lozells on the Villa road and it was slap bang in the middle of Aston Villa's ground and also West Brom. To be honest, I probably lived a little nearer to the West Brom ground than Villa. I went to Holte School where everybody followed Aston Villa and that is when I first started going to the local ground with my brother in 1972. I noticed a lot of skinhead bovver boys at the game who used to kick it off all the time, and at first as a kid, you do shit yourself.

I seen guys who used to paint their Doc Martins silver, and it was exciting and such a buzz, I started going down the Villa as much as I could.

Q. When did you become one of Villa's main heads, and how?

A. To be honest, I had no intention of being a thug; I would go down the game wearing two scarves or what ever. The Steamers put on a coach to Everton in 1978, they had a bar on there but I wasn't into drinking. One of the Steamers says to me that I'm gonna get done, I ask what this guy's talking about, and he mentions the two AVFC patches Danny has on the back of his jeans. The coach pulls up at Goodison, and the Steamers all leave and head off up the road to the game. I was walking round Goodison with a few younger lads, and we were getting a hard time from the Everton lot. Mobs of Everton were slapping groups of Villa around the ground, when Brittle, who was also on the coach, bumps into Danny while he's outside Goodison. Brittle looks at Danny and the situation is moody as hell for the 10 or so Villa outside the ground. Brittle says, "If any more come, we're gonna stand

and have it." Everton seen us as proper supporters, but that is when I myself become aware of other lads who were willing to not be made a fool of. When we started developing as a crew, you had people like Dennis Clarke who loved us, but a number of the Steamers didn't take to the new crew. Because we were making a name for ourselves, some of the Steamers didn't like it, but it was also similar to the C-Crews dislike for the later emergence of the Villa Youth.

Q. What clubs and pubs did you drink in in the late 70s 80s?
A. I used to drink in the Crown and Cushion with Bulldog when I was into my jazz fusion dancing at the Birmingham alldayers, also Samantha's, and the Rum Runner, which was on Broad Street on a Monday night when it was pure jazz funk.

Q. What was it like being one of the only black supporters following Villa's firm home and away?
A. I was going to the Villa in the real dark days when in the late 70's we went to Middlesboro with just 500, and the police put us in the corner of the ground, and all the singing was mainly aimed at me from Boro because I stood out a bit. We left the ground, and in those days you got no escort it was just every man for himself. I would chat with some of the other black lads from Villa at the home games, and show them my battle scars. A number of these guys, who supported Villa but only at home games, used to ask me, "What the hell are you doing going away, are you insane?" I become friendlier with Brittle and then used to travel on our own coaches now, that's when it escalated.

The one game in the 81–82 season, we went to Ipswich and we went to the seaside and had a big row with Tottenham. In those days we didn't have a name for the mob, so we called ourselves the Sea or the C-Crew.

Q. I thought that the name derives from the section of the ground the firm used to sit in at Villa Park?
A. We did sit in that part of the ground, but we wanted it to be funny, a sort of play on words.

APEX TO ZULU A2Z!

Q. Why did the Villa Youth hate you?

A. We just didn't get on mainly because we operated slightly different to them that's all really. I can remember the one time when we were drinking in the Cabin, and a scuffle has broken out between the Youth and a few C-Crew, and Patterson has been slapped and fucked down the stairs in the pub.

Q. When would you say it changed for Villa with regards to drinking in pubs in town?

A. The way I see Villa–Blues and the pub situation, and this is only a personal view. Town has always been mostly Blues and it's always been like that as far as I can go back. Blues have always had the majority of town round by Edwards and John Bright Street, Broad Street and in the early 80's, if we were going round by Edwards then we were going for the ruck, because we had no other reason to go round there.

It was just a way of life; you lot man, fuck me. If I had to do anything in town and it come to after 1.00pm then I know that there is gonna be a firm on the ramp outside McDonalds. And I know I'm gonna get hit, or I'm gonna hit somebody.

Q. The time when you were rushed by four teenagers in 84 on the ramp, it was the Junior Business Boys, Me, Smurf, Hamilton and Rankin. You dropped your shopping bags on the floor and we all just piled into you on both sides and bounced off ya. Do you remember?

A. (He laughs!) Whatever, yeah. It was a way of life at the time and for anybody who was on that scene in the 80s, it was a buzz and a half. Throughout the week, town was yours, but everybody who was into Villa or Blues looked forward to when Saturday comes.

From the early 80s for many years, there was a price out on Danny's head, and if anybody heard that Danny was at it in town with a firm or not, then people would walk around town in search of him come rain or shine.

A. Cuds was established in the early 80s and the Apex were still around, and I can remember going to the Villa–Blues match at Villa Park. Somebody says to me, "Have you seen this?" A guy passes me a little calling card which says. "Black Danny Wanted, Dead or Alive,

DAVID C GEORGE

Birmingham City National Front. Listen to the joke, you know when I got to the Holte end of the ground, it was like confetti on the ground. No word of a lie, it was all over the place.

Q. What did that make you feel like?
A. You know when you're young, you're fearless man, so when you're asking me what it felt like to be hunted, of course I knew I was wanted, man that's just the way it was.

Q. Best dressers at the Villa early 80s?
A. You mean people like John Daniels, Whitehouse, Patterson.

Q. Name any the main heads at Birmingham City that you've had a straighter with?
A. In the late 70s, Villa were going to Blackburn away and Birmingham had an FA cup match away on the same day. Birmingham and Villa were all intermingled on the station, and it was just a matter of time before something happened. On the station I met Cuds for the first time, and the verbal started instantly. Cuds started bouncing up and down ready to have it on the station but nothing happened. In 79 we used to walk round town in huge numbers and the police would tell Villa to go one way and Birmingham to the other, but we would always meet up around half an hour later and have it with Blues. One day at New Street, Cuds was on the station on his own, and I came down to New Street with a few Villa heads. We've both looked at each other, something was said and we both ran into each other. A few fists were traded between Cuds, and me but another Villa lad joined in and Cuds chinned him and the guy stepped backwards. Cuds had to back off and do one because he was on his own really. A crew has now come out of the Nightrider in search of us, and we were in Oasis buying a hat or something and a huge black guy who was with Cuds was a monster of a man called Reven. Just the look of this one guy was enough to make most people think again about doing anything. We all pulled blades, and blues had to have it on their toes. Another time we wanted it with Blues, so we walked up Bull Street past Blacks outdoor wear store and up by the back of Rackhams at the time. We

bumped into Cuds and a firm of all black geezers. Cuds has fronted Villa with the rest of the Blues lads, and Villa didn't know what to do. I thought to myself, fuck this, I'm not gonna run. The rest of the Villa ran and one guy passed me a blade before he took off. I was surrounded and under some serious pressure when I tripped up and fell on my arse backwards and got stamped into the floor near Pigeon Park.

What Danny also didn't realise is that when somebody pulls a blade on a mob of proper Blues heads, then they normally get done with the same blade that they tried to use on themselves so he was very lucky indeed.

Q. What would you say the main differences are between the mentality of Birmingham City`s firm and Aston Villa's in the heyday?

A. In the heyday, yeah Birmingham City were more organised in the sense of making money. Going to away games, looting and taxing anybody they came across, posting stuff back to themselves. Villa were more into stealing clothes and looking pretty.

Danny asks Morph and myself a question
Q. You see it all depends on what you get into football for, regardless of the rucking, I'm a Villa fan. Ee aargh lads, if I was to walk through town waving a white flag and said allright lads, I've had enough fucking about, I'm gonna join your crew," what would you think?

A. Depends!

Q. You'd think, oh, you're a fucking turncoat or whatever and I would never get the respect that I would down Villa?

A. You're right, because people would be wanting to test you even more than they did when you were with Villa, mate, and it just wouldn't work.

Morph's reply
Well, it goes two ways, because even the fact that Fidgy switched (Morph looks at Danny) He was a big name and he was riding with you at the time, but you know what, I couldn't disrespect him because on his day he is a proper good lad.

DAVID C GEORGE

When the Zulu was formed, some people misunderstood why we took the name Zulu, or accepted the name Zulu, it was explained to them that it was to piss everybody else off with the name, and also and more importantly, it was the coming together of all tribes under one banner, and it would be called Zulu. But it was about nashy bashing. Turning over racists, it was that, Georgie, I'm telling ya. The Irish lads remember their windows getting put through because of the IRA and all those goings on, and they wanted to get back at any racist mobs who wanted to have a go along with the black and white lads who felt the same about racism.

Danny
Is that right?

Morph and myself in unison
Yeeee!
A. That's why we hated Villa, that's why we hate Villa to this day because the main crux of Villa's so called hardcore element is that, Red Hand of Ulster and Combat 18.
Q. Fowler, yeah, I don't like Fowler. I don't know if you know but over the last few years Villa firms don't talk. The season Villa got to the FA cup against Chelsea yeah, we're in a boozer, me Lloydy, O, Say. Someone says Fowler's over there, yeah, and the geezers with fucking Chelsea. So I've gone, I ain't fucking having that, so I've gone to walk over and people are saying naagh Danny it's Wembley, but I thought, fuck it mate, I'm going over. We've walked over the road and gone up to Fowler with Chelsea and we've gone, we're here, we're Villa C-Crew, what ya saying, ya dickhead? There was all these people pulling us away and stuff. He's got these two black geezers in his firm.

Myself. They must be really retarded?
The one geezer tried to put a hand on me, and I've just pushed him out the way. Oshay was giving Fowler loads but then it all got quashed and whatever. When Blues got into the Premiership, right, there was all this talk about the C-Crew and Fowler's firm coming together. I said to the lads, can you do me one favour, do not join up

with Fowler at Rocky Lane. So Fowler's firm was at Rocky Lane, and we were in Moseley. I've been in Belfast, right, when the Orange Men are marching, right, and I've seen some of Fowler's boys.

Morph
This is why a lot of the right wing elements have turned on Blues at England matches saying, "Where are all your black lads?," and it's due to the many racist northern and southern firms all wanting to beat black people up. In ten years' time when, say, your son who wants to go to an England match, you don't want idiots like Fowler shouting at players because of the colour of his skin. This is 2006.

The main areas that the Villa C-Crew came from in the early 80s were Erdington, Halesowen, Kingstanding, Great Bar, Bromford, Sutton Coldfield, Castle Vale, Northfield, Perry Barr, Ladywood and a sprinkling from Chelmsley Wood.

A few of the best Villa dressers on the scene were Russell Clinton, Eddie, Static, Brittle, Whitehouse, Ravenhall, G Little, Rat, Big George, Ed Patterson, Belch, Baxter, Davies, and Macco, but by far the best-dressed Villa firm were from Halesowen.

In 1983, a young sixteen year old called Joe used to travel abroad with a few mates to Italy and Germany stealing some of the finest garments available, then bringing them back to Birmingham and parading round with the Aston Villa's C-Crew looking the business.

The Villa's C-Crew in the early eighties had numbers of around 200 strong, but as anyone will tell you, when there is a firm, there are always hangers on. This would bring the numbers up to around 300.

The main Villa pubs in the eighties were The Windsor, The Cabin, The Old Contemptible, Cagney's, Le–pub and Sara Moons.

Popular nightclubs were Millionaires, The Elbow Room and sometimes on occasions some of Villa's top boys used to drink in Boogies, which was a stronghold of Birmingham City fans, so quite risky for any Villa fan to frequent, but some of the C-Crew did underground black-market business with some Zulu's and could bowl about town on occasions.

1984–85 was around the time when a number of pubs in Birmingham city centre and further afield saw the emergence of Aston

DAVID C GEORGE

Villa National Front stickers that popped up out of the blue. This was due to the new connections that some Aston Villa fans had made at England matches with Chelsea Head-hunters right wing element.

This made any clashes with Birmingham City Zulu Warriors and Aston Villa C- crew very intense, emotional and political.

In 82, around eight Villa C-Crew were travelling to an England game in Switzerland. They were at the National Coach Station when a number of Birmingham's Apex clocked them as Birmingham were playing at home on that day. Villa had on some proper nice clobber from your Farahs slacks to your Diamond Pringles and Adidas shoes.

A firm of Birmingham around the same size as Villa's C-Crew, but slightly younger, confronted them in the buffet area in the coach station when the lot goes up in the air. Tables are flying everywhere; bins are flying at Villa while all the commuters are sitting there half way through their meals frozen to the spot. A couple of Villa are slashed up pretty badly and there is blood all over the floor. The handful of Apex are now walking towards the ground through the Industrial estate past the Forge Tavern public house when the police land on them and get them all to line up against the wall.

One of the Villa C-Crew gets out of the car, and as he does, he nods subtle like towards the Apex. He walks down the line of Blues fans and turns to the officer and says, "It wasn't any of them." He then gets back into the car with the Old Bill, and they drive off with the small group of Apex all exhaling at the same time.

The Aston Villa Youth were the younger version of the C-Crew and had numbers of 180–200 strong. Originating from Cardinal Wiseman School in Kingstanding, where a group of the closest friends had a tight bond with regards to looking after each other. The Villa Youth did come from the same areas as the C-Crew but not having the same reputation as their elders. The Villa Youth was formed around 1983, which was slightly before their archrivals, The Zulu Juniors and the Junior Business Boys. The Villa Youth were a band of young Aston Villas supporters around the ages of fourteen to sixteen year olds wearing designer clothes, and were known for generally causing hassle in their local areas and at home and away matches. Spraying walls in snooker halls and making sure people knew who they where as very young teenagers.

Years later around 1989, some of Villa's young C-Crew boys became entrepreneurs on the acid house club scene at the Kipper club in Birmingham which was the smaller room of a larger club in Birmingham called the Hummingbird. One of Villa's good lads at the time was Brendan, who was well respected in Villa circles and was one of the gamest youngsters supporting Aston Villa. The main differences between The Villa Youth and The Zulu Juniors are the types of people who wish to be in a firm and move as a unit. With the Villa Youth, you had a lot of youngsters whose families had a good bit of cash and they would generally come from nicer areas. Now I'm not saying they were all flush with money, but areas such as Sutton Coldfield and Lichfield are not exactly lower working classes, are they. When your numbers are made up of 60% fashion parade and 40% proper firm, then what's going to happen when it's on top? Exactly. A large number of The Villa Youth were into looking good but only a small contingent was game enough to get the job done. From meeting most of Villa youth's top boys throughout my days of debauchery on the club scene, I noticed there wasn't the same incentive to put the cat out as there was at Birmingham City. Don't get me wrong, because I know that some of those Villa lads were game as a piece of wild venison, but just not enough of them to be a real threat to the Zulu Juniors or The Junior Business Boys.

The C–Crew themselves didn't travel with the Villa youth to away games at all and generally The Youth were left to fend for themselves. There was also another mob of Villa who were all dressers that travelled to away matches with numbers of around 60–70. They didn't have a brand name and were like-minded individuals who were game to kick it off, but didn't follow either the Villa C–crew or The Villa Youth. It was very rare you would get all of these Villa firms marching together as they all had different agenda's. This was the main difference between Birmingham's City's mentality and Villas way of thinking.

Black Danny was one of the most notorious characters relating to Villa's older firm the C-Crew but did not have the respect through all of the ranks of the different Villa firms. Gary Little, who sadly died a few years ago. Static, Whitehouse, O'Say and Brittle were all well known to be some of Villa's top boys, and if you saw all these characters together, I guarantee you a firm would not be very far away.

Derby Days

During the late 70s and early 80s, the Aston Villa C–crew were a force to be reckoned with. Birmingham City on the other hand had no real organisation with regards to moving as a crew, and had bands of people who would try to fight Villa, but never had the numbers. The C-Crew in the early 80's used to bowl into town searching for Blues fans in huge numbers and to be honest, they were scary. Blues were printing flyers and passing them around to their fans telling them it was "Time to show Villa what was what." Success breeds results and prestige, prestige breeds a larger fan base, a larger fan base means you have more people who would be keen on fighting for the name of the club they support and for the reputation of the City.

The year the C–crew came into the Kop, both Nap, and myself were there with several other lads when we clocked their firm going in. We had left town having searched all the main Villa boozers that were known at the time with no joy. On sighting their firm, we sent one of the younger lads to go and get Cuds and the rest of the firm. We walked into the Kop with Villa standing just in front and to the side of them. Their firm included Black Danny, Brittle, Langley ECT. They all looked very confident when they came in and at the time, we were smirking looking over at the Villa lot thinking, in a few minutes you're going to get splattered, when all of a sudden it was us that were taking a whacking. I got attacked from behind and was punched in the face a few times as I scrambled down the terraces to get away from the C–crew. In the melee, Napp broke his leg and the police intervened with Villa getting the result mainly due to the fact they came into the ground at 2pm. Quite rightly, the C–crew were given credit for what they achieved during the early 80s they did have a proper good firm. I got to know a few of their lads and bought my first Fila top from a Villa lad after they played in Brussels in the semi final of the European cup. Black Danny was rated back in those days and became a big scalp to have on your CV. Smurf and Georgie rushed Danny on the ramp outside McDonalds, and when I heard this, it warmed my heart, as the pair of them were only sixteen. Never the less, lets not be mistaken between being a good lad at the football and being a tough lad. Danny has been done on a few occasions including getting a slap off one of his own lads from Bromsgrove when they were arguing over who should sit where on one of their coach trips to an away game. He had bottle in abundance as we caught up with some of his lads under one of the subways by Corporation Street. We outnumbered them at least two to one with a lot of the proper faces present on both sides. As we walked towards him and his firm sitting in the middle of the subway, I remember BF from Chelmsley saying, "Alright lads?" Danny didn't bottle it but instead threw something up in the air shouting, "Come on then."

Panic set in amongst Blues causing a stampede in the tunnel that led you from one side of the subway to the other. It soon dawned on Blues that they had far to many stragglers on this night that were not real lads (clearly the cause of the panic) We re-organised ourselves but couldn't find their firm again.

Even though Birmingham City has never won any major honours within the football game, I can still safely say what they do have over Aston Villa supporters is a sense of humour. Since 1875 Birmingham City fans have yearned for success on the pitch but it has never come. You have to have a sense of humour following Birmingham City, because if you watch the way they play a lot of the time, it is a fucking joke. To be a Blues supporter means more to Blues than what it does to be a Villa fan. For instance, since promotion into the top flight, Aston Villa and Birmingham City has met six times. Aston Villa has only beat Birmingham twice, once at home and away, and the simple reason for this is that we really want to win. On the 19th Mar 2005, Blues played Aston Villa for the sixth time and won 2−0 at home.

Real Aston Villa supporters hate Birmingham City because they see Birmingham fans as scum and beneath them, with regards to the success they themselves achieved in the eighties, but since then, they have failed to live up to those glory days and are now worried and jealous that their arch rivals seem to be getting bigger and stronger each season. With the hiccups of more than one goalkeeper, and the buying of many a player just doesn't seem to cut the mustard, Aston

Villa do not seem to have the vision or the know-how to step up and be a real threat to us on or off the pitch. I have read some of the comments made referring to the first Zulu book that came out written by my friend Caroline Gall. For me, a lot of the people who are slagging Birmingham City are Villa fans, or people from areas such as Warrington and places like Carlisle. In response to these people, I would just like to say that if they have ever been a part of a firm that has consistently had it with all of the best firms in the country, then it is obviously hard for someone who watches Carlisle or Villa to understand what a proper firm with proper lads is capable of doing in many parts of the country. If you can name a time when Aston Villas C-Crew have ever give it to Chelsea in London? or Millwall, or Tottenham, or Pompey, or Cardiff, or Man Utd, or Liverpool, or Stoke, or Middlesboro, or anyone who is capable of giving you a right hiding, then please lads, write your own book on your fantastic firms that nobody gives a shit about. By the way, it is easy to become a book critic sitting in your house with your fat stomach, but it is a lot more difficult to get a reputation if your friends and your firm are only into beating up small numbers of fans and claiming it as a victory, jog on, you sighs.

Snooty Fox – Solihull 83

Solihull is the area of Birmingham where a number of middle class youths thought that they were a proper firm but most never really made the grade. A friend from Chelmsley Wood called Wilson, got a bit of a slap in Solihull by some local lads with a firm called the ICF, the Inter Cheswick Firm. At the time, Wilson had a lot of respect locally and also at the match when watching his team Aston Villa. Around 100 Villa Youth landed at Solihull Station with a tall red headed lad called Brendan bowling at the front. Wilf, Rankin, Mulally, Brownie, Wilson and Hutton, with another 15 good Chelmsley lads were with me as we stood outside the station. The Yew Tree firm were also in town at the same time, but we didn't really have a connection with them in the early days, so they were in the background on this day. This was not a normal situation to be in because we were standing in the middle of the Villa Youth without anybody being cut or knocked clean out. On this day, everybody was up for kicking the living daylights out of the Inter Cheswick Firm, who at the time got on everybody's nerves. The Villa Youth in the beginning were not the enemy, but over the coming years, they became our main rivals. We walked down the main high street in Solihull and approached The Snooty Fox wine bar. The Villa Youth and the Chelmsley Zulu Junior firm bowled into the Snooty Fox. Sitting in the corner was a handful of ICF chatting as around twenty youngsters approached the two tables of lads. "Is your name Check?" was the first thing said to the rather large chap sitting down with his friends. "Ye, why?" Smack! A thirteen stone, thirteen-year-old lad from Chelmsley called Brownie, chins Check who looks shaken and very nervous. They where told who we were, and we left the wine bar with not one piece of furniture being wrecked or any of his friends being chinned, so they where very lucky that day. I chatted with Brendan for a while outside he was pretty switched on at the time and a proper good lad. He left with most of the Villa Youth, but the Chelmsley lads stayed in Solihull for a few more hours, just in case the Inter Cheswick firm needed convincing again. Around half an hour later, one of the Solihull lads from the Snooty was collard by a Chelmsley lad who enjoyed wearing weight lifting belts. I've never seen somebody being flogged before, but I think that this was closest I would ever get. The guy was whipped all over the floor and screaming from the heavy-duty leather belt being used to take the skin off his back. The best of Solihull's lads in months to come now joined with Chelmsley Wood, Highgate and Kings Norton Juniors and became part of our crew for a time and some still are friends.

Pigeon Park 84–85–86

Pigeon Park was usually the venue for meeting with the Villa Youth, but a much of the time it was so hot for old Bill, that you had to get in and get out quickly. Villa Youths numbers far outweighed the JBBs with the Blues crew having numbers of around 60–70 good heads. Villa on the other hand had numbers of 200 easy, but we had something they didn't have. We had people who were willing to butcher and maim anyone who came near them and would stand against anything that come. Villa would come from the far corner of Pigeon Park near the bus stops in huge numbers, but we knew that when you see the whites of their eyes, that is when you separate the wheat from the chaff. Villa would always rush the JBB, and back us off at first, but after the bottles and bricks and everything else had been thrown, then you know who you can really trust and who is reliable when the shit goes down. All the JBB were reliable even though our numbers were a lot smaller. When you get right into the core of the Villa Youth, there are about 30 or so proper good lads who would have it bang off with you, but the rest are just there to show you what clothes they've got on, and what new swear words they have learned. Smoggy has clashed with Villa near the Fire station with sporadic fighting all over the streets. Sparrow and Smoggy with around another 30 Blues have stood to around 60 Villa near the University. Big Gary steps forward and fronts Smoggy who doesn't move an inch. Sparrow says to Gary, "I wouldn't fuck with him mate, because believe you me, he can put the cat out." Gary and Smoggy clash one on one and for a few minutes it's pure knuckle. Little gets a pisser to the chin from Smoggy, who is no slouch when it comes to straightners and ends up on his arse. What must it feel like when Blues Juniors are taking out Villa's top boys for fun?

JBB Vs Villa Youth Crown & Cushion 1985

We wanted to show the Villa Youth that the Junior Business Boys will go anywhere to fight them, and through the years we did. From Falcon Lodge in Sutton Coldfeild, Lichfield fair, Tyburn Road traffic lights in Erdington and Solihull shopping centre, the JBB would travel around the Midlands to have it with the Youth anywhere. Today, the Juniors were off to the Crown & Cushion in Witton on match day to have it with the Villa Youth. We travelled there only 30 handed by bus from the city centre, and got off a stop before the pub. We bowled round the back of the pub onto the car park. One of the Juniors walked round to the front of the pub to see how many chaps were in there, and there were around 50 Villa Youth having a drink in their local. We marched round to the front of the pub and rushed the door, smacking everybody who looked or smelt like a Villa fan. Then more Youth pilled out of the door hurling glasses and stools at us. After sidestepping the glasses, we rushed them again and they managed to lock the doors of the pub so we couldn't get in. This is just before Birmingham were playing Villa up the road, and the pub itself lies on a busy main road with tons of traffic, so we had to get the hell out of there before the dibble landed. People were waking past the pub on the way to the game and must have wondered what the hell was going on at the time, but sometimes, you have to put your bollocks on the table and hope that the public don't get to scared and call the police before you've eaten your pudding and paid for your meal. Most of the JBB were small lads with big hearts and to look at them, you wouldn't believe what sort of shit we got up to. When people see a group of youngsters with the average height of 5ft 6, dripping with designer gear and frowning through red eyes, it used to shock the hell out of many fans up and down the country. From my experiences down the football, it was never the obvious person who was the one to watch out for, but the one who you haven't noticed at all, until it's too late. If it's going bang off, mob to mob, then the worst thing you can do is concentrate on the person in front of you. Always use the green cross code if you've got any sense. What I mean by that is that you should look to your left and your right when it's bang off, as well as in front, because I guarantee you that when you're focusing on one man, then a next man will mess up your program good and proper.

The Sara Moons disaster 1984

These things happen occasionally and this was one of those days. The Sara Moons pub is situated in Birmingham City centre near Oasis market. Villa had a good firm in Sara Moons and were waiting for blues to come to them. On this day Villa were playing at St Andrews, but yet again, we have to bring a mob over to them. Blues bowled over to Sara Moons 150 handed with even numbers on either side. Villa steamed out of Sara Moons and ran Birmingham back into the city centre. I'm not sure why everybody ran, but I think they didn't expect Villa to even want to have a go. How wrong we were on this day. It was horrible to see this happen, but I have no excuses as Villa did what they had to do. I stood outside McDonalds sucking on a strawberry milkshake, and talking to Brains, with Villa's firm snarling right in front of us. We didn't move, and they were not interested in us anyway. One of Blues top lads was so pissed off for Blues running that he walked to the ground with Villa's firm. Villa were saying his name all the way to the game, but nobody approached him at all. If Birmingham City and Aston Villa's firms were to have twenty fights within a year, Villa would probably win one, and on this day they did. No excuses.

Fire Station Ambush 1983

It is very rare for Birmingham City and Aston Villa to play home matches at the same time, but on this day the people in charge must have been using Valium, or they must be just plain stupid. Birmingham were playing Crystal Palace at St Andrews, and left the match around twenty minutes into the second half. 400 Zulu's now walked over towards the Villa ground to meet them as were planning on coming into town for a drink. The Zulus walked down by Birmingham University undetected and got under the subway near the fire station. The subway near the fire station is absolutely huge, with a least six different exits leading into a huge open area. In the centre there are bushes dotted all over that Birmingham took cover in. There are now 400 Zulus in bushes waiting for Villa to walk through before they get into town. This is Gorilla warfare at it's best, when firms don't even know that you're there, and your numbers are heavy, and your firm is proper.

A few lookouts went up top and waited for any sight of Villa's escort.

Blues were pumped up on this day, as we were once again showing Villa what it is to be No 1 in Brum. As Villa approached the subway, everyone got ready to jump out and have it, but first they waited for the whole escort of Villa to get downstairs in the centre of the subway. Villa only had a handful of police with them, and most waited at the other side of the subway as they were on motorcycles or horses.

Blues now stand up and roar, ZUUUUUUUUUUUULU! Villa were in disarray and scattered to every exit after getting smashed all over the place downstairs. They didn't know who was who, but to any blues fan, we can smell Villa fans at a hundred yards. Blues are by far the number one firm in the Midlands without a doubt. Here is something for you to think about if you're a Brummy. Why the hell would you want to support a football team who have a large percentage of fans that are connected to C18 and BNP?

This is a multi-racial city and we love it that way, which is why Birmingham's firms are so dangerous.

Coventry Chaos 1984

The Junior Business Boys were eager to show the rest of the Midlands who was top dog when it came to youngsters with front and kicking it off in the early eighties. On this day we travelled to Coventry to have it with Cov and then have it with Villa. Birmingham City didn't have a game on this day and got to Coventry on the train 40 handed with six of the older lads who were keen on cracking a few heads. We got off the train in Cov and bowled into the centre searching for Coventry, but couldn't find them for love or money.

We ended up having a drink in a pub and relaxed for a while in order to get hold of Villa's firm. After three quarters of an hour we walked back up to the station through the subways and noticed that Villa had just arrived at the station. We quickly went back under the subway and got ready to bum rush Villa as they were walking straight towards us. No tools, no weapons, just hands and feet, we came running out of the subway with both fists clenched roaring, ZUUUUUUUUUUULU. Villa shit themselves and turned and ran back to Coventry station, but if they would have stopped and taken a proper look at our numbers, they would have realised they outnumbered us about four to one.

Villa were jumping the barriers and running back into the station and a few decided to have a go and stand. A short Brummy guy who wears one leather glove was smacking Villa fans all over the station and flashing his gritted teeth, he reminded me of the Begby character from Trainspotting. Black Danny, who never made it through the barriers, was being stamped on by one of blues older chaps. He got a right hiding. The Juniors caned everybody on our side of the station and then beckoned the rest of the Villa to come through the barriers. They declined. These days Birmingham were hot to trot and made no bones about wanting to put the rest of the Midlands firms in place. None of them were in the same category, but this doesn't mean you can't come unstuck, because this can also happen when you least expect it.

Villa Youth Tenerife 1987

The Kingstanding firm are in Player Los Americas looking at these young London kids dancing in the middle of the strobe lights and having a good time. The Villa crew were enjoying themselves and dancing to tunes such as the Pasadenas and Salt & Pepper. The London lot were wearing really bright clothing with their jaws going backwards and forwards like an old fashioned typewriter After Tenerife, the Villa lads went onto Ibiza and were invited to Amnesia club, which was way out of the centre at the time. 20 Youth now enter Amnesia and had a proper good night out that stayed with them for a long time. They knew that what was going on in Ibiza was something that was going to become very big, and they were interested in the whole scene from the get go. From playing all of the crazy drinking games and meeting many people from around the country at Beach parties, the Villa lot really had a good time. From slapping some London lot at a Beach party, the DJ's also from London at the time were now taking more notice of them, and they became friends. Belcher was a Villa lad with an infectious personality and a lot of confidence for someone so young. He decided to stay in Ibiza when all of his friends went home, as he wanted to find out more about the scene.

Leaving his job as a spark in the UK because he wasn't being paid the right amount of money for his skills, he quickly evolved as one of the first people to really be on the Acid House dance music scene along with Chames, bringing the spirit of Ibiza back to grey overcast Birmingham. In 1988, Chambers was living in London and was on the phone regularly telling me about these strange all night parties where people swung their arms around like zombies and had bulging eyes. When you're looking at most of the newspapers of the time absolutely slagging off the whole scene, with police desperate to smash your head in for being ripped to the tits and wanting to dance and drink water, it is no surprise that all of these people had to do a reverse in thinking when the scene became so popular that TV advertisements, Radio the pop charts couldn't get enough of it. This was the biggest ever-underground music scene since the sixties, and we were loving it.

In 1988, I was persuaded to go to a do in London with Chames, Woody from Liverpool, Adel and Debra both from Wigan. The four of them drove to Chelmsley Wood to pick me up and at the time on Chelmsley, most people were drinking in Woody's bar and listening to Lovers rock and Sound systems played on tapes behind the bar. We are on our way to London when we have a high-speed blow out that gets fixed by a police officer was kindly helped us out. After landing in London we entered the first place, which was called (Unit 4) where we met Zarkoff from Birmingham who was working on the door. The place looked like a huge underground storage facility, with loads of strangely dressed people waving their hands in the air. The next place we went to was called the (Car Wash) in Vauxhall. This was an underground car park with loads of fancy motors all in a row with a few smaller rooms going off the main room. I sat down next to Adel, Woody and Debra, as we were all Acid House virgins. After a few hours of persuasion, we all decided to enter the world of moffit; so all four of us end up swallowing a Californian pill and a Tangerine Dream trip. At the time, D–Mob had a white label track out which was ripping London to pieces. The track was called ACID and was so catchy that the dance floor would go berserk whenever the tune was played. After around twenty-five minutes we all came up for the first time on our Californians, sat in a row looking at each other with astonishment on our faces; mouths wide open doing slow double eye blinks.

I tried to talk, but failed to form words that made any sense. I just about got up off my arse, and my legs were shaking like a shitting dog. My heartbeat was going ten to the dozen, when I quickly grabbed hold of the wall and tried to get my bearings. My head was shaking like a Thunderbirds puppet, and my eyes were spinning like washing machine on full cycle. This was the first time I had ever experienced rushing before, and to be honest, at first I was all over the shop. My body was feeling waves of niceness flowing through me from my feet to my head and as the wave rolled up my body, you cannot help but take in a slow deep breath and scan the room. I slowly walked over to Zarkoff and said to him, "What the hell am I going to say when my

DAVID C GEORGE

mates ask me what it was like?" Zarkoff smiles, shrugs his shoulders and says, "Fuck knows." This was my introduction to the world of Acid House, and many years later, this scene would change the face of youth culture and nights out for millions of people across the globe. This was the beginning of the big change in Birmingham's night life, as dancing all night fuelled by class A drugs was a huge money maker for some of the people who were on the ball from day one and embraced the new way of late night entertainment.

When arriving back from London in 1988, Birmingham lads from my neck of the woods were frequenting the Mackadown in Kitts Green and listening to tracks by Billy Ocean singing, "When the going gets tough" and smoking weed at the back of the room with the Lea Hall firm. I've bowled in there with Chames wearing the latest clothes from London and trying to explain what I had just experienced. Dancing round a warehouse with some of Tottenham's, Arsenals and even Millwalls lads all giving it what for on the dance floor. As you can imagine, it didn't go down well at with most people thinking we were from the planet Mars, but you have to understand that at the time, there was no Birmingham scene what so-ever except for a little club that the young Villa C-Crew had up just started putting on called The Kipper Club. At the same time in Chelmsley Wood, Hoyte who was a good friend of ours used to play a lot of the London tunes by Ten City, Yellow, and The Thompson twins, "In the name of love" and "That's the way love is" tapes in his house over near Whitesmore School, and this was our version of the Kipper Club in a council house. All the people who were first switched onto the rave culture will know what I am talking about, as the people in Birmingham blanked us because they didn't understand what was going on, and were not interested until they realised they could make a shit load of money from it. Coventry gets a big shout out from myself, as I was introduced to Reflections nightclub, which stood across the road from The Tally Ho public House. Neville used to stand on the door of Reflections, with Peewee on the door of the Tally Ho. Neville would let myself, and Chames into Reflections for free, and it was a real eye opener. It was as though Coventry had kidnapped a chunk of London, and held it hostage in the centre of Coventry. These were truly the beginnings of the rave scene in Birmingham and they were great days I shall never forget. While Coventry was rocking its socks off and producing outdoor raves in country mansions with Doc Scott and Mann Paris, the majority of Birmingham were none the wiser, and had only heard of raves when reading the Sun newspaper. After months and months of the buzz and the word going round, Birmingham people start to get switched on, but it took some doing to convince a lot of people this was going to be fucking huge. People started to DIY and put on club nights all over the place which evolved into every Tom Dick and Harry having a go. Most of them were shit nights out because the people didn't really know what they were doing, and the reason why they were doing it, but there were some gems out there that will never be forgotten. You know which ones I mean.

Rocky Lane 2002

Another day, and another mission to go and find Aston Villa's firm again. The main problem with this is that it is very difficult to move in large numbers around Birmingham anymore. Aston Villa were playing at St Andrews, but this makes no difference with their mentality on Villa coming to us for knuckle. To be honest, Villa never come for Birmingham City unless they have just won a major cup, or they have come off the train at New Street from an away game they've managed to win. Due to it being so on top, most Blues fans are not interested in meeting Villa because they would rather have a drink and read the paper, than have a helicopter following them across the city. The idea of having a thirty second fight and being arrested doesn't seem to appeal to the majority of Blue noses, this only leaves the people who don't give a fuck about who is watching, and if there is a strong possibility of being arrested.

Around 50 Zulus walked over to Rocky Lane to have it bang off with Villa's firm of around 150. Now this is a risk that blues are willing to take time and time again for Villa, which should give you an idea of how much we also hate them. The Police are clearly filming the whole row, as Birmingham and Villa's firm dance in the main road and exchange house bricks and bottles at close range. Fists are thrown but no real injuries were reported. Once again, Villa classes this as a result, but if you look at the video footage, you will clearly see that it is just a standoff. If fifty Villa were to take on Blues proper firm, there would be many hospital beds full that night. A lot of Blues fans were arrested for this fight against Villa, and to be honest it ruined blues firm a few weeks later in the same year as we were travelling to Westham away.

Lichfield Road 2005
Ry. Northfield

People who are not from Birmingham, won't appreciate the rivalry that is there between Birmingham City fans and Aston Villa supporters. The types of people who follow the teams are very similar in lots of different ways, but being a bluenose gives you a certain confidence that Villa used to have way back in the early 80s that they have lost. We get the usual call for a meet with the Villa lot and a few names of pubs are mentioned that we all go and visit around thirty handed in taxis.

As were walking down the road in Aston, we've heard a huge roar with voices shouting, "Come on, were here." We saw silhouettes of geezers coming towards us. There must have been around a hundred Villa now coming towards us and let out another roar, which sounded as though there was a small army coming at us.

Blues were now jogging towards Villas firm on the Lichfield Road when all of a sudden as we got close to them, the artillery hit us first which came in waves of bottles and glasses.

Blues stood only 30 handed and kept on moving from side to side so as not to get hit by flying debris. The glasses stopped and then instantly we are hit by a second wave of just pool balls flying at high speed, then pool cues came shooting past our heads like spears.

Blues now clash with Villa, and have it toe to toe with them and it is vicious as hell. People are being bashed to the floor and kicked in as standard. The noise and the adrenalin running through your body is amazing, as it's up in the air, but you have to always remember your objective as you can easily lose the plot and start to operate by yourself which is the wrong move to make in a mob fight. People are getting back up and going in again and again, with blood all over the place on people's clothes, faces, on the floor, and all over people's hands. Birmingham had taken only the Young Guns up to the Lichfield Road, but we made a good account of ourselves as Villa were in a proper good battle with us. The man in all white who was standing at the front of Villa, was somebody everyone wanted to get hold of, and we all went for him and came under another rain of bottles. As the old bill have turned up, Blues have run one way and Villa the other, but we still wanted it bang off but the night was over, until the next time we dance with the Voile. Villa never come over to our manor because they know and so do we. The last time Villa tried something like that was when they came over to the astro turf in Highgate all those years ago and got bashed and had to do one sharpish. We are the people who are loyal to the cause and that is what we do, we don't need to brag about who we are, as we are already know who we are, and we are Blues. Full hammer..!!

Keep Right On!

A Classic 80's Blues song used to wind up the Villa
Gary Shaw, Gary Shaw
Gary, Gary, Shaw
When he gets the ball he does fuck-all
Gary Gary, Shaw.

If you look at the history of the city of Birmingham, it will become apparent Aston never wanted to be a part of Birmingham for a very long time and the feeling Aston people hold against real Brummies is still as passionate as it was hundreds of years ago when Birmingham as a city was becoming more successful. Aston was separated from our city due to its wealth and historic and political past.

Still to this day, Birmingham City fans will fight Aston Villa fans anywhere and anytime, and time and time again have proven this over 25 years. If I were to count the amount of times in the last 25 years Villa have actually turned up to where Birmingham City are to fight, then It would only just about get into double figures. For everybody out there reading this, we are Birmingham City, not Aston City.

DAVID C GEORGE

Villa youth outside their ground – 1985

Original Villa youth – 1985

APEX TO ZULU A2Z!

Villa Youth in Kingstanding – 1985

CHAPTER 5

Brummy Characters

BY FAR ONE OF THE GAMEST and most respected people to ever deserve the accolade of, devastating is the one and only, Fat Errol. Fat Errol has stood on for Birmingham's firm so many times that he deserve this appreciation from me, and every other Blue nose who has had the pleasure of his company. From having it with Errol in Coventry, London, Manchester, Wolves and Pompey, I can safely say that this man is truly a Birmingham legend and, in my opinion deserves the key to the city. A true gentleman who should never be forgotten and earned the right to be classed as a true Terrace Legend. Another character that was one of the most charismatic and clever individuals to ever bowl into St Andrews was that of Morph. Morph was a man who had a warm smile every time you met him and would usually be the person way back in the early 80s who would come up with tactics and ideas of getting round city centres and finding the opposition. He played a key role in strategies and techniques to get the job done and is a well-respected head in Birmingham. Another who that stood on for Birmingham and came from off the town is none other than Barrington. Barrington was one of the main heads on the town that had evolved into a proper lad known all over Birmingham, and always had away fans wanting to go home ASAP.

Cuds is definitely one of the most well known lads connected to Birmingham City and is one person who has well and truly earned the respect of all people who know him well. His tenacity and courage has had many a football casuals lips flapping from North South East and West in England. Cuds is one of the people who can move a crew when need be, and can also hold a line when it's ups in the air and proper bang off. A true gentleman and a proper Blue nose through and through with the right attitude to be looked up to by many people in Birmingham and further a field.

The General is a well-respected man at Birmingham City for the right reasons. This bloke is a real gentleman with the heart of a lion, who has throughout the years earned a real reputation as a proper geezer. Troganite is also another well-respected man who some people have classed as a nutter. He is far from this most of the time, but can equally switch it on when necessary. What he has is a lot of balls and a lot of respect for having it wherever throughout the decades and easily makes this list of Birmingham's lads. Cockney B was a slick dresser who was a proper head back in the early 80s, his trade mark style and his animated posture when it's about to kick off was unforgettable, this guy could fucking motor. Brains is a proper geezer and a dresser who has been one of the most consistent in Birmingham since the Apex onwards. This man has got some fucking style that most could only look at and admire. One of the gamest individuals to have ever entered St Andrews gates, Brains is a true Bluenose casual. Cockney Al is a man who has entertained hundreds throughout the years by doing what he does best. I have known this guy since I used to collect golf balls for him at the ripe age of 11 at The Belfry with a good friend of mine called Wilf RIP. Al is an original Trooper head who deserves recognition for his services. Balla is the Begby character from Trainspotting. If you wish to know anything about this guy, then forget the sweaty sock accent and change it to a Brummie, then you have got Balla. A good lad who has stood through the tests of time and deserves to be on this list of geezers. The bread van Bros are unforgettable when they were doing the do in the 80s. I've seen the pair of them hold the ship and keep it afloat when the waves were as big as houses. They should never be forgotten for their sterling work as true Brummie soldiers. Selby was a casual with some serious style and as game as you like. A lot of people are not aware of this lad but in his day, he was very clever and gamer than a lot of heads who were about in the early days. A true gentleman with a good heart and well worthy to be on this list. Tony .G RIP, was a true terrace legend. This guy would bowl through the Holte end wearing a Birmingham City hat with not a care in the world. He was also one the gamest geezers at St Andrews and The Happy Trooper respectively. Loved by all and rated as one of the best, Tony Gardener will be missed by all who knew this real stand up man. Sherry is also a man with a big heart and has taken our Roman soldier Zulu horns of the bull line, to many parts of the country with many successes. Known by many for his colourful language and personality, he is definitely a man who makes this list hands down. Chesty is also another character who has made a name for being loyal and very game. Coming from the rough working class Smethwick area, he has established himself as a main head and is not shy when things need to be done. I've seen this man have it proper on numerous occasions including Boro away when he went so far into The Frontlines firm that we couldn't even see him. Respect is due. Black Stuart is a geezer and a half. I have had the pleasure of knowing this man in the early days on the town and at games up and down the country. He is undoubtedly a proper head with credentials that are known throughout the manor. Respect is due. Fat Gregg was a true soldier who has earned his stripes way back in the day and is a character that many people enjoyed his company when he's around. If there was a war on, and some members of your Platoon were getting awards, then this geezer would be given the Iron Cross as standard. Noggin is a true Brummy character that has been around longer than Fred fucking Perry. A proper, proper geezer with all the trimmings and some. Satty is another well-known character that is as real as they come. Through many years, he has been a person who has been a geezer for a considerable amount of time with Blues and is a character a lot of people respect in Brum. Convey is a proper character many people know as a proper lad. From the early 80s, Convey has been a community casual with the gift of being very clever and on the ball which has earned him a good reputation for the right reasons. Fat Gary was a very keen geezer back in the day and as game as you like it. This man wasn't shy when it came to fronting firms quadruple your size, but sometimes it had to be done. Keep Right On! Blue Army. Lanks & Sharky were two charismatic characters from early back in the day who evolved from knowing many different types of people from different manors. They both should be well on this list of chaps, as they are well known to the people who know. Highgate man dem, big up..!! Nuff said. Duffy has the true Irish eyes and the respect off all geezers who have had the pleasure of his company. From being a young skinhead and frequenting The Crown pub as a nipper, he embraced British Youth culture and took it to his heart when it metamorphosed and evolved into many different highbred cultures. He is a stand up man with a warm personality that makes this list of Brummies without a doubt. There are many, many, other characters in Birmingham who can make this list, but for me personally, I wanted to give my respect to a few of the faces & heads that I remember who were a part of the Birmingham spirit that lives on to this day.

Keep Right On!

Throughout the fifties to present day, black people have had a huge influence in street culture, music and style. Caucasian people embraced the music and the style of black people and black culture, combined with their own as soon as the media and record companies of the time diluted the music and made it more accessible to the white population. From inventing The Blues, Rock & Roll, Jazz, Motown, Soul, Gospel, RnB, Disco, Hip Hop, Reggae, House Music and being the pioneers of the DJ – two turntables and mixing and scratching, black people are the originals of popular music and are responsible for a huge amount of style seen on the streets of the UK and the rest of the world today. Many caucasians have always been fascinated with the black man and feared him both sexually and physically. Even from the first meetings when Europeans spoke of the black man in a derogatory way in order to dehumanise him, this mentality is still strong in many areas of the UK and the world today. Society tries to define people's character but doesn't do a very good job explaining what we as the public are thinking. For example, why is it that people are supposed to be good or bad and not both? Human beings are on the whole capable of compassion and cruelty depending on circumstances and situation and choice, but this does not mean these emotions cannot fluctuate

DAVID C GEORGE

now and again just like any other human being. These days, many Caucasian girls want their skin colour to be as dark as possible, and want to have a backside that is firm and sticks out like Jennifer Lopez. Some also even have injections into their lips to make them fuller, and use slang words that derive from the black community. Even down to dancing. When a person of colour does something well, then he puts his own identity into what ever it is. Black people have always had an uncanny knack of being able to pull off particular coloured garments that their white counterparts could not. From the dressers I have known throughout the football and the alldayer scene, I can safely say the black influence in Birmingham style was very potent indeed.

Early shoplifters in Birmingham were very much into the idea of having a particular garment that was extremely rare. This was called one cut. If you found an item that was one cut, you would lie your face off with regards to where you got it from, and also the price. If it came from London you got it from Leeds, if you got it from Manchester, it came from Brighton. This was going on for years in Birmingham and across the rest of the country until people didn't even bother asking where garments came from, because they knew that any real casual is not going to tell you where to get hold of the same clobber he had got on.

APEX TO ZULU A2Z!

CHAPTER 6

Junior Business Boys

Zulu Apprentices + Zulu Juniors = Junior Business Boys

HOT YOUNG TEENAGE DRESSERS in 83–84 were McConnell, Little Stig, Hamilton, Gizmo, Brooksie, Delaney, Elvis, Roachy, Faye, Crock, Golding, Smurf, Applehead, Coaly, Rankin, Boo Boo, Little Darren RIP, Peggy, Smoggy, and Malardo.

    For me, there was no felling when stepping out of your house early in the morning, dressed from head to foot in mint clobber, knowing full well the people you grew up with and who supported the same team and were exactly on the same hymn sheet as yourself. I am proud to be a Brummy, and felt a lot of pride and excitement knowing that people who are usually from similar working class backgrounds are going to be on your case all day looking to take your teeth out of your mouth without an anaesthetic. Defence of your people is one of the reasons why firms evolved and became popular, along with the realisation that when you move in huge numbers, it becomes easier to rob and steal from anywhere you want to have an earner from. Clothes shops, Jewellers, High Fi stores ECT. Most people were not however thieves, but if someone smashes a shop window, and it turns into utter chaos then other people obviously become tempted to make a bit of cash for free. Just the same as way back in history, when people sacked towns and villages for profit. Just like many troops do when a war is taking place. This is human nature. We all live in a society that is based on lies, and corruption with wealthy families who have been brainwashing us for hundreds of years. The government has always worked by making you think that your choices in life are your own, but I would beg to differ. This is a huge pantomime that we live in, but most of the working classes are the props used by the real performers who are the Blue chip companies, landowners and government that have blagged us silly for years.

Early 83, Rankin is sitting in his house sporting a pair that of Levis, Adidas Munchen, and a Lacoste T shirt. Fernanda, who was Rankin's Dads partner, asked Carl how much his T-shirt was. "£50" was the reply, and then Fernanda said she could get hold of tons of them for less than a pound. Only two months later, I'm sitting in Rankin's Dad's pad, next to a huge box of crocodiles, a pile of stripped T-shirts and a tub of super glue. This was the get as many snide T-shirts on the market time. We sold snide T-shirts at school to the younger school kids and also Armani jogging tops, which looked fantastic for snides. The only problem was that people who washed the T-shirts kept complaining that the badges kept falling off. Our reply was, "Well what do you want? Get your mom to sew em on then." Not many could afford the real stuff in the early days, and most of the best clothes thieves kept most of what they stole.

I was standing outside St Andrews in late 83 with a few lads from Chelmsley Wood called Roachy, Rankin and Delaney who were very good friends of mine. We were all still at school on Chelmsley Wood, where our school uniform was non-existent. In upper school office, there was a glass case on the wall, with a brown uniform shirt and tie all crisp and fresh sitting in there. The only thing was, we didn't have to wear the uniform for some reason, which meant that we could turn the school into a football casual catwalk. The best dressers to come out of my year at Whitesmore were Hopkins, Rankin, Wilson, Dyson, Pickering, Roachy, Delaney, Craig and Crowther. At St Andrews, we were waiting for the gates to open, as we had no dough to get in the game. Three lads are approaching in the distance with a much younger lad. They were all dressed well, but I could not take my eyes off the young lad bowling up to the gates with three lads at least four years older than him. His name was McConnell and he was the hottest young dresser to come out of Bordesley Green, standing around four feet tall and holding a push button handle brolley. This guy had a pair of red Adidas Munchen, Armani jeans and a red WCT Fila that zipped up on the side.

I didn't know it then, but this guy was to become one of my best friends over the coming months and a friendship between fellow young dresser Blues fans was about to come to life. Friends and myself would be standing outside the home end, with groups of likeminded dressers from other areas of Birmingham. We would stand about outside the game admiring each other's clothes and talking about the football match. Another group of guys who were very much into early Giorgio Armani and Nino Cerruti, also used to stand outside, but none of us actually knew each other very well, so we would give a quick nod at someone who was standing outside the gate after half time. Four guys from Highgate, Basall Heath and Edgbaston. Smurf, Dean, Hamilton and Paul dressed slightly different to the style we were used to, but they did look the part. Bright tracksuits and Farah slacks with kickers were all over the place like an epidemic but as kids, we knew we looked tidy.

A young lad approached us as me Roachy Delaney were chatting. His name was Smurf. Smurf asks for a light on a cigarette and starts talking. The average age of this group of lads is 15 or younger and we got on instantly. As the gates opened, the Chelmsley lads walked down to Smurfs friends and we all shook hands then walked into the game. Combined with the other groups of youngsters outside the game we walked into the Kop end near the clock and all stood together talking. There were a few people pointing and staring at us, but we didn't really understand why. Years later I was told that when we first walked into the ground all dripping with clobber, we looked the bollocks. Kings Norton also had a good firm of Juniors that used to be called The Nutty Norton Turnout, which derived from a gang of lads from Kings Norton boy's school. They changed their name to

The Zulu Apprentices and evolved into The Junior Business boys with all areas coming together as one crew.

I suppose in a way it must have looked quite impressive to see such a group of kids so well dressed and supporting the local team, but to us at the time, clobber was more important than our girlfriends.

APEX TO ZULU A2Z!

The main areas that the Junior Business Boys came from were Lea Hall, Chelmsley Wood, Yardley, Acocks Green, Bordesley Green, Small Heath, Westheath, Highgate, Balsall Heath, Edgbaston, Kings Norton, Damson Wood, Handsworth, Sheldon and Leamington Spa.

Everybody around Birmingham City had herd of the Villa Youth at the time, but nobody had really had it bang off with them before. The Yardley firm at the time were coming up with the name The Zulu Apprentices with calling cards to match, the Highgate firm were also calling themselves the same. Chelmsley Woods firm had calling cards and were called the Zulu Juniors, which made things a little confusing at the beginning. I remember standing on New Street and seeing a young guy with far too much hair. His name was Stig. He was standing on the train station in a yellow Head ski coat and giving out calling cards to every young Blues fan who walked past. I stopped and had a look at the calling card, and said.

"What the fuck is this?" Apprentices! "What the fuck are you on?" "We are not fucking trainee carpenters or builders" "Sort it out?" Stig and Jeff both looked at me with shock on their faces, as I didn't know either one of them. As I walked away, Stig says to Jeff. "Who's the fucking nig nog?" And Jeff says, "That's Trogg's younger brother. Believe it or not, that is how I first met the Yew Tree firm and to this day, they are some of the best lads to ever represent Birmingham City home or away. A small group of Chelmsley chaps used to drink with the Yew Tree juniors and also Solihull and Small Heath and on occasions, we would have running battles outside the pub in Yardley with each other. The best fights we had were against Small Heath who would always come down to The Yew Tree to fight us. Even though we knew each other and were friends, we wouldn't pull any punches of kicks if we were rowing each other so sometimes this would end up in broken noses and black eyes. Coley was always a loon on these occasions and would hurl house bricks at your head from 10ft away. He was a character everybody respected as a good lad and as game as they come. When fighting our friends from Small Heath, a mob of around 15 of them would jump on the 17 bus and duck down as they are coming past the Yew Tree then get off around the corner and rush us outside the pub. Those were great days for me and for everybody else. Frazer from Small Heath punched so hard that no one wanted to trade fists with him, so we would hurl half house bricks at him continually so he couldn't get close. Mob up, and then run them back up the road to Small Heath fighting all the way. Malardo, Smoggy and Archie were also big hitters, but we also had our own. Crock, Applehead and Cotts and Boo boo could all bang, but so could the rest of us. I was more interested in accuracy and speed than power, but this is one of the reasons we all respected each other as friends.

The main differences between the Junior Business Boys and the Zulu Warriors was age and respect. Certain lads in the Juniors have now become an integral part of the Zulu family and are well respected, but it wasn't always this way. On numerous occasions in the early 80's walking into town or looking for other rival firms, you could hear a number of the older lads complaining that they didn't want a bunch of babies following them around town. The thing that made some of the older lads uncomfortable was that they didn't trust all of the Juniors to stand if it went off, so we had to prove ourselves in hostile situations, and we did. There is no way in this world you would be trusted by the Zulu Warriors, if you haven't put your self on the line North, South, East and West of Birmingham. In our City, you don't get respect for nothing. We were the younger version of themselves, so it would be like disowning your own children if they didn't show us the ropes. The Juniors would sometimes travel to big away matches on earlier trains than the Zulu Warriors, and go shoplifting and doing reconnaissance reports before the older firm got there.

When standing outside the Knightrider or Boogies, the Juniors would march up to New Street and sit in the cafe behind the barriers and wait for away fans to land. When away supporters came up the stairs onto the main concourse, we would approach them and find out what their plans were. It didn't always work because some firms were scared of their own shadow and would charge at you making as much noise as possible in order for the Police to arrive. When firms came into New Street with Junior teams, we would always be looking for an opportunity to spank the youngsters and put the fear of God into them. London had been using this technique of terrorising away supporters in small numbers for years and we had just taken a leaf out of their book. There is nothing worse than getting to a train station very late and there are only a handful of you, and you have to get to the ground when there are still people waiting for you to come out of the station. Sometimes when really good dressers came in late usually from London, we would wait for them to get outside and jump into taxi's, some of the taxi drivers used to let us beat up away fans before they left in the cab, leaving them in a crumpled heap on the floor of the taxi, without a few their nice garments. Welcome to Birmingham New Street.

A list of Juniors who could hit you so hard, you forgot what team you supported.

Crock – Yew Trees finest
Evans – Sheldon's Proper geezer
Frazer – Small Heath massive
Brownie – C/ Wood Trooper
Ozzy – Highgate's Martial law
Smoggy – Bordesley Green click
Cotts – Yew Tree KO merchant
Herman Bro's – Stechford Double Combo
Boffy – Tile Cross gent
Smurf – Highgate massive.
Malardo – Small Heath banger.

Three lads who were rated very highly within the Juniors camp and throughout the Zulu's were Elvis & Smurf & Coaly. Elvis was one of the gamest geezers bowling round with he JBB in the early 80's and always moaned if he had to chase people up the road when a fight was about to kick off. This guy was very naughty on his day and would never leave you even if the whole world were coming to take your face clean off. He was undoubtedly a proper head from over twenty years ago with real backbone.

Smurf was the original Tasmanian devil who could fucking motor like a Ferrari.

He was a proper head way back in the day and became one of my best friends throughout these days. He should be remembered for what made him special back in the day and that was his character and his courage. Coaly is a proper geezer, hands down and make no mistake about it. From sleeping in Rackhams overnight for an earner, to chinning geezers all over the country, this guy is a proper head and a good friend of mine. Big up your chest Keith, as you are not forgotten mate. Respect is due. By the way, the incident coming back from Lichfield in the first Zulu book with the fire extinguisher was Coaly and not Cuds as suggested, I don't know how they got it wrong but I have just corrected it.

Mozza; Council estate kids

In the early to mid 70's, Birmingham City Council decided to deal with the population increase by building on green belt land in the south of the city. As a result, several new housing estates sprang up. I was fortunate enough to be educated in life on one of these estates, which was Hawksley in Kings Norton. It was full of all the usual salt of the earth social misfits, a working class community that stuck together unless it affected the earner. From the age of seven to twenty five, it was home. My school friends were a mixture of car thieves, burglars, druggies and bullies. It was during my school days that I met several lads from other areas of Kings Norton, eventually opting to hang around with the Westheath lads. This then led onto me becoming one of the 11 Kings Norton Junior Boys. The young football lads in Kings Norton totalled more than thirty with the older Kings Norton firm commanding up to eighty lads who were known and respected down the game. The Kings Norton Juniors tended to do their own thing at games in order to prove themselves more than anyone.

Introduction To Violence

My granddad got me into the Blues at the tender age of six, and by the time I was eleven I was attending game with schoolmates Haggs and Drapp. At twelve, I first came across the ICF when we played Westham at St Andrews. They came and sat in the railway end, which was the home section of the ground. They were kitted out in designer sportswear such as Fila BJ's, Lacoste, Ellesse and Tachinni. Blues scored a late equaliser and Westham came onto the pitch to front the Kop. Outside the game, everyone waited on the park for Westham to come outside, and come out they did. In those days Blues weren't always compact as a firm with areas still opting on sticking together in smaller groups. Westham marched across the park in one solid mass and together, put anyone and everyone on their toes. I was scared shitless and ran for ages but knew this was what I wanted to be when I grew up. Being together with my mates against whomever.

The Corduroy Jacket Caper 1984

In the 5th year at Whitesmore Comprehensive, Eamon Delaney and me with a number of other heads Rankin, and Wilson used to travel up to Manchester on weekdays and weekends on a regular basis, having a mooch and generally dossing about. Manchester had a number of good sports shops and casual designer boutiques we used to visit on the regular such as Wardrobe and Zip which both had quality garments by the truckload. We certainly didn't have the money for the clothes we wanted, but we needed to think of a way of making some good dough. On our rounds through the Arndale, we spot a spotted a shop selling cord jackets with hoods. They didn't look much but we tried them on anyway for a laugh. The only thing that made the cord jacket look better than it was was the rest of the designer gear we were wearing. Looking in the mirror in the shop, the jacket looked quite tidy when worn with Tacchini bottoms and Adidas Wimbledon. The only people wearing these jackets in Manchester were old ladies who were shopping, pulling one of those checked trolleys on wheels, and a few local lads. The cord jackets were checked on the inside lining and looked terrible, but if you zipped them up near to the top, they were half decent we thought. The jackets were worth only £6.50 and we bought one each but didn't think much of it at the time until we went to school on Monday. Worn with a bit of designer clobber, most people thought that the jackets looked proper tidy, so when hearing this, we laid the shit down with a trowel and told kids at school that Manchester's hooligans were all wearing this up north. This was the biggest crock of shit we had invented to create a buzz about a £6.50 corduroy hooded jacket worn by pensioners in Manchester.

We told people that the jackets were worth £20–£30 and lads at the time from school were all getting money from their parents to give to us so we could go to Manchester and pick them up a brand new old ladies' jackets. That was it. We were now travelling up to Manchester buying as many jackets as we could fit into Head bags in every colour known to man. Eamon was known to carry a great big fuckoff suitcase off the train in Manchester Piccadilly to go shopping with. We could now afford to bowl into Zip and Wardrobe, and pick up two new pieces of clobber every week for the next four months. Pub lunches, pints of beer and smoking cannabis were all on the menu, and for a couple of fifteen year old school kids, this was fucking Top Drawer, Proper Sharp, Straight Through Bread, Shogun Assassin. The corduroy jacket phenomenon spread across the rest of Birmingham like wild fire, which made us laugh out loud. People from Perry Bar to Kings Heath were now sporting corduroy hooded jackets, but most people didn't know how it all started. The Villa Youth were even seen wearing the £6.50 cord special, and combined with their hair permed at the back and four sovereigns on one hand, they thought they looked the part. For us, the whole cord caper was a fluke, a blag that seemed to stretch and evolve into other areas of Birmingham. To this day, I don't know of any other firm in the UK that wore the corduroy jacket with the hood, so in that sense we were being innovative for the time. Style is something you have or you don't have, and that's a fact. Many people who attended football matches were sheep with regards to what makes of clothing they would wear, but if you have got a touch of style, you can make a £6.50 corduroy jacket look like the trendiest piece of clobber around if worn with the right accessories.

Wrap a Burberry scarf loosely round your neck, slap on your C-17 baggy jeans and a pair of Nike Internationalist, and you're away. Splendid, splendid. As far as I'm aware, Eamon was the first person in Birmingham to sport a pair of Adidas green Trim Trabb which he got from a sports shop in Manchester and pissed me right off because we were both hunting the shops for them, as Tottenham had shown us how cool they were the season before. Shawy, Ellerman and Avery all had a tickle on the corduroy jacket scene, but it was only after a few months of good earnings from this business, they got switched on to making some good cheddar from it themselves.

APEX TO ZULU A2Z!

1st Jan 1985 Sheffield United BBC – away

Sheffield is another place that finds it extremely difficult to tell the truth as their firm can only manage results against firms when they are at home.

The difference between Birmingham and Sheffield is vast when talking about firms, even though Birmingham has only played a handful of friendly European games throughout its history. Birmingham have a reputation Sheffield could only dream of. When Birmingham tend to come up against firms like this, then if the Blades get hold of a much smaller group of fans, they will kick you till you are unconscious and keep on kicking you while you are out cold. When confronted by the full firm, these same people will be the ones who all want to run away, because they are not used to fighting a proper full firm with a proper pedigree. Have a quick look at The Blades book and you will notice they have never lost a fight. How can this be? There are a number of other firms who claim to be in the X-men who have never lost fights before, so let's see what they say when the truth comes out. Yawn fucking yawn. People would think a little more of you if you told the truth, lads, but to make yourselves sound amazing, you opted to lie through your teeth. Tut, tut, shame on you and your amazing firm that has over the years done nothing in Birmingham, nothing in London and a little in the north. You should be ashamed of yourselves for putting out a book that should clearly be placed on the fiction stands of all crap bookstores.

Mozza

On the 1st January 85, we played Sheffield Utd at Bramall Lane. The word was that everyone was getting the 9.00am train from New Street. The trouble was that most of the firm were still in bed nursing hangovers from the night before.

20 Juniors and around 25 of the older lads caught the 9.00am train to Sheffield as the advance party. We got to Sheffield and walked out of the station with no old bill in sight. We were milling about deciding what to do, when this geezer comes bowling up the road and walks straight through the lot of us, arms swinging in the classic window wiper style. One of the Yardley lads, little Stig, decides on whacking

him. This local lad jumps back into the road and says, "You want it, if you want it wait here." He then runs off across this island and up a side road. We waited for about five minutes and decided this was a blagg, headed off towards the town centre. Behind us a roar went up and around 100 Sheffield lads now come

charging out of this side road and across the island at us. Blues grouped together and looked at the older lads to take the lead, but no one seemed eager to lead the line. Finally Clive & Fats flew into them, closely followed by Smurf and M.Bray of the Juniors. The rest of our firm followed suit as we stopped Sheffield dead in their tracks on our side of the island. Fighting was erupting right across the road, and for a few minutes it raged back and forth with each firm regrouping every now and then before charging back into the thick of it. Finally we regrouped one last time and the roar went up which gives every Bluenose an extra bit of oomph when the charge is on. We ran into them and they broke, but before they had a chance to regroup, we attacked them again and this time they were on their toes. Even though they had double our numbers, Birmingham held it together and got the result.

The old bill had been arriving for sometime at the scene, but was unable to get a foothold between the warring factions. Now one side had collapsed, the police moved in and around us to get us all together. The older lads couldn't believe it, one of them saying, "Fucking hell, there's only 20 of us with a few kids to back us up." Another lad said, "What you on about, they were gamer than us."

The old bill escorted us to the ground but it was still only mid-day, so they left us outside the ground with three hours to go before kick off. One of the most clued up lads said to everyone present, "They'll be back to check on us" and as sure as spit is saliva, a van comes crawling around the corner, parked up for a few minutes then sped off up the road. We decided to catch a bus back into town, as there were only about twenty-five of us left due to the fact that Birmingham lads had jumped the escort at every opportunity while we were walking to the ground.

We noticed a few cars going past with lads in, then shortly out of a side street around 40 Sheffield came at us. As most of our 20 or so were Juniors, we didn't stand much of a chance. We had a go but just didn't have the weight of age to deal with the situation and we ended up on our toes. Their numbers seemed to be swelling as our lessened. About five of us now ended up back at Sheffield train station in the rail bar. We watched as Sheffield flooded the concourse. We armed ourselves with plastic cutlery, we knew this was no good, but we needed to hold something due to the numbers now coming after us. The first few started slowly coming through the glass doors, smiling sickly, we were about to be annihilated and there was nowhere to go. A Yew Tree Junior called Crock appeared from nowhere and smacked this smiling Sheffield lad right on the chin, then suddenly the back of The Blades firm seemed to just get wiped out. They had just been hit by a much stronger force. The second wave of Blues' firm had just arrived and Sheffield were kicked off the concourse and ran outside onto the forecourt. Thank fuck the days when British Rail trains ran on time. This later train had arrived with 300 of Birmingham's finest casuals. The few Sheffield who had come into the bar stood frozen while it was our turn to smirk. We didn't land on them but we could have wiped them out no problem, but they knew what they had just seen and the potential was enough.

Georgie

Blues took a good firm of around 300 good lads to Sheffield on this bank holiday and landed around an hour and a half before the game. Myself and a number of juniors used to jump the train on every occasion, but this also meant people had to wait for you for an extra ten minutes or so before you found a way out of the station. This is what happened on this day. Blues had carried on across the road into the centre of Sheffield and around ten of us waited for the rest of the fare dodgers to arrive from the station. We now walked into the centre and up a hill, passing a corner pub on the right. There were a few lads standing outside who were definitely Blades, but they didn't say a word, which I thought was strange. Most of the twelve Brummies were 14–16 years olds with around four older lads from The Yew Tree and Bordesley Green. When we passed the pub and started to walk up the hill, the pub behind emptied into the road and there were now around a hundred and fifty Sheffield United's firm shouting us and calling it on.

We knew we didn't have the numbers to stand and trade toe to toe, so one of the older Yew Tree lads told every body to start jogging. As we reached the top of the hill in the shopping centre with pint glasses bouncing all around us in the road, Selby tells us to wait a while and let them get a little closer, before we start to jog down the middle of the shopping area. When Sheffield got around 30 feet away, Blues start jogging again. Sheffield centre was pretty empty on bank holiday, except for us, and this group of Blades who were trying their best to catch up and do us some damage.

What still makes me laugh, was the fact that before we had walked past the pub full of Sheffield United, Blues' firm had gone the same way ten minutes before and Sheffield must have stayed in the pub, which gives you an idea of the sort of place we were in. Blues now were half way down the centre of the shopping area, and the two brothers from Bordesley Green, Selby from the Yew Tree and a guy named after the famous American diet, Atkins, all stood and so did we. Psychology was used again by Blues firm knowing that the further these lads have to come and get us, the more knackered they would be when they arrive, this was the genius of Selby. We now tooled up and picked up advertising boards and potted plants commandeered outside a gardening store. We waited for the first lot of Sheffield to catch us up because in a firm you always get loonies who want to get into it before every one else arrives, you get people who are running faster than anyone else to kick it off. Blues made as much of a line as they could then, all of a sudden, a flare gun is set off by Blues, which stops Sheffield in their tracks. All you can see is a bright green light flying up the centre of the shopping precinct and the Blades part like the Red Sea to let the flare carry on up the street. Blues are still standing and waiting for the fastest runners from the Blades to get to us. "Crack," one guy gets levelled, and then "Slap," another gets an advertising board wrapped round his head. Blues are now running from side to side lobbing plant pots as if they were taking a throw in with a football, shouting, "Come on nen." The rest of Sheffield's firm of lads arrive and as they do, Blues let off another flare gun, which hits one of the Blades. Blues take a left out of the centre across a dual carriageway bridge that goes up and across, then up and across then across. As we are going up and across, the Blades are not bothering with the bridge, but are instead jumping the fence of the busy dual carriageway and running across the road to beat us to the other side.

Police sirens are now heard and they catch up with us, and escort Birmingham's firm of twelve to Sheffield United's ground. As we are standing outside the ground, Sheffield's firm walks past us and the usual verbal exchanges are flung around until we see the geezer who was shot in his leg bleeding and hobbling past us trying to look as main as he could. We all burst out laughing at him and the police then shove us into the ground to watch the game. Octopus had written on the wall in the away end of the toilets, Zulu Juniors BCFC, which made me laugh because we had only been in the ground for two minutes.

Mozza

Around 60 of Blues' top lads decided they were going to go into Sheffield's Utd's seats. So half an hour before the game, the Birmingham lot practised there best Yorkshire accents and entered the ground. They got into the upper tier of the side stand and sat near the front, but we were then moved by Cuds, who got us to sit right at the back of the stand instead so we would be fighting downhill as it went off. Sheffield Utd's firm were coming in the seats, clocking us and then disappearing back down under the stairs. It was obvious they were firming up under the stand, and shortly the roar went up, and in they came. Everyone was chomping at the bit to get at them, but Cuds was cool as he ran the show. "Wait, wait! Now! Our roar went up, ZULUUUUUUUUUUUU! And we charged down the seats into them. We were just too tight and organised for them, and after an initial exchange of punches, they were off. Some of them even jumped into the lower terraces to get away from the Birmingham firm.

Georgie

As we got to the front of the away stand, we were told that around sixty Blues were sitting in the Sheffield seats where all the Blades sit in the top tier waiting for them to come in. If they thought they had fun in the centre fighting mostly juniors, then let's see what they're like when they meet the older crew. Blues are now sitting in the middle of Sheffield United firm and the crazy thing is that a number of the Sheffield lads were nodding at the Blues lot thinking they were with them. At the away end of the ground where most of the other Blues fans were, Birmingham fans started pointing in unison singing "Zulu's gonna get ya – Zulu's gonna get ya." A flare gun is fired from the Birmingham end into the Sheffield end of the ground.

Blues made their presence known by standing up in the middle of the Blades firm holding their arms out on either side, and shouting "ZULUUUUUUUUUU" and wading straight into Sheffield's firm punching everybody in sight. Sheffield fans were running across the tops of the seats to get out of trouble and the away end of the ground all cheered as Blues ran amok in Sheffield's seats, sending many of the Blades jumping into the lower stands where they were safe. The police now came into the seats and started to smash everyone and anyone over the heads with truncheons then they escorted Blues through the seats where they still had to battle Sheffield United fans to get onto the pitch. The sixty or so Blues firm were now bowling round the side of the pitch and waving to all the Sheffield firm in the seats, as the Blues away end were singing and pointing at the firm singing "Zulu, Zulu, Warrior, Zulu, Zulu, Warrior." It was another monumental day for Birmingham City who won the game 4–3. When you do everything best on a football day and you know it, there is no better feeling in the world. One of their lads gets shot with a flare gun, The Blade gets run out of their own seats in their ground, Blues get escorted round the pitch waving to Sheffield's firm, and we win the game 4–3. What a fucking beautiful day. Somebody get me my sunglasses and an ice-cold beer.

Brighton & Hove Albion away Oct 1980

Travelling into Birmingham early in the morning, the Trooper mob combined with chaps from Northfield, Alum Rock, Stirchley and Billesley caught the train from New Street to London.

A well known lad from Northfield with a few of his friends were using West Midlands bus passes all the way to London and on to

Brighton without any ticket collector even batting an eyelid. When asked for a ticket, the Blues lads from Northfield, especially Mcquaide, used to flash their bus passes and say, "This is the working man's pass mate." The reply would be, "Oh, OK." These were the days when the National Exhibition Centre was just an idea, and in to get into Birmingham you had to travel into town on either bus or local train. The Birmingham mob were entering the crossover of styles but were still favouring the Brogue and Gibson shoes, Pilot jackets and Harrington's with Levi jeans and Fred Perry T- shirts. A small mob of Blues arrive at Euston 70 handed and instantly spot a bunch of lads with funny haircuts that are long on one side and short on the other, what we would call wedge heads. They had Slazenger V necks sweaters with round neck T-shirts on with gold chains hanging out, and Farah slacks. Due to this firm wearing a lot of red, Birmingham thought it was Arsenal, but it turned out to be a mob of around 25 Cockney reds. Birmingham rushed them on Euston station and smacked the shit out of them before catching the underground train to Victoria to get to Brighton. It was quite an uneventful day for Birmingham so they ended up hitting the pubs to sink more than a few before the game. Mcquaide, while drinking in a large pub in Brighton, decides on taking his trousers down and standing on a table in the middle of a Brighton pub. With tattoos all over him and two eyes tattooed onto his arse cheeks, he looked like something out of a sideshow. The 70 Blues fans that had been drinking for most of the day were so bored with the match that they all sat down in the stand. Saint John Ambulance carried Troganite out of the ground due to him suffering from alcoholic poisoning from drinking Snakebites all day. After the game, Birmingham travelled back into London Euston, having a few scuffles here and there but nothing of much interest. A mob of black guys from London were on the Tube and didn't take kindly to seeing a mob of white skins and decided to let their feeling out. What they didn't know is that the group of skins that travelled to away matches from Chelmsley Wood were anti racist against the right wing elements, or idiots from London who couldn't keep their mouths shut. The black guys from Chelmsley steam into the black guys from London and give them a right hiding. Even worse was to come because the lads from London now get off the Tube and get bashed again but this time by everybody from Birmingham, leaving them on the platform floor.

Birmingham now catch the train back home and are walking through the carriages, when they spot the Two Tone band, Bad Manners, on the train. The Birmingham lot sit down with the group who are off to Coventry City centre to play a gig. The Birmingham lads fancied a drink on the journey home, but the buffet car is locked with the shutters down and the Birmingham lads are pulling at the shutters to steal some beer. They manage to force open the shutters but not all the way and are getting some of the smaller skins to try to sneak under the slightly ajar shutters. Coo Coo? No, Troganite? No. None of them would fit through until a 12-year-old skinhead called McCormick, who was a lot younger than the rest of the lads, got under the shutters and started passing four packs of beer through the opening. The Birmingham lot sat down with Bad Manners and listened to Buster Bloodvessel singing a melody of their hits, while the Birmingham lads plied the pop group with stolen beer from the buffet car.

Brighton away 6th Oct 84

Sitting in a pub in Castle Bromwich having a drink in the afternoon with a geezer called Plug. Plug was a good lad from the local area who was as bored as me. We were contemplating jumping the train to go to Brighton, but it was also if we could be arsed to just get up and go the night before. We knew a load of Blues fans had already gone a few hours before, and we were in two minds whether to sit there and get smashed or to go and have some fun in Brighton. We checked our pockets for dough and both had enough money for the train, but didn't want to pay, so we didn't. We got on the train to London and arrived around ten thirty on Friday evening, caught a tube to Waterloo, then got on the train again free of charge and landed in Brighton at about 11.30pm. Brighton's nightlife was in full swing and so were some of the Junior Business Boys. We were told local lads were chasing five Blues fans around the streets of Brighton with kitchen knives for the past half hour, and it turned out to be some of the Yew Tree Juniors. Elvis took a bit of a slap by some locals in a bus depot, until

APEX TO ZULU A2Z!

Birmingham now grouped up 30 handed and went to deal with this situation. A guy from Kings Heath also had the hood of his corduroy jacket pulled off in a minor skirmish, but there wasn't too much to report the night before except that we had to sleep on the station, as we were too late to get a B&B. At around 1.00am a few cars pulled up full of Blues fans. One guy had thrown up all over his Farahs and was trying to find the toilets to wash the crap off his slacks. We all got some rest for a few hours and some slept in the cars and some on benches and it was a grim night but hopefully after a breakfast in the morning, we would be ready for a new day. Birmingham lost the game 2–0 and had a little scuffle in the ground, but the best was yet to come. Birmingham's firm of around 300 now bowled round to the away end at Brighton to get some knuckle. They arrived near a tunnel singing, "We love you Brighton we do, we love you Brighton we do, we love you Brighton we do, Oh Brighton we love you." I still cannot believe this trick worked, because from my knowledge, Brighton had hardly any black fans, so you would think that they would have cottoned on to us. A few juniors clocked some younger Brighton dressers near the tunnel in the scene from the movie Quadrophenia, and they were severely dealt with and taxed of a leather and suede jacket that didn't button up and was placed over the head like a cagoule, which was quite fashionable at the time. Birmingham now ran though the tunnel, and a Blues fan fell over and was repeatedly kicked all over the floor before the rest of Birmingham realised he was also a Blue nose. In the distance, Birmingham could see Brighton's firm standing outside the home end, and started singing again towards the Brighton lot who didn't take much notice of us coming out of the tunnel because we were all singing about their team. As we get at least twenty feet away from Brighton's firm, Birmingham let out a huge roar, ZULUUUUUUUUUUU! Brighton are slapped outside their main stand and scatter into the distance. Birmingham are now escorted to the train station and are standing outside waiting for the train, when a police car pulls up with the guy who lost his leather and suede jacket getting out with them. The young teenage Brighton lad is sporting a huge black eye, and is now walking down the line of Blues fans trying to pick out the guy who bashed him and robbed his jacket.

DAVID C GEORGE

Sorry pal, your jacket was now on the way back to Birmingham, and was sold on the train for £30. Cheers by the way.

The Gov'nors & Man City Snipers away 10th Nov 84

Manchester is the third largest city in the UK and has heaps of passion and pride within the local people. This was a day for everybody to be looking sharp because Manchester City's Gov'nors have a reputation for coming straight at you for knuckle, especially at home.

Birmingham land at Manchester Piccadilly 500-handed for this journey. On this day Blues firm was heavy duty with most top boys from individual areas of Birmingham all representing. I know people say there is only one top boy at Blues, but to my knowledge there are several people in the same category, but some are not as well known as others. As we leave the station, we bowl straight down the road towards the shopping precinct, keeping an eye out for dibble. I'm not sure if I can explain this feeling properly but I will try to explain it to those people out there who have never been involved with a proper firm. There is a feeling you get when your walking down the road in a foreign town with your friends, and you look to your left and right and you get an overwhelming surge of adrenalin through your body, accompanied by the feeling that nobody is fucking with this today, and we are in your town, full hammer.

On my left is the Kings Norton firm, on my right Highgate, in front is the Bruckshop crew, Lea Hall, Acocks Green, Bordesley Green, Quinton, Chelmsley Wood, Yew Tree, Handsworth, Maypole, Billesley and everywhere else I've missed out. The Bruckshop crew were part of Blues firm who used to go to a few home and away games for a laugh and to kick racist's heads in, but the main reason they were there was to have an earner. As we are bowling into the precinct, a number of the Bruckshop crew are pulling gold chains from local shopper necks as they walk past them. The Bruckshop crew take Blues' firm into the Arndale, which wasn't actually on the agenda. Blues are now in the Arndale 500 handed, and a jeweller's window goes through. The alarm goes off and the Arndale security tries to stop 500 Zulus in a shopping centre. Birmingham are now trying to get out of the Arndale up a set of escalators, but are being stopped by a security guard near the top, who must have watched far too many action movies.

He holds out his truncheon and tells everybody to get back, and then he loses his truncheon and gets thrown off the escalators onto his face. A few Manchester City lads were in the centre, and come a cropper, as they were collared by Birmingham fans who were now all over the Arndale trying to find a way out. As we get to the top of the escalators, the Manchester riot police rush into the Arndale holding huge plastic shields and wearing equipment that made them look like storm troopers from Star Wars. Blues are now escorted out of the Arndale with a huge police presence, and are walked all the way to Manchester City's football ground. Around seven of the Juniors were not in the escort and were walking behind Blues' firm as we walked towards Moss Side. We got near Moss Side; then the seven of us took a diversion and got to the stadium before Blues arrived. We entered newsagents, which is across the road from Man City's ground to buy some refreshments and stand and wait for Blues firm to arrive. As we are chatting, we see a huge firm at the end of the road walking towards the ground with a number of black lads at the front. This was our mistake, because we immediately thought this was Blues firm. Wrong! It was the Manchester City Gov'nors bowling straight towards us 400 handed, with some black geezer with an Afro, right at the front with his hands behind his back, and his neck grotesquely stretched forward, flashing his gritted teeth. We all tried to keep calm in this situation, because the worst thing you can do when things are on top, is to run like a yelping dog, so we all kept it tight and backed off round the corner. As we turn the corner, Blues escort arrives down the other street, which was a godsend, but Man City were still right in front of us and getting closer. Man City's Young Gov'nors arrive now about 20 handed and are standing on the opposite side of the road from us looking for some action.

One Manchester guy steps into the road and asks for a straightener with Skully from Birmingham, and Skully being Skully obliges by running straight into this lad and putting him on his arse, but as this is going on, five more of Man City's Snipers join in and start kicking Skully on the floor. I'm holding half a can of Tango in my hand which I throw at one of the lads from Manchester and bounce into the road to defend my friend, but as I do this, I was unlucky enough to be grabbed by a copper on a horse, who decided on taking me for a jog on tiptoe around the ground by the scruff of my neck through Man City's firm.

Fats grabs an umbrella from Elvis and goes straight into Man City. It went right up in the air outside the ground with The Gov'nors and Birmingham Zulu's and the police let it go off for a while before stepping in. Birmingham were clued up when it came to pyrotechnics, and had created acid smoke bombs to throw at Man City, or to drop on people who had been spanked and gone down to the floor. Coaly was pretending to be my brother, which was funny in itself because he is mixed race and looks nothing like me. He was pleading with the police officer to let me go, and the reply was. "Fuck off you little black cunt, or you're next." The police officer now has me standing in the middle of Man City's firm waiting to be arrested. Some young Mancs are walking past me and giving it large, but to be honest by then, I was only concerned with going to watch the game. As they put me in a room and sit me down, the police tell me they are arresting me for violent disorder. As I said previously, the police are very much the same as lions on the plains of Africa, and when they wish to eat, they go for the easy prey in the herd. A sixteen-year-old guy in the middle of a full-scale brawl involving around 200 fans, and they manage to get hold of a teenager who looks around the age of fourteen. Give that Old Bill a cigar. I lied about my age to the police officer and pretended to cry saying I was thirteen had lost my Dad near the shops. The officer must have thought I was too young to beat up and arrest, so he let me go and I walked round to the away end at Maine Road making sure I wasn't being followed. What I noticed in Manchester is that the police are very much into making their Manchester fans look better than they are. If Man City fans are kicking you all over the floor, the police will turn a blind eye, but if you as an away supporter show any glimpse of retaliation, they will come down on you like a ton of bricks.

Some of the Snipers had a style of dress that was alien to us Brummies, that of the tweed jacket with the huge Levi flares. I had seen this style a few times throughout the day and thought it suited the little manc dressers, but I don't think that style would have gone down to well in

Brum, even though the JBB did sometimes slip on a pair of whopping great flares occasionally, to the disgust of the older Blues lads.

Second's Away – Round Two Manchester City away.

The next occasion Blues went to Manchester City, around twelve Juniors had a van outside New Street with a driver. Kelly from Small Heath was with us, but that's another story I wish I had known the ending to before he'd got in the van. We had had it with the Gov'nors and the Snipers on our last visit, and even had a tickle in the Arndale, but this time we drove straight to the ground and parked up the van and went in search of the Man City Snipers in small numbers. This is what made the Junior Business Boys a proper firm in the eighties, because I don't know of any, and I mean any, firms of youngsters twelve handed that would attempt this around Birmingham City's ground. There were no tactics from us on this day, as all we wanted to do was park up, and walk round the ground and just hit em hard.

Black Stuart, Boo boo, and Lawless were all there as we walked past a pub full of Man City's lads, but they didn't come after us because our average age was 16, so they were not interested in us, which was a relief. As we carry on past the pub with our hearts in our mouths, we bump into a small mob of Man City Snipers. They are standing outside a bus stop talking when one of the lads from Manchester gets a smack in the mouth and as this happens, they all look round to see only a small mob of Junior Business Boys standing in the main road with their arms behind their backs saying, "What ya saying then ya Mank fuck, let's av it?" Fair play to the Snipers though, because they did have it with us and it was toe to toe battling, on one occasion the Snipers backed us off across the road until we got outside a newsagents, then the tables turned again. Blues picked up crates of milk bottles and ran at Man City Snipers who took foot up the road, which we were relieved about, even though we had brought it to them on their manor. As we are standing there smiling and stroking each other's egos, Lawless looks up the Coronation Street style road, with the washing lines straight across it and says at the top of his voice. "Eeeerrrrr, lads there here." As we all look up, we see at least 70 Man City Snipers now calmly walking towards us covering both sides of the pavement and the middle of the road.

Boo-boo is rallying the troops as the twelve of us line up in the road to take on the Snipers. Lawless was worried and should of kept his comments to himself, because when you are so outnumbered by another firm, the last thing you want to hear from one of your chaps is negativity.

The Man City Snipers are now about twenty foot away from us and they all just stop and look at us. We are all moving from side to side bouncing up and down on the balls of our feet with our hands up and fists clenched, but the Manks don't move. Then a tall black Sniper pushes his way to the front of their firm holding a huge kitchen knife, we turn and run with Snipers right on our heals. Black Stuart is reluctant to run and is at the back of us slowing down drop kicking any Manks who come near him as he is laughing at them. We get onto the main road and the scene is like a classic sketch from The Benny Hill Show.

Two vans full of police now skid at the side of us and take charge of the situation by sending the Snipers the other way, while we were told to get into the ground. The police now drive off and the Juniors walk round by the football ground to pay into the game. As we get to the turnstiles, we realise they are not even open yet, so we stand outside having a chat about the scuffle. The only thing is that this was the old ground situated in Moss Side, and unfortunately the layout of the ground means the Snipers entrance into the game is right next to us.

Manchester Snipers have now emerged from a side street with even bigger numbers, and are coming straight for us. It might sound strange to all of you there who think the police are doing a good job, but the police were there in vans and cars outside the ground watching this go on. Blues Juniors have nowhere to go because behind us was a brick wall and in front was around a hundred Snipers. This was do or die time. We lined up against the wall with our heartbeats going like the clappers, we looked at each other for a couple of seconds, and without saying a word, our faces changed from fear, to fuck it. Personally, I thought that if I am going to be mullard on this day, I will tear someone's throat out with my teeth before I die. We rush the Snipers swinging lefts and rights outside the ground, and they back off. Man

City Snipers come again and I'm shoulder to shoulder with Boo-boo as we rushed them again and they back off, but just like a fly at a barbecue, they just wont go away. We simply didn't have enough lads to bum rush The Snipers properly, but we thought that if we are going to get a kicking, then we are going to make sure we all take a few Manks to the hospital with us. As The Snipers come again, I'm collard by the Old Bill who drags me off into a van parked outside the ground, then he and his partner sit there watching it still going off. I can only think these two police officers were making bets on who was going to get beaten up as they didn't seem that bothered about what we were doing until we flash the whites of our gritted teeth and retaliate. I am now driven away from the ground with two police officers who are telling me we shouldn't be fighting at football matches, even though the pair of them must look forward to it as much as any casual in the country. The one copper tells me he's going to teach me a lesson which turned out to be him dropping me off in the middle of a housing estate about three miles away from the ground, and kicking me out of the van while laughing.

I'm not sure what area it was, but it was the type of place similar to where I was from in Birmingham. This must have been the Manchester equivalent to Chelmsely Wood, and was not supposed to survive around here. I walk up the main road and spot a bus stop with a huge queue of lads all City fans talking and generally having a laugh. I stand at the back of the cue and take out some money, but then realise I didn't know how much it was to the ground. As I knew all these guys were football heads, I just waited to hear what the guy in front of me said, and just put in the right change without saying a word.

As I'm sitting upstairs on the bus, I also realised I didn't know where to get off the bus to go to the game, so I waited for the majority of City fans to get up and off when everyone else did. I had got back to the ground and missed only ten minutes of the game, which wasn't bad really, considering I could have been lying in a puddle of blood somewhere with footprints all over my head, or arrested.

Manchester City Vs Birmingham City

Birmingham took around 100 lads to Manchester on the train and were relaxing and taking it easy. As Birmingham approached Stockport, Sooty gets a phone call from another Birmingham lad who has just landed at Manchester Piccadilly.

He says, "You lot are going nowhere mate, there's fucking hundreds of riot police with dogs and everything." Police on horseback are all waiting for your arrival at the station. Birmingham's firm decided to get off the train in Stockport instead of getting off in Manchester, and all caught taxis from Stockport into Manchester.

As they were leaving the train in Stockport, Blues numbers had swelled to around 250 good lads and were now on the way into Manchester with no police presence at all. A Brummy lad has just explained the situation taking place in Manchester when the Birmingham train pulls in. "All of the riot police were ready to start on the Birmingham fans including the dogs and the coppers on horses, they were getting ready for treating people like absolute shit for the simple fact that they will try and defend themselves against people who want to fight them." As the train pulls up in Manchester, the riot police were ready, dogs ready; horses were ready to make Birmingham's day a complete nightmare. The police are all standing there with dogs barking all in a row waiting to see the brummy firm get off the train, but no. The only people to come off the train were a couple of old ladies and some school kids. The police had made a huge blunder that must have cost them hundreds of thousands of pounds. Defending yourself in the UK is seen as a crime and should not be tolerated, but you can also say that as a working class person following Birmingham City, what is the alternative? If you're wearing designer clothing at a football match that makes you look as if you're a casual even though you're not, you are in for a rude awakening. The idea back in the day was to wear the garments in order to stand out to other like-minded casuals and thugs. It has now got to the stage where everyone from the milkman to the lad selling the Big Issue dresses like a casual and the style has been battered good and proper. The thing was to put on your best clobber to show the other firm you are better than them in every way, including, style of clothes, courage, your songs, your team and even the way you walked. This mentality is exactly the same when a military army meets another army. Testosterone and competition are extremely high indeed. Birmingham met up at a hotel in Manchester and it was rammed solid full of Blues firm. Manchester City knew we were in there as a few of them were walking past. Blues now marched 300 through Manchester centre and up to the ground. We got into the ground where it banged right off in the seats with the old bill because they are another gang who love to cause trouble. A police officer loses a few teeth while it goes mental in the ground. After the game the police tried to keep Birmingham in the ground when Sooty was already standing outside.

Man City were in small numbers all over the place outside when the doors to the away end have burst open, and a huge firm of Birmingham now came bowling out of Man Cities ground. Blues were standing on a huge car park when a fight has broken out with the old bill. Blues firm now gets split up into two groups, with Sooty, Claude and The General all in one group. There were 60 to 80 lads in the one escort when Man City have had a go. It went up in the air with people smacking the crap out of each other all up the main road. As Birmingham walked down the road, Man City have made themselves known and it's gone off big time.

The police have come and split us apart as Birmingham carry on marching up the road. As they reach the next corner, Man City have come again and this was just head on. Bang, bang, bang as people were being filled in and kicked in the face while still standing, this was proper. The Man City firm were game as fuck and this has to be said about The Gov'nors because they do properly come and have a go when they want to. Birmingham carried on walking and had it yet again with Man City when loads of fruit and vegetables were thrown at them outside a convenience store. You may laugh, but have you ever had a potato thrown in your face at full pelt? Birmingham now walked up to Manchester Piccadilly where they herd that there was a pub near the station that was full of their boys. There was about 200 manks in the pub with a proper good firm but we couldn't get at them due to old bill. Birmingham now sees an absolute massive firm standing outside Manchester Piccadilly around 500. The 60 Blues lads are now being escorted toward this huge firm, which they were not very happy with as they thought it was The Gov'nors. The whole of the street outside Manchester Piccadilly was rammed full of this firm and the old bill didn't hesitate to walk our much smaller firm up there. As Birmingham got close to this other firm, it turns out to be all Birmingham's mob that got split off from their firm outside the ground.

Oldham Athletic away 84

First game of the season in 84 and the sun is smiling over Birmingham's masses. Birmingham has put together a good firm for today but not for Oldham Athletic because Oldham was simply not in the same frequency as Man City or Man Utd, who were the firms to be bothered with. Everybody has on their best clothes to go and represent for Birmingham today, and all the people who turned up on the day were well dressed. If you go to an area in the country where most people talk out of their noses, and sound as though they have a cold all year round, you know you have to expect the unexpected. Blues get to Manchester Piccadilly and there are two Man Utd heads waiting for blues on the station. One black guy and one white. We instantly knew they were Man Utd because the black lad had a huge pair of flare jeans on with cord shoes, with a shirt buttoned all the way up to the top. They are giving it a bit of mouth and checking on our numbers trying to arrange a meet for later after the game. Birmingham's firm bowl across to the next train station in Manchester Victoria, to get to Oldham, but before they go, they decide to go and have a bit of a mooch to see what they can see.

Blues firm is 350 strong for this day, and the fountain near New Street must have been completely empty. Every knuckle dragger, crook and brawler from Birmingham who supported Birmingham City was in Manchester and looking for some serious action with The Gov'nors or The Red Army. Man Utd were also playing at home on the same day, so there was a strong chance of us bumping into each other before the day was done.

A centre punch was used on a jeweller's window in Manchester, and trays of gold went missing before we got into Oldham. Some Oldham lads were in the pub where a firm of Birmingham decided to have a drink, and the one was wearing some nice clothes, when Davies has asked the lad to strip off, leaving his Fila tracksuit and Tachini T-shirt on the bar. "I'll have that, and that as well, he says. The lad looked at Davies as if he was joking, but he wasn't. The Oldham lad left the pub bare chested from the waist up.

The Birmingham fans had a good mob out on this day, with the town Zulu's combined for this excursion. As Birmingham reach Oldham's ground they break open a fence and march into the away end with the rest of the Birmingham supporters cheering them as they entered. A game of roughhouse football was taking place in the ground on the terraces, with a football being kicked all over the stands. Someone had booted the ball over to a group of old bill standing in our end of the ground, and many people went over and started kicking the old bill and then trying to explain they were only after the ball. Alex from the Yew Tree gets pissed and goes into the Oldham end of the ground and gets a bashing before being dragged out by the old bill. I could say more about this character, but he has chosen his route in life, which differs to my way of looking at things, so lets just leave it at that. A few Birmingham lads were talking to a girl from Oldham near the fencing, separating the away end from the home end. She was sporting a lot of jewellery, a good few rings and chains ECT. A Birmingham lad was asking her to pass her gold through the fence so he could try it on, and believe it or not, she did. The Birmingham lot stood there with this girls gold sovereigns and chains on smiling, when the stewards came along and got the gold chains and rings back off them and gave them back to the local girl. Birmingham won the game 1–0 from an own goal by Clements. After the game Birmingham fans gave it to the old bill up and down the main road outside the ground. It was missile heaven, with the old bill having to retreat at least four times when they were under fire. I don't think the local police were ready for a firm like Birmingham as they lost control of the situation for a good half hour until we got to the station that takes us back into Manchester. A police sergeant came to talk to the Birmingham firm before we caught the train back into Manchester, and he was just standing there insulting the Birmingham fans saying, "In all my years I have never experienced what had taken place here today." Just as he was about to carry on speaking, a brick has been thrown which

161

slaps the sergeant on the side of his head, knocking his flat hat off. The Birmingham crowd cheers and the sergeant goes mental, "Get these lot out of here right now." The police now start ramming the blues fans with the horses on the station while the rest of the police are on the embankment. A blues lad picks up a 4ft plank of wood in his hand and calls one of the officers. "Oi." As he turns round the plank of wood is propelled forward and hits the officer side-on slicing his face wide open. The officer is holding his face while shouting to other's, "Get that black bastard." The Birmingham lad ducks into the crowd and takes his tops off and vanishes into the middle of the crowd while swapping tops with another blues fan. A police dog goes mental and grabs hold of the front of a Birmingham lads trousers, resulting in punctured teeth marks in his testicles. Blood was pouring from the lad's balls while were waiting for the train. I'm not sure what happened to this poor unfortunate guy who was in the wrong place at the wrong time, but he will never forget the scars on his knackers and the pain.

Birmingham now arrives back into Manchester with a huge escort of police, but around 30 blues escaped the escort and went walkabout around Manchester, This is when Ozzy was scouting a hundred yards in front of our small firm and was pinged

by one of the Man Utd who had met us at the station in the morning. Ozzy was seeing three of everybody, and was proper dazzled by this Mancs Judas tactics.

A short while later, Birmingham did bump into Man Utd who were keen to kick it off with Birmingham but the police were there to make sure nothing occurred.

Rankin was thrown into a meat wagon and driven away with a van full of Manchester old bill. The Manchester sergeant has now got into the van and said to an officer, "Have you nicked him, what did he do?" "No, no," replied the officer, "He didn't do anything but he was there." With this, the sergeant has now put on his big black gloves, looked at Rankin with his knotted eyebrows and says in a broad Manchester accent, "Right then, next time you come to Manchester, "WHACK..! Be on best behaviour." He has now punched Rankin full force in his face which nearly knocked him clean out, then dropped him off at

APEX TO ZULU A2Z!

Manchester Piccadilly station walking sideways into the station trying to get his bearings. Carl was only 15 years of age at the time and had just left school.

The Inch High Posse Vs JBB's 86

Stechford fair is in full swing, with mobs of heads from different areas of Birmingham standing about and chatting. A firm of young black geezers from Handsworth called the Inch High, had robbed a couple of guys of sovereign rings on the fair, and had chinned them in the process. I used to love days like this, when people from other manors turn up and start to push their weight around not knowing who, or what they are dealing with. A couple of white guys wearing some nice clobber with a bit of jewellery must be idiot season for stupid muggers. I get a phone call at the Trooper pub from a pal at The Malthouse, who asks me if I can get a firm together in half hour, in which I say, I'll have a word with em, and then walk up to the Malthouse. As the lad who phoned me is a proper good mate, I got 25 lads from the Trooper up to the Malthouse to meet Lea Hall. As we get to the Bell chippy, the Malthouse pub empties onto the car park with the Lea Hall firm doubling the size of the Trooper on this occasion. We all get on the 14 bus and fill it front to back; a chap explains the plan to everybody from Lea Hall and Chelmsley Wood. As we get off the 14 bus opposite the petrol station, a Lea Hall bod tells it how it is. "Right, we're gonna go down there to the entrance of the fair, tool up and line up, then walk through the fair and spank the lot of them." I must admit that this sounded good, but when we got to the entrance to the fair, there were a number of Inch High who had already clocked us. ZUUUUUUUUULUU! We now rushed into the fair with eyes spread wide and gritted teeth, and bashed any mobs of Inch high we could get hold of. It's funny that when you collar some lads who speak patwah most of the day, when the shit has gone totally ill, how quick their English accent comes back to them. A couple of Handsworth boys got stabbed in the arse with kitchen knives as were running them out of the fair. The police are nowhere to be seen, which sends a few people Doo Lally. A guy from the Trooper picked up a bin, and hurled it at the off licence window. The worst thing was that

DAVID C GEORGE

the fucking shop was still open anyway. East Birmingham is a black and white manor and will never be intimidated by people who have a ghettoised view of the world that only works in a small network of business.

APEX TO ZULU A2Z!

Spin-off calling card with bad spelling

A fantastic Torquay Welcome in 2006

Early 1983 Zulu Juniors calling card used in Chelmsey Wood

Original calling card used by the Birmingham Juniors

DAVID C GEORGE

Canning in Manchester – 1984

Blues at Man City – 1984

166

APEX TO ZULU A2Z!

Birmingham having problems with a full train – 1984

Birmingham lads in Bolton – 1985

DAVID C GEORGE

Elvis, Bod, Stuart and little Stig – 1985 Scarborough

Daks-Burberry and Aquascutum were all the rage – 1984/85

APEX TO ZULU A2Z!

Birmingham 1984/85 style

Blues at Man City outside the ground – 1984/85

169

DAVID C GEORGE

Highgate Juniors and (Shrk)

Blues in Manchester heading towards town – 1985

APEX TO ZULU A2Z!

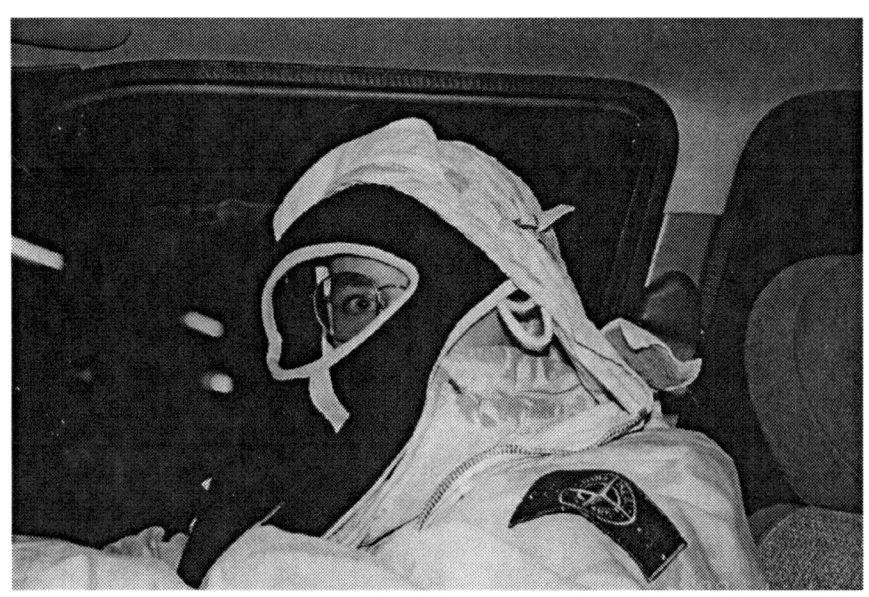

Eamon loosing his bearings – 1991

Warwick Juniors – 1984

DAVID C GEORGE

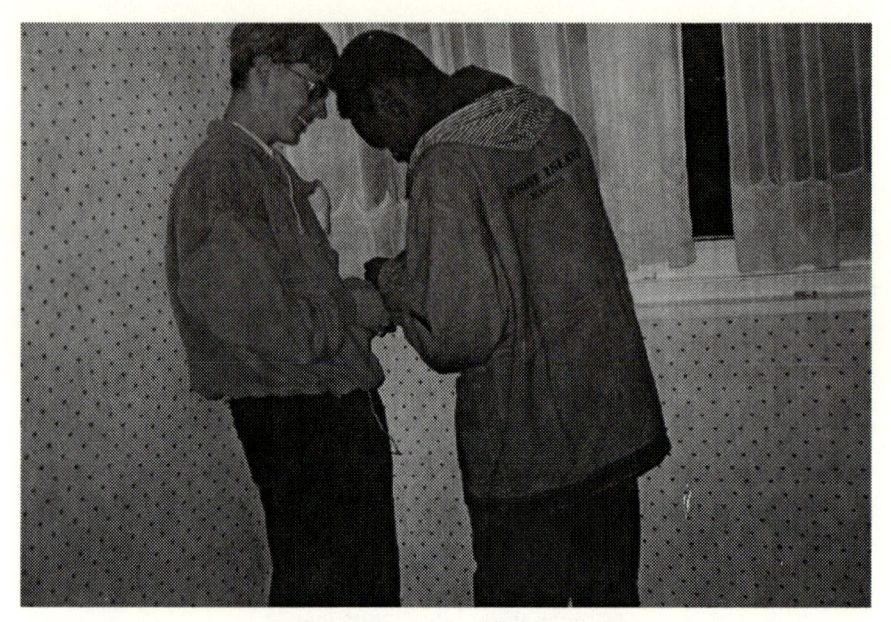

My 1st stone island. 1987 with Eamon

Blues in Manchester – 1984

APEX TO ZULU A2Z!

Blues in Scarborough

Juniors outside Man City ground – 1984

DAVID C GEORGE

Man City Chaos – 1984/85

Travelling away – 1984/85

APEX TO ZULU A2Z!

Blues at Man City – 1984

DAVID C GEORGE

Blues in Manchester

Blues on the move in Manchester

Junior Business Boys outside Navigation – 1985

1984 Style: myself and Roachy

CHAPTER 7

The History of British Fascism (Northern & Southern Racists)

THE FIRST ACTIVE FASCISTS appeared in Britain after World War One. The most notable of these groups was the British Fascists (BF) its founder, a woman called Rotha Lintorn-Orman, set up the British Fascists in 1923 due to her belief that immigrant workers were accepting lower wages, and were also responsible for the over crowding and the creation of run down slums in cities. The (BF) ideas of imperial unity were complemented with organised military groups. Some of it's divisions were even trained in Jujitsu and unarmed combat.

In 1931 a new personality was to take centre stage in British Fascism, Sir Oswald Mosley. Mosley had left the Labour Party after being disillusioned with their socialist views and formed the New Party in 1931. A gang of thugs that were called the Mosley Biff Boys supported the party.

The New Party then evolved into the British Union of Fascists (BUF) and was an attempt to unify all the British fascist groups. The most popular form of dress for the fascist was the black shirt uniform worn by Mosley and his motley crew, but British fascism was to become very unpopular in January 1934. With the rise of Hitler in nearby Germany, Britain created the anti-fascist movement despite publicity at the time from Lord Rothermere whose Daily Mail headline read "Hurrah to the Blackshirts." Sympathising with the Nazi's at the time and believing this fascist form of politics was the way forward

DAVID C GEORGE

for Britain shocks me to the core. Adolf Hitler and Goebbels attended Mosley's second marriage to Diana Mitford, and was also suspected of funding the (BUF) along with Mussolini in previous years.

Organised British fascism is rooted in the mix of social Darwinism, eugenics and scientific racism, and also retarded people who eat food with their feet.

Men are loyal to strong leaders and Birmingham's firm has several people in this category. There is one name that stands out, but strength and leadership have always run deep in Birmingham's City's firm to this day.

The Zulu Warriors in the 80s were aware of which teams in which part of the country were likely to be racist. For instance, if you go further north than Birmingham, there are hardly any black fans except in Manchester, and most of them didn't really go to football matches in big numbers. Areas such as Leeds – Doncaster – Barnsley – Hull – Blackburn and Liverpool ECT were all prime hot spots for racist fans and we knew it. When Everton used to sing, Everton are White, Everton are White aloooo – aloooo. You didn't think they where talking about lemonade did you?

If Birmingham City were playing one of these backward neanderthal teams, every black fan and every other blues fan with backbone would turnout en masse and land in any of these little god-forsaken towns early in the morning. The worst thing for any racist firm to see would be a 500 strong firm of dressers, bowling out of their train station, with at least 150 black fans dressed better than them and confronting them in their own town.

Bright coloured jackets, expensive umbrellas to rap around their heads, and a smatering of CS gas, smoke bombs, Stanley blades, Jiff bottles full of ammonia, flare guns and a good right hand would be what is necessary to show these fools what's what. A number of Birmingham City's frontline are avid martial arts students and the most popular art was and still is today, Taekwondo and boxing.

The main difference between Birmingham City's firm and most other mobs at the time was that Birmingham's firm educated themselves to the techniques of street tactics, they used philology. Most people who read this will probably laugh, but it is true. If you come from

178

an area such as Blackburn or Leeds for example, where most of your community is Caucasian, it stands to reason that your lifestyle and your way of thinking does not include ethnic minorities. Therefore if you ever see a person of colour at a game anywhere around the country at a football match, the simplest thing for them to do would be to shout racist to wind you up.

The difference was that Birmingham City's black, white and Asian crew already knew the score, and were prepared for this nonsense through travelling with Blues in the late seventies as kids, and had already secured a tight bond with regards to who they are and not what colour they are. Birmingham fans would joke amongst each other on a regular basis while travelling to away matches in the back of removal vans or on the train. It was a normal thing for us to take the piss out of each other, but it was never used as a political platform to air your views but just as lighthearted banter. A typical bit of early 80's Brummie banter would be: Your mom sells weed in church! And a quick reply would be: Well your mom's tits are so veiny, that they used them for the blueprint of Spaghetti Junction. If this didn't have the whole of the van or carriage on a train rolling about laughing, it would carry on until somebody slips up and runs out of lyrics. This was always one of the best times of the day, when everybody is relaxing and having a laugh with each other en route

Well-used 80s Brummie slang
Nitto – Don't be stupid
L-rig – Girl spelt backwards
Shaping – Loosing your bottle
Draipsing – Mugging
Lunn Polly – Get Away
Wetting your hood – Sleeping with a girl
TYD – Trapp you div
Wrag Order – In a bad way
Nit-Nit-Gerra grip – Don't be stupid, pull yourself together
Nause – Irritating / Nauseating
Reg – Friend / Pal
Cheeza – Idiot / Fool
Charv – To sleep with

DAVID C GEORGE

From my experiences of home and away matches in the mid 80's, I would say Birmingham City's hardcore element was very necessary to eliminate pests from our City and keeping it to a level that most decent ordinary Birmingham folk could go about their normal lives. You may be reading this and thinking we are also the problem, but I would say, that if your City or town does not have a central defence mechanism within it's hierarchy of working class youths, what you tend to get is groups of youths from other parts of the country, plundering and pillaging on their visits. The police are not there when incidents occur, and only arrive when it's already at boiling point, therefore can not deal with situations when they need to be dealt with. Fear of the unknown works very well for outsiders intent on unsavoury goings on in our City, and to this day, people related to footballs hooligan culture, across the whole of Europe are aware of the threat of the Zulu if pushed into a situation that may lead to violence. Compared to the Roundheads of the English Civil War, the Zulus are a part of the old guard in our fair city, and by any means necessary will defend the city of Birmingham against people who ridicule and despise the Midlands working class man. Very similar to the African Siafu, the flesh eating killer ant from Tanzania. It has a similar job description in its place of origin. Siafu has to battle on a regular basis in its chosen environment in order to survive just as the Zulu has to battle to maintain it's rightful presence within the City. If you see Siafu or the Zulu Warriors up to full strength walking towards you, the simple thing to do is to get the hell out of the way, unless of course, they are coming for your crew.

Southern racist firms in the 70s–80s were different to their northern counterparts because for them down south, being racist was their life and not much else mattered. Teams such as Chelsea, Millwall and a number of West Ham United supporters, have always been in this category and it was a main part of their lives. Combat–18, The National Front & BNP are all based around the East end and South Bermondsey areas of London since their conception in 1923. In the fifties, fascists headquarters were also based in Notting Hill, over in the West End, where a huge amount of fascists used to travel round in large numbers and bash black people within an inch of their lives, sometimes killing them. The confused Teddy boy of the 50's, who used to listen to black Rock n Roll, were the main group who used to enjoy beating black people up and chasing them round the streets in cars and vans. It was called, Nigger bashing. Most of the public in Notting Hill at the time enjoyed this behaviour, and used to follow the Teddy boys around the streets with hundreds of people looking to bash black people to death. Sometimes, the local police used to point out black people to the mob, in order for them to be attacked. These were certainly hard times for black people, as the law was also against you and enjoyed the same primitive behaviour as the local lawless people. Respect goes out to the men from Brixton at the time, who brought a team of die hard black men to stand up for the locals of Notting Hill. When black people start to defend themselves, white people used to say we were causing trouble, but if you didn't stand up for yourself back then, your days would be numbered on this earth, or you would be a cripple.

With most of Chelsea's hardcore racist firms coming from areas such as Cheam, Croydon, Hampton, Vauxhall, Slough and Tunbridge Wells, they have flown the flag of anti Irish and anti ethnicity for at least two decades. Birmingham has had many altercations with Chelsea throughout the years and in 78 at St Andrews, even tragically ending in a Chelsea fan being head butted and losing his balance while a fight was taking place on Digbeth High Street between rival factions, causing him to fall into the road and ending with his head being crushed by a double-decker bus. The lad from Chelmsley Wood who was arrested and did his time was called Terry Sherlock. Chelsea have run Birmingham in the 70s at Stamford Bridge it is true, and have even come onto the train at Euston and bashed blues again just for good luck. It must be said though that at the time, London teams were far more organised than Birmingham could have ever dreamed of, and would take full advantage of situations if they came about. Some you win, some you lose, and that's life.

1979, twelve blues fans were travelling to Liverpool to watch Birmingham play at Everton. At the same time, the unemployment march was taking place through Liverpool, which involved around 100,000 people.

DAVID C GEORGE

Eight lads from Chelmsley and four lads from town arrived at Liverpool Lime Street at 2.45pm. Liverpool were playing Sunderland away but there was a huge mob of scousers that never went to the game, and were waiting for late blues fans to arrive.

As the train pulled up into Lime Street, Blues were looking out of the carriage windows as Liverpool fans are now coming down the platform.

The one scouser says to the blues lads as the train is pulling up. "Where's Genocky, where's Genocky?" Dex is first off the train and walks up to the Liverpool fan and says, "Listen, ... fuck Genocky, We're from Chelmsley Wood, we've come ta give it ya, Smack! The Liverpool fan gets a full on punch in the face, and the twelve Blues fans walk up the platform. The rest of the Liverpool fans now run into the arcade on the station and come steaming back out of the doors with heavy numbers. Blues jump the barriers to confront Liverpool, and are surrounded by Scousers trying to cut them with Stanley blades. There is a full-scale brawl on Lime Street, which spills outside into the street. Blues are heavily outnumbered and it's looking on top, so big Mickey Cooke, picks up a taxi rank sign with a lump of concrete at the end, and starts swinging it around his body. Anyone who came close was going to get a concrete lollipop wrapped round their head.

The unemployment march was at the end of the same street, and a couple of police officers who saw the commotion, now come down the road to stop the row outside Lime Street. The police put the twelve blues lads into taxis and they head off towards the game at Goodison Park. When speaking to a few Liverpool lads later on in the day, they said that 150 Manchester City had come to Lime Street a week before, and none of them would leave the station.

In 1982, Birmingham were drinking in the Knight Rider public house in town around 7.00pm. There was an altercation with a number of townies and security guards at the top of the ramp near McDonalds. Around twenty Blues fans walked up the steps from the pub to find out what was going on, and as they did, around 40 Everton had stopped off in brum before their next train and had walked up the escalators to have a bit of a mooch. As they got to near the fountain, they stopped and started pointing at the black dressers who were standing down from them near McDonalds. "Darkies fucking darkies" is what they were saying amongst each other before they realised they were in the wrong place at the wrong time. The Everton fans rushed at the twenty or so Blues fans while pulling out their trade mark stanley blades. Blues stood, and when Everton got close enough, Blues made their move and bounced straight into Everton, who turned and run, some throwing their blades to the floor and sprinting back down the escalators into New Street. Having run down onto the station, Everton then ran out through the glass doors and scattered. Blues by this time had also decided to go their separate ways and were only about 8 handed when Everton started to mob up outside on New Street car park, now realising Blues slim numbers at the time. Everton now came looking for the eight Blues fans, and down by the Knightrider pub, they collard Morph and surrounded him in the road. Punches and kicks were thrown at him ending with him using a car bonnet to roll over so he didn't end up on the floor. After a minute or so, the Everton fans left and walked off. Morph got up off the bonnet of the car, which was now dented. He had a few bruises on his face as he shouted at the Everton fans. "Is that it?" There were a few townies looking down off the ramp who cheered and clapped their hands at Morph who had survived the group of Everton fans efforts to try and fill him in. While this was happening, the townies that were so keen on arguing with security guards were not keen on defending another brother from a group of outsiders. Which gives you an idea on the diversities black people have in Birmingham with regards to what they think is true and just behaviour. To be fair, Birmingham hasn't had that many run-ins with Everton, but we are aware of their work as a firm. Another incident took place involving Everton was at Goodison Park in the early 80s, when Wire was listening to a number of Everton mouthing off to the Birmingham fans near the fence. Wire has gone to the toilet and took a dump in a Daily Star newspaper. He then folded it over and went over to the fence where the Everton fan was gobbing off. The scouse lad sees the newspaper in Wire's hand and says in a broad Scouse accent, "Wot's da, a Millwall brick?" Wire smiles at the Scouser while holding the warm contents of the newspaper out in front of him and replies, "No, its Birmingham shit" Wallop! The shit is flung threw the fence at the scouser whose face and clothes are covered with warm human doings.

What makes me laugh about a number of these so-called footie books is that some firms claim to have never lost a row in their lives. If you look at the situation realistically, it would stand to reason that the more fights you have, the averages of never losing a battle are very slim indeed. I am not pointing the finger at anyone in particular, but you know who you are. Think on. Even Jackie Chan's been turned over, so lets all take a deep breath at the same time shall we? And relax..!! You are not the fucking X-Men. We have all lost fights here or there but as I said previously, that is life.

BNP Away

K.   Morning Georgie
G.   Kingy you twat
       You've shaved your head
K.   It's a Suede head
G.   We've got Burnley away
K.   I thought we'd bring the BNP round to our way of thinking
G.   Our way of thinking it's all in your mind you mug
       Your ten and half stone punching above your weight
       You're a junkie not a thug
       Lost in the illusion that they're flapping and running away from you
K.   I'm front line mate
G.   Exactly you cunt we are all standing behind you
       A thousand strong on a good day
K.   Au contraire Georgie I understand what's on my side
       The way I look at it
       The pen and the sword
       The persuasion of the pugilist
       And the power of the written word
G.   Kingy I can't get me breath
       What you gonna do talk them to death
       You end up on your arse getting beaten and slapped
K.   You know it don't work like that

APEX TO ZULU A2Z!

G. Yeh I know how it works
    I knock em out and then you rob em blind
    While there out for the count
K. Yes well it funds the trip
    Pays for the van
G. You waltzer pushing window licker
    Your flying mate
    You wanna lay off that wan
K.G. Oh ram it you loser here's the lads.

Kingy.

CHAPTER 8

Millwall Rivalry: Millwall Vs Birmingham City 1971

Johnny H

THE HISTORY BETWEEN BIRMINGHAM CITY and Millwall FC goes way back to the early 70s when ClockWork Orange was the movie that was on the lips of every teenager. The train took us to an overhead station; I think it was New Cross Gate. Around twelve of us got off the train and there was no Birmingham fans to be seen. Nobody wanted to no us at all, it was as though we had some disease that all Cockneys knew about, and we didn't. Jimmy Kennedy, Milko, Ribbs ECT. Got up the stairs and out of the station, and you know how things influence you as a kid? I've never seen spray paint like it in me days. In massive four-foot letters on a nearby wall it said, "THIS IS THE LAST CHANCE FOR YOU TO SHIT OUT AND RUN." It had shit out with an arrow pointing back to the station. Another sign next to it read, "CBL THE DEN OF NO RETURN."

So nobody wanted to know us and if you're with Johnny Heron, you're fucked. About twelve of us were in this pub looking out of these windows, and the whole train load of Birmingham was chased up the road by a mob of Millwall all tooled up to fuck. We lost 3−0 that day, and you know they were all men, no listen. They were all fucking men. I had tools on me that day and I was still scared. We never forget what has happened in the past with this lot, and the feeling is still there to this day.

The Bushwhacker Situation

On 29th December 1986 Birmingham City played at home against Milwall, for the first time in years I could remember. Millwall were the team every other firm in the country had heard of the reputation from going back in the seventies. The Millwall Bushwhackers or The Treatment had been talked about for years in Birmingham as being the one crew they would like to bump into and now the day was here. Standing outside Boogies wine bar with three Juniors and Natty, having a drink. Boogies Brassiere was full to the rafters with Blues firm and DJs were flinging down some quality tunes, also across the road in the Grapes. A guy comes running up the hill from New Street and runs into Boogies wine bar, his face was red and his left eye had taken a whack. Leaning up against the door out of breath he says "They're here" Blues finished their drinks and a buzz of electricity and excitement went round the bar. Boogies had three floors all large enough to hold at least 150 lads on each. I looked around the room through a teenagers eyes and saw crews from all over Birmingham City dressed to impress, but also very well capable of throwing down the gauntlet. Some lads had opted for the wearing of a bit Best Company with a spot of Aquascutum. Others had gone for the hooded leather with cashmere scarf lifted high upon the face, Barber wax jackets, New Man jeans and Bruno Zeppi shoes. Standing outside again now, and three lads approach the pub. They were quite tall and their faces I had not seen before. As we looked at each other, we realised this was it. Three Milwall fans were standing in front of Boogies and fronting us and inviting everyone in the pub out of the bar. The double doors of Boogies Brassiere flew open and a stampede of bodies came flooding into the street, some carrying bar stools and pint glasses. It rained bottles for about 5 seconds as Blues let out a roar "Come on nen," "come on?" The first group of Blues fans bounced up and down in the road, grotesquely stretching their necks forward looking up and down the street to see where the rest of Milwalls firm was, Birmingham then charged at the three Bushwhackers.

DAVID C GEORGE

The three Millwall ran down the hill past The Grapes and across the road. Blues were now emptying out of Boogies and the Grapes at the same time, and bowled down the hill towards New Street near the zebra crossing. Millwall had well and truly arrived, standing across the road from us now, with numbers of around a hundred, some with beards covering their faces and most of them wearing hooded wax jackets or baggy leathers, and not a kid in sight. A number of Millwall had large pieces of wood in their hands that were probably found at some roads works nearby. Millwall looked dangerous it must be said, but we wanted to see what they were like away from home, against The Zulu, against us.

Millwall bounced into the road, red and white planks of wood held high and roared. "Wall, Wall, Wall" bricks and other missiles were thrown only a short distance and at first, Blues backed off a little giving Millwall too much respect, but they couldn't back off very far due to the sheer numbers that had now come out of Boogies Brassiere & The Grapes. Blues backed off about a metre before Blues frontline got their act together, they blocked pieces of wood and bricks with their elbows thrown by Millwalls boys. I'm standing shoulder to shoulder at the front with "Flowers" from Ward End now, when Blues started to bounce in unison, and then a mighty roar was let out that all of Millwalls firm at the time would remember. Very loud – "ZULUUUUUUUUUU!" Blues now ran across the road and jumped with legs high into Millwalls firm, who were totally overwhelmed by heavy kicks and big punches flying at them in waves of aggression. Birmingham used the horns of the bull tequnique which is an old Zulu battle tactic without them actually knowing. The horns would flank around the sides while the main body would attack the front. Millwall spread out and tried to look for a way out of the situation, but it was true from the start that it just was not going to be their day. Clusters of Millwall were being bashed everyway they turned. Four Millwall were knocked out cold, one had wet himself while being kicked all over the road, and the rest ran back to New Street as fast as they could to ask for an escort to the ground. Some Blues fans followed Millwall back up to the station and proceeded in terrorising the now scared Millwall fans until the British Transport Police turned up to save their bacon. I saw a youngster from Birmingham kicking one of the Millwall fans in the stomach, and leaning over him and snarling through gritted teeth. "Welcome to Birmingham, you Cockney cunt." He took the Londoners jacket off his back, turned and walked back up to Boogies & The Grapes.

When meeting Birmingham City's firm with very large numbers, it is difficult for anyone to get a result, especially if you're from Millwall and have totally underestimated the main firm from the Midlands. Some of Millwalls firm ran through New Street and up the escalators and got to the ramp outside McDonalds where a firm of Birmingham caught up with them. Bins were bashed off Millwall fans heads and Blues just went into them again. A huge Millwall skinhead was standing there while it's complete and utter chaos in front of him with Millwall fans being attacked. He says, "Somebody pass me a tool," again! "Somebody pass me a tool?" A Brummy lad smacks him right on the jaw and the Millwall lad doesn't move an inch, he looks at the Birmingham lad and says yet again to his Millwall crew who are well under the cosh, "Somebody pass me a tool" One of Birmingham's top lads has rushed forward and roundhouses the Millwall skinhead, chest-height into the railings, and he has dropped to the floor on one knee. The skinhead gets back up and says, "Somebody pass me a tool." Whoever that Millwall fan is, he could not be the full ticket because he had so many punches put on his chin and kicks to his chest that didn't even affect him at all. The police now arrive and the skinhead bowls off down the road with just a few lumps on his face.

At the same time, another group of around forty Millwall had got down onto Digbeth and believe it or not, were being pointed out by an under-cover police officer to the Birmingham fans. Birmingham came at this group of Millwalls firm, and they were game as fuck without a doubt. An Asian lad from Birmingham pulled out a blade, and was seen by the police, so he threw the blade onto the floor under a car without the police seeing it. A local cafe was open at the time, and a woman who didn't look as if she had all the tokens for a pop up toaster came to the glass door. As the Birmingham lads are standing outside the cafe, one the Zulu's asks this woman to take the blade into the cafe. Believe it or not, this is absolutely true, leaving the police without any evidence for an arrest. As they are talking to a number of Blues fans in the road, another lad from Acocks Green is arrested then they decide to let the guy go as they could not find the blade. A police van comes screaming around the corner, knocking over the two police officers and the Asian lad before he's arrested.

Millwall Away 1986

Travelling to Millwall away the same season in 86, after the Bushwhackers had taken a beating in our City, Birmingham Zulu Warriors were up to full strength. 650 proper good lads landed in London by train, vans and cars. We met up with everyone else in Victoria in a couple of pubs near to the underground station. As we walked towards the pub we were confronted by a sea of Blues elite hit squad. The firm was proper top drawer, full hammer. Because Blues firm was so big, they had to leave the pub in numbers of around fifty and wait on the platform that goes to New Cross Gate. The whole platform is absolutely packed to the point of being unsafe. The train pulls up and everybody tries to get on but with the sheer amount of blues fans trying to get on, we had to leave about 100 behind because there just wasn't anymore room for them. The conductor tries to shut the doors of the train several times, but to no avail.

Some lads had to get off because Blues firm was too big to fit on the train. I looked around the train and everybody was smiling, this was it, this is the one. Sometimes when you're bowling with a firm and you're with the right people, you get a feeling of invincibility and that was the feeling running through everybody's veins on that day. Blues now land at New Cross Gate and before leaving the station they, zip up coats and jackets, leather gloves on, hoods up and eyebrows dropped. It's time to roll. Blues bowl straight out of the station onto the high street, they look left and right and decide on right. We are now walking up the road in New Cross and a van begins to kerb crawl at the side of us. Two of Millwalls lookouts are sitting in the van and nodding their heads at the sheer size of Blues firm.

They drive off to obviously tell the rest of the Bushwhackers that the Zulu's have landed, and we certainly had.

As we walk further up the road, there is a grass verge on our left with around twenty Millwall at the top. Only seeing one or two blues fans walking at the front because they hadn't emerged from the high street, the twenty Millwall mount a charge and begin running down the grass verge.

Five seconds later, they have all stopped running and are just standing there looking at the size of the crew they were foolishly about to run into.

We were not bothered about these twenty, they meant nothing to us, and we wanted the main crew. Blues carried on walking but around 15 Zulu's slowed down and lagged behind to get a bit of action, because they were gagging for it to bang right off.

Blues had now reached the arched tunnel just before the Lions Den, and the Police were telling everybody they were going to be searched one by one, before being let into the ground. As we walked through the tunnel, you could hear the sound of metal objects being thrown onto the floor. Hundreds of Stanley blades, CS gas, screwdrivers, Jiff bottles full of ammonia and hammers were covering the floor. The Police were not happy with this situation, but if you have ever been to Millwall, these types of precautions have to be taken. It is very rare that Millwall fans will just try to beat you up, as some of them are known to carry machetes and other savage weapons to disable and destroy away fans. On this day Birmingham City were well and truly prepared, and most still had tools on them even after they had been searched. We are now standing outside the famous Lions den and the Police have erected makeshift metal barriers to hold us on one side of the road before we go in the ground. Some of blues lads were standing on the opposite side speaking to a couple of Bushwhackers. This Millwall lad said it was the biggest firm he had seen come to Millwall in over ten years, and a Blues fan said back to him, "These are the divs mate, the proper firm will be here in twenty minutes" The Millwall fans jaw hit the floor, but the Brummy lad was just winding our southern spoon player up for a laugh. Not really getting much of a tickle with Millwalls firm, Birmingham entered the Lions Den to watch the game. Millwall sang their No One Likes Us; We Don't Care song, which echoed through the ground while Birmingham's firm sang, the trademark A Who De Aagh? Zulu! A Who De Aagh? Zulu! Also the famous The End Of

DAVID C GEORGE

The Road song, but they also mocked the Millwall by singing as loud as possible with high-pitched voices repeating the name, "Millwall, bom, bom, bom, Millwall bom, bom, bom. Birmingham fans started to get bored because of all the hype they had heard about Millwall, we were expecting an all out full scale battle with Millwall knowing full well they had been well and truly turned over at our ground. One of Blues lads started to collect newspaper and empty packets of crisps and pile them behind the refreshments hut in the away end. All of a sudden, there was a huge billowing cloud of smoke from our part of the ground. Birmingham had set fire to the refreshments bar in the away end of the Lions Den and Millwall fans reacted by singing, "Your gonna get your fucking heads kicked in." Blues won the game 2 – 0 and were kept in the ground for around twenty minutes before being escorted by police to New Cross Gate station. If people are foolish enough to think it's only the capital that has tasty firms, then think again. Birmingham had sold only 800 tickets for this game and had a firm of over 600 lads ready to take on the Bushwhackers in their backyard. Nobody had eaten breakfast on this day and everyone had come to chow down on Cockney flesh. The Police had put Birmingham's firm on the train at New Cross Gate and were now travelling back into central London. As we were pulling up at London Bridge Station, we noticed the platform was already full of lads. Millwalll were waiting for us and there was no way for the police to stop this, as the doors were about to open and the few Police on the train were just lost in a stampede of "ZULUUUUUUUUUU!" Blues and Millwall clashed on the platform at London Bridge and it was ferocious. Everyday civilians who were also standing on the platform screamed as they were caught in the middle of a vicious brawl they couldn't seem to get out of. It was utter chaos for a couple of minutes until Birmingham bashed Millwall up the stairs and ran them up the road outside the station; until more Police came to herd Birmingham fans back down onto the platform and into central London. Birmingham's firm was very much up for this one, and had now managed to slap Millwall home and away, which as any casual in the country will tell you is a great achievement that only a handful of good firms can even repeat or dream of, in their whole life of football experiences.

APEX TO ZULU A2Z!

Millwalls Revenge

In all the years that Birmingham have had altercations with Millwall, there has only been one incident where Blues have got run, and this was it. Before the game, Blues had taken a firm of around 250 to London Bridge to take on the Bushwhackers, which was a third of the usual size. Blues were having a few cheeky drinks in a local pub before they headed off to the game. It was a tidy firm Blues were carrying with them, but what they didn't have was any get up and go with regards to going and finding the opposition. A car pulls up at London Bridge with the Bushwhackers checking our numbers and trying to sort out a rendezvous. Blues agreed with Millwall that they would meet after the game, and the car shot off up the road. After the game, the police take the masses of Blues fans back to the train station, and they each have a choice to either take the train to Euston and fuck off home, or take the London Bridge train and get it on with Millwall. Most Blues fans were not keen on going to London Bridge. So the Die Hards went to represent the congregation. Around 40 to 50 Blues lads went to London Bridge to wait for Millwall, but to me, this was not how it should have been. There should have been around 300 hundred at London Bridge, but most could not be arsed to fanny about in London waiting for the spoon players.

A Blues lookout comes running down the road at London Bridge station and says Millwall are coming this way with heavy numbers. Millwallls firm must have been at least 500 handed, and tooled up enough to make you wish you hadn't come to the Smoke at all. A few Blues chaps see the size of the Bushwhackers firm, and start to turn over the green shutter bins in their path to slow them down a bit in the tunnel. A number of Blues fans are hurling bottles and bits of old junk that's fallen out of the bins, but it's no use. Millwall are still coming, and the situation is not looking good. Millwalls firm was proper tidy, with a combination of both black and white in the firm. Blues decide to do one at the last minute, and get chased up the street.

Blues small firm scatters all over the place, some running across train tracks, and one Brummy guy was unlucky enough to be electrocuted on the power lines. A small contingent of Blues make a stand on the stairs to have it with the Bushwhackers, and it goes bang off. Millwall fly into Blues and Blues fly into Millwall. A guy from Bordesley Green gets CS gas in his mouth at close range, and ends up throwing up chunks of orange bile all over the stairs. The Blues who stood on the stairs had it right up in the air twice, before they could see any crime enforcement officers around. As Millwall were rowing Blues, a firm of them sneaked round to the other side of the steps to cut the Brummies off. If this would have happened, then it would have been a nightmare and a half because Blues were only 10 handed.

As the sirens could be heard in the background, a few Blues lads were walking up the street trying to work out what they were going to do if they were to turn a corner and bump into the Bushwhackers again. A Bordesley Green lad says to Kluvert, that if Millwall come again, "pretend that you're Nigerian?" Kluvert, who is mixed race, turns and says, "How many mixed race Brummy Nigerians do you know?" Fair play to Millwall on this day, as they have shown they can be a formidable force at home, but on their journeys throughout the UK, it's is not always the same story when they are away.

Birmingham City Vs Millwall Oct 93
Sooty

Everybody is aware of what happened in the ground when Birmingham were ripping out seats in the top tier of the railway end, and bouncing them off Millwall fans head as it was all over the news up and down the country. Birmingham knew Millwall were going to get a mad escort into town after the game, so Birmingham got into town before they arrived. Birmingham got a small 60 firm together and laid low in a bar waiting for Millwalls escort to come up the road.

60 is a decent size firm but it is also small enough to keep off side until the time was right. Birmingham also had another firm of the same numbers that was also off side who were also waiting for Millwalls escort to come through town. About 150 Bushwhackers who were heavily escorted are now walking up Digbeth and past The Old Bulls head pub. Birmingham brought one of its firms out at the top of Digbeth for the police and Millwall to see them. As the police have seen Birmingham's firm, they have now charged forward to stop the Birmingham mob getting at the Bushwhackers, but little did they

know that this was exactly what Birmingham wanted. The police have now left the Millwall standing on Digbeth High Street unprotected and all looking up the road at the chaos taking place, when the other mob of Birmingham now get into position around the corner from the Millwall fans. Birmingham's other firm has now come charging from around the corner and hit the back of Millwalls escort hard, sending panic all through their firm. The Millwall are all running up the road towards the police in shock, as they did not expect to be attacked in such a way. They were totally unprepared for this ambush. Birmingham clattered Millwall up the main road for a couple of minutes and then did one.

Millwall vs Birmingham City Division 1 playoffs 2002

Second leg of the Division 1 playoffs and Millwall got a draw at our ground leaving the score 1 – 1. I was on my way over from Kingston Upon Thames looking to meet up with blues at London Bridge Station.

As I get to London Bridge, I see a train on the platform packed to the rafters with blues lads, so I try to get on the train. Unfortunately with train being so full, I was told by the police to wait for the next train, which would leave me missing 15 minutes of the game, but I didn't really have a choice.

I'm now standing on the platform waiting for the next train to Bermondsey when the station now starts to fill with Millwall fans. I had a look round and spotted a number of Bushwhackers who were obviously running late and were all keen on getting to the game as soon as possible. The train pulls up and I get on and sit down facing the walkway down the centre of the carriage. As I look up, I see two lads at the end of the carriage very familiar to me, so I approach them to have a quick chat. As I reach them with a relieved smile on my face, I ask the two lads which part of Birmingham they're from, and to my surprise, they both frowned and spoke in the broadest south London accents I had heard all day. "Wot you fakin talkin about, we aint fakin Brummies." When hearing this information, time seemed to stop for me and realising I had just made the fuckup of the century, on a manor that is so hostile that Charles Manson refused to go there, because he said the occupants of Bermondsey are far too violent, I thought to myself that things were about to get worse before they get better. I turned and walked nervously back up to my seat facing the walkway and noticed around twenty Millwall lads now congregating at the end of the carriage. I thought to if I'm going to get done, I'm gonna go out like a hundred pound firework. I also knew that if they were proper Millwall, they would of turned me over straight away where I stood.

The train now pulls up at Bermondsey and I put on my leather gloves, and stand up while the train screeches to a halt. I bowl off the train and jog up the steps rather than walk, because I didn't want to be caught out on the stairs. As I reach the top of the stairs, I have Millwall lads on either side of me trying to trip me up, but I carry on bowling down the walkway, with the window wiper arms coming out of nowhere. The one Millwall lad said, "Cam on nen Zulu, wot you sayin nen, where's ya boys now nen ey?" Realising these were not people who were proper heads, I simply carried on bowling, dropped my eyebrows and told the lot of them to fuck off at least four times. London lads had shown Birmingham what front was all the way about back in the early eighties, and I was just bringing it back to the capital for them to have a look at. If people who think they are lads have to ask where your boys are, when the game has already started and we are coming off a late train, it gives you an idea of the calibre of these individuals. I mean, was it worth me saying, "They're in the ground watching the game you fucking dickhead" "Where are yours?"

As I get to the end of the walkway there are a group of around fifteen police officers waiting at the bottom of the next small flight of stairs.

Seeing this, the Millwall lads stopped nausing my ears and walked off across the road and stood there waiting for me. I stopped and had a word with the Old Bill because I knew that as soon as I walked towards the ground, I would be rushed by a group of idiots who find fun in beating up one person on his own. I said to a police officer, "I need to get to the ground," and his reply was, "It's that way." I thought fuckit, because the police are not really up for protecting you from away fans a lot of the time, and they usually like to turn up when the fight is already over, or in full swing. I decided to try and get to the game and headed off up the main road. As I got only forty yards, the Millwall lads started crossing over the road some with their hands in their jackets. The police now called me back to the train station and advised me to get a taxi. If anyone has been to Millwalls New Den, they would realise the ground is about 800 metres away from Bermondsey station, which for me seemed ridiculous that I have to catch a cab to go this short distance. Time is ticking and I could hear the game from where I was standing but couldn't get the short distance to the New Den. These Millwall were still standing across the road waiting for the opportunity to carve me up, so my last resort was to try to flag down a taxi. I had more chance of group sex with Destiny's Child in Netto supermarket than getting a taxi near the New Den. So I'm now back with the Old Bill who happen to all be from Birmingham, and the one officer leans forward and looks me dead in the eye and says. "Is your name George?" I looked at him and said, "Well if you know me that well, then we might as well get engaged." The other police officers burst out laughing, but by now I had missed a good twenty five minutes of the first half. I'm standing there with the dibble who are all having a laugh amongst themselves, I've got some depraved Millwall on the other side of the road waiting for me to make a move, and my ticket is at the turnstiles at the New Den.

Just then, five Blues lads come bowling out of Bermondsey station with window wiper walks that are very familiar to me. I shake hands with all of the lads and now bowl towards the game. As we are walking down now six handed, the mob of Millwall all of a sudden didn't fancy their chances, even though they still out numbered us three to one, but these were five of the older lads of Birmingham who if you see them, you would automatically know they are no mugs. I call Kluvert who informs me what entrance I need to go to, and we all get in the game.

The game is even stevens really and could go either way, but the worst thing for all 1,800 Blues fans who made the journey was that Aston Villa's Dion Dublin was on loan to Millwall and was playing well. I was sitting in the top tier behind the goal watching the game, and the smell of skunk was potent. Near the end of full time, the score was still 1 –1 so as we got into added time, Steve Vickers sent a cross over to Stern John who buried it in the net. Blues were in Wonderland, the atmosphere was incredible.

The ugly element of Millwall now stood up in the seats doing impersonations of monkeys, and then stroking the one finger across the throat to give Blues an idea of what was going to happen after the game.

As the ball was picked up out of the net and placed back into the centre of the pitch, the ref blew his whistle and the game started again, but only after what seemed like another minute and a half, the game was over and Birmingham had beaten Millwall to face Norwich in Cardiff's Millennium Stadium for a chance to get into the Premiership.

Millwall now try a pitch invasion, which doesn't seem to go very well, and are now baton-charged off the pitch by mounted police. The Millwall fans now start the Nazi salute they love so much, but they hadn't counted on Birmingham fans having a greater sense of humour than our spoon playing whelk eaters from the south. All Birmingham's black lads now congregate at the front of the top tier and start doing the Nazi salute back at Millwall who are now very frustrated and pissed off because.

1. We stopped them from having the closest chance of getting into the Premiership ever.
2. Their Nazi salute was tired, so we spiced it up a bit.
3. They tried a pitch invasion and got only two yards.
4. We sang two songs that must have killed them dead on the spot.
5. We're going to Cardiff; we're going to Cardiff
   You're not, you're not
   We're going to Cardiff; we're going to Cardiff
   You're not, you're not.
6. Cheer up Mark McGheeOh what can it mean
   To a fat Scottish bastard
   And a shit football team?

The second song was repeated for at least ten minutes non stop after the game by the whole of the Birmingham City fans, as we don't like racists at the best of times, especially when they use tools on you that you would normally find in a dense forest to chop through bamboo.

Birmingham now congregate downstairs waiting for the gates to open and are standing outside penned in by riot & mounted police and are puzzled by the amount of time it's taking for us to be able to walk to Bermondsey train station. As we are standing outside, we can hear what sounds like a riot a few streets from us, and a helicopter with a huge spotlight is shinning onto the floor. The Birmingham lads have a firm around 350 strong, and it was a good crew, and they were asking the police why they had to stay outside the ground for so long. People were mumbling through the crowd and thinking of a way of getting onto the streets to have it with the Bushwhackers. A mounted officer leans forward with his riot helmet on and says we are being kept there for our own protection. This comment pisses at lot of people off, and a lad leans back with his right arm and punches the horse right in the mouth, sending him reeling backwards. Blues now start pushing the police backwards, saying, "Look around you, we know who Millwall are, we will walk, we don't need a fucking escort." Blues keep on pushing the police but are forced back by a number of arrests being made. After around an hour of standing about, we are now able to leave the New Den and walk up the main road. As we turn the corner everyone's jaws hit the floor. The ground was covered in broken slabs, every car on the street was burnt out, and their local was a smouldering shell. It looked as though we had gone back in time to the London blitz of the Second World War. Blues lads were walking through the carnage and picking up bricks and tools lying all over the floor and stuffing them into their jackets. The police had riot vans on either side of most of the escort, with riot police with shields walking on the outside of the vans.

As we are walking towards the station, there are roads on our left each with Millwall boys just waiting for us. A burning settee was thrown at us, but they couldn't lob it very far. A Brummy lad joked, "He should have gone to Specsavers" Blues firm is right at the front of the escort and we are surprised how easy it was to get back to Bermondsey as it is just up the road. The police now stop Blues escort, as there are around 500 Millwall standing in the road right outside Bermondsey station.

The police officer says to us, "When you get to the station, I want you to go straight onto the platform and onto the train." "I don't want you hanging around, just go straight onto the train, OK?"

DAVID C GEORGE

Blues lads flip the hoods up on their coats, and place the gloves on their hands and bowl towards the station. Blues average age in the firm was late 30s mid forties and the crew were seasoned pros. These were a lot of the same people who had given Millwall a hiding on two occasions before, so were not afraid of taking them on again. When seeing the Bushwhackers close up, I noticed most of them were kids who lived locally and just enjoy wrecking the place if they get the chance. The police were not there to fight Millwall, but the Zulu Warriors were, and if 350 lads would have rushed Millwall, a few people would have been hurt, but the residents of Bermondsey would have kept most of the cars and the pub intact. The police didn't have the resources to deal with Millwall properly, as something else was going on across the other side of London the same night. A lot of Birmingham are carrying the tools they have picked up outside the ground. Millwall start to shout, and Birmingham fans can't hold it down any longer and now rush forward past the police and charge Millwall. Millwall back off, but it was a combination of police and Zulus that backed them off.

Blues are now standing outside the station and the police are ordering Birmingham fans to get on the train, but blues have got other ideas.

The Zulus have mobbed up and are standing in the road outside Bermondsey train station for about five minutes, calling it on to the Bushwhackers who just stood there watching about 150 yards away. For a firm that was so keen on wanting a piece of us earlier, and we are standing here not moving onto the platform, they didn't seem very keen in clashing with us. It also must be said it had to be on the Bushwhackers minds to make petrol bombs before the game had even kicked off, because there is no way you can come out of a ground, and have that many tools at your disposal if they hadn't had it planned already. They must have sat down and had a conversation where they all agreed there was a strong chance of them losing the football match, therefore if they did, they should trash their own pub and burn the local's cars and have a major tantrum.

Carling Cup Millwall Vs Birmingham City 2005

Of all of the well respected firms in the UK, Millwall are certainly up there with the best, but with regards to organisation and actually fighting toe to toe with no tools, Millwall score very low indeed. As much as they have some real stand up people who live local and support the team, when it comes to travelling away from London, Millwall are not what they are all cracked up to be. Since Stern John knocked Millwall out of a chance of getting into the premiership in 2002, Birmingham have never met Millwall, so today is going to be interesting.

After Birmingham's the first book signing, the feeling was that Birmingham need to show Millwall what we can take into London when necessary. 70 blues lads went into London early and had an afternoon of drinking while the main bulk of Blues' 600 strong firm landed in the afternoon. This was not your run of the mill firm that was out today as we realised nobody in London likes Brummies including the police and the Bushwhackers. More old school heads were with Birmingham on this day because Birmingham will look after their own. As much as the police tell us they were there for our protection, this is just not true, as most of the police are there to beat you up and collect their overtime pay. All you need is a lot of people who don't take any shit, add some of the gamest black & white lads from all over Birmingham and you have police who treat you like vermin because you are a stand up guy who doesn't take shit from the police or Londoners. It is a known fact that the police enjoy beating people up at football matches, and have been smashing people's faces in for over 30 years or more. As a football supporter, you will notice all of your rights as a human being go out of the window. If the police could get hold of enough money to convert shower rooms into gas chambers without suspicion, I think they would. I think they should have also had a good look at the crew that just rolled into London on a dark Tuesday evening 600 handed. As Lanks clearly stated, this was a dirty crew; with some of the biggest brummy black geezers from the Jurassic period London had ever seen. Many good lads from areas of Birmingham were all representing, including people capable of shattering your cheekbone with one punch. Tolkien was right when he wrote Lord of the Rings, as Brummies are from Middle Earth and we are also The Precious. The football is one of the only places where your human rights are completely taken away from you by the police, and yet nobody says a word. Watch how the police cover up their badges when a fight takes place.

The police escort us out of Euston with a heavy prescence and march us up the road to another station. As we are standing outside a hotel surrounded by police, the smell of weed was very strong indeed. We were waiting for a special train that was put on to take us over to Baker Street to meet up with the 70 Blues lads who went into London earlier in the day. A black guy who was stopping in one of the hotels is just about to leave when he turns round on the doorstep and views at least 600 people looking at him including 200 police.

He pauses on the top step and says to the crowd, "Thank you for turning up" Everybody cheers, he then goes into a speech, which sounded similar to an Academy Award acceptance speech. "I'd like to thank my manager for supporting me, and also God" everybody cheers again, and this guy trundles off down the street with his overnight trolley on wheels.

Birmingham are aware that the reputation they have will also bring a huge number of police officers on duty who are keen to beat somebody up. Talking to one police officer at Baker Street, I realised that he wasn't as stupid as he looked.

He realised why Birmingham had to come to London in numbers like this due to the reputation of both firms. Birmingham had nothing to worry about on this day, as the firm was heavy duty. When travelling through London Bridge station Birmingham fans were walking very quickly as this is normally the place where Millwall will come and try to have a go. Instead, some over-zealous police officers decide on beating some of the Birmingham fans for absolutely nothing whatsoever. Birmingham's firm now steams into the police who are all wearing riot gear while carrying telescopic coshes. The police look nervous and are shouting at Birmingham fans to get back, but there was no reason for Blues to get back, except that the police wanted to fight us before we got to the ground. Birmingham steam the police again who are now looking very nervous and backing off as they didn't think Birmingham would defend themselves against attackers. If you come with bad intention, Birmingham will fight you whether you are backward and from Bermondsey or a police officer who loves to beat up away fans. Turning off the escalators and starving us and having no access to liquid refreshment was the police methods to gain control. Arriving at the New Den, Birmingham enter the ground and walk up to near the top of the stairs and wait. Birmingham filled the stairs all the way back to the turnstiles with their firm and waited for everybody to get into the game. "Wait, not yet" could be heard… then "Now" "ZULUUUUUUUUUUUU" Birmingham make an entrance into Millwalls ground they will all remember for a long time. The firm was incredible. It spread across the seats like a virus and kept getting bigger and bigger. Millwall had two firms in the ground that even if they had put the two crews together would still be smaller than Birmingham had in the seats.

Birmingham managed to scrape a win a Millwall on penalties and were then escorted back to Euston with a heavy police presents. As we arrive back at Euston from the tube, Smurf approaches a police officer and goes into a loud fake African accent. "Hello, good evening, I am wanting to go back to Africa to find the true Zulu's could you help me please?" The officer has a red face and doesn't know were to put himself, until hundreds of Brummies who know Smurf all start pissing themselves laughing. This is the thing about Birmingham supporters that some fans will never understand, and that is that we are crap, we have mainly been crap all of our existence, and it does matter who owns Birmingham City or plays football for the team. Hardly any of them are real Blue noses in their mindset except for the fans, and that will never change.

DAVID C GEORGE

Birmingham taunt Milwall with a pisstake Nazi salute – 2002 Playoffs

Blues escorted to station – 2002 Playoffs

APEX TO ZULU A2Z!

Milwall start to play up
– 2002 Playoffs

Blues arriving at Milwall
– 2002 Playoffs

Blues kept away from rioting Milwall fans after losing the game

DAVID C GEORGE

The front of the Blues escort at Millwall – 2002

Blues vs. Millwall – 2002

Millwall vs. Blues – 2002 Playoffs

CHAPTER 9

Middlesborough Away 84
The Mighty Few

8th Dec 84 Home – 6th May 85 Away

MIDDLESBOROUGH, THE INDUSTRIAL NORTH and an absolute shithole. If you were to take a shit in Middlesborough, you would have to apologise to the shit for leaving it there. This place was grim as fuck and the KLF were absolutely right. It is grim up north. The place was full of big ugly knuckle draggers who worked on the docks and had no idea how to write their own names or dress themselves properly. Welcome to Middlesborough. In 1975, Birmingham played Middlesboro in a cup game at St Andrews which we won 1 – 0. Several years later, Mooney, Big Glynn and Big Cookie were drinking in the Yellow Rose in Boro and got talking to a monster of a man who was a local supporter. He asks the three Blues fans if they went to the game in 75 at St Andrews, and the three looked at each other and replied, "No why?" The guy says that when he left the game at our ground with his friends, he was walking down Cattle Road and was punched in the face and thrown off the bridge, which doesn't surprise me in the least. Middlesboro and Birmingham have always had a rivalry since the mid seventies when they came into the Kop at St Andrews and also in 86. We know Middelesboro is a tough northern town, but also they realise Birmingham City are the Midlands chaps from the industrial working-class streets.

DAVID C GEORGE

I arrived on a special and was taken with a huge number of blues supporters off the train and straight onto buses towards the ground. Being that I didn't go to Scarborough the night before, I thought it would be safer to go straight to the ground rather than having a mooch on my jack through the centre. We arrived at the ground and paid straight in. Blues were sitting behind the goal and singing their hearts out which put a huge smile on my face. I hadn't seen any Boro as of yet until near the end of the game. Birmingham's firm of around 400 tidy lads were standing in the seats with a foot on the seats in front pointing and singing to the Boro fans, "On the pitch, on the pitch on the pitch"

The police came and lined up in front of us just in case we attempted it, but I don't think we wanted to go on the pitch in the first place due to the number of Boro that had flown in front of the goal, and were now standing behind the police and goading us to make a move. Boro's firm was fucking huge and game, but they had not yet seen what Birmingham can do if put into a situation of violence. It was a goalless draw 0–0 and we left the ground after the game.

We left gagging to bang it straight off with Boro, but the local police had other ideas. A road full of buses awaited Blues fans and most were forced onto the free transport back to the station. The road to our right was barricaded with metal waist-high fences. Fat Errol was standing on the other side of the barriers and a small number of Blues firm were looking to join him to go on a mission. Blues then kicked down the barriers and around 70 good lads went looking for Boro. The police outside the ground saw this and stopped us immediately, but we said we had come in vans and that they were parked near the centre. The police let us go, but to this day I recon they knew we hadn't got any vans, but were expecting us to get our heads well and truly caved in.

As we are walking up the road, Boro fans are leaving the ground and we had walked round to the other side of the ground for some knuckle. The home fans are all over the place and The Frontline boys are in small numbers and haven't got together yet. Trevor can't wait and flies into them straight away and gets collared by the old bill. The strange thing was that the police officer held him down on the floor and said something in his ear, let him get back up and let us off again.

We now are on a large main road and I'm walking with some of Birmingham's proper top boys and some of the gamest juniors around. From Highgate to Yew Tree, Bordesley Green to Chelmsley Wood, Billseley to Ward End. This firm was proper top drawer.

In the distance at the end of the road, we could see a huge group of lads coming towards us. Make no mistake; it was The Frontline with numbers of around 700–800 strong. Some of Blues' top boys were rallying the troops and getting everybody to tool up, make 3 lines and get ready to have it proper. I'll be honest and say I thought we had bitten off more than we could chew, but I also realised the lads I was with had no intention of running anywhere. We pulled down fences, we had crates of milk bottles but I seriously didn't think we had enough for this huge firm coming towards us. If you have ever seen the beginning of the London Marathon, that will give you an idea of what was coming towards us. A guy from Bordesley Green was shouting through gritted teeth and walking up and down in the road on tiptoe frowning and saying. "STAND! Mek a line, no one fucking run, lets fucking do it." I turned to big Stig and told him this was going to be a fucking mad one, and he looked at me while pulling on a fence saying, "Fucking electric, isn't it?"

Boro are now very close and the sound of their firm roaring towards us was heavy. Blues stood their ground and the first wave of Frontline clashed with The Zulu Warriors and Juniors. Middlesboro's frontline were big and fucking ugly and I know for a fact that if Blues had run that day, they would still be buried up there. Blues held the line and dealt with the first wave of Boro. A number of people from either side were floored, but it was Birmingham that stepped forward and changed gear. This was the first time I had seen Cuds drop some serious roundhouses leaving a number of Boro sprawled over cars.

Cotterill had his Aquascutum jumper caught on a low spikey metal fence and was being pummelled by two Boro lads; I stepped in and slapped a guy round his face and kicked him in the chest. Cotterill had to leave his jumper on the fence because it was in rag order.

Middlesborough didn't know how to get the job done and stood where they were, they didn't run but they didn't move forward either.

DAVID C GEORGE

A number of The Frontline standing further back were throwing house bricks, but the only problem was they were standing too far back and every house brick was hitting their own lads on the backs of their heads. Blues moved forward again and held the 3 lines, any one of Boro who got caught out when Blues stepped forward were well and truly wiped out by the second and then the third line of Blues. Game as fuck, and military tactics are some of the main reasons why Birmingham City has always been in the top five of firms for the last 21 years.

The police turn up after around 3 minutes of full-scale brawling round up all of the Zulu's on one side of the road. Middlesborough's firm is so big that it is now in front of us, at the side of us, and behind.

A police officer is looking at the blues firm and shaking his head, and it turns out to be the same old bill who let us through when we said we were in vans. He obviously cannot believe how many of us have just taken on the full firm of Boro and are still here to tell the tale.

The local police and The Frontline firm, who are not happy at all, are now escorting blues through Middlesborough back to the station on foot, which took forever. On the doorsteps as we were bowling through Middlesborough, were a select few big burly northerners literally standing on their doorsteps with their children, shouting racial abuse at the Birmingham fans. This was very surreal for me, because the scene sounds so cliché about the north and their views that I had to speak to a few black lads walking back to the station." Did you see that?" Was what I kept saying, because no matter how surreal it sounds, this was the reality we were in, and thank God for civilisation, because from I having seen up there, had made me realise how nice it is to come from a city that is rich in ethnic diversity and doing very well from it.

Blues firm have yet again shown why they are rated so highly and have also shown Middlesborough a thing or to about dressing, because most of them did not have a Scooby Doo.

As we arrive at the station, we are told the last train back to Birmingham had already gone, but they said we could catch the next train to York and see what we could do there. We got on the train and landed in York, and as soon as we stepped off the train, the York police bundled us all into waiting vans and told us our sort were not stopping in York for the evening. The police dropped us at the side of the motorway, kicked us out, and said. "Birmingham is that way" and drove off. The lads had now felt the full hospitality of the north, and were eager to get the hell home, but our journey was far from over. We were now walking along the hard shoulder of the motorway thumbing lifts, and a few lucky bastards got lifts after a few hours. After a number of other people had got lifts, it started to get dark and around fifteen of the JBB got off the motorway and walked into a local village police station. Most of the juniors never paid for most of what they indulged in throughout the day, including train tickets, food, drink, and even tickets for the game, and would find it more difficult to get home from an away match sometimes due to their ages and financial backing. Being thirteen to sixteen, it is a lot easier for other crews to take an interest in you because a lot of older people saw us as a soft touch. If you can imagine being a character from the film, The Warriors, with crews all trying to outdo each other to become the top dog, this was the feeling throughout the eighties.

On the way home, a couple of guys walking with us on the motorway were lucky enough to get a lift all the way to the Midlands. A couple of people, one a professional stripper and her manager who were also travelling all the way to Leicester, picked up Jeff & Applehead. The one girl was talking pure filth as soon as they both got in the car, and Jeff and Applehead declined the stripper's advances due to their young ages. The stripper was a stunner, but the idea of having sex with a stranger in a moving car, with the manager driving, didn't appeal to either Jeff or Applehead. On the way to Leicester, the car pulled up at a service station and they bumped into Coaly and Stig who had got a lift in another car. After Jeff explained to Stig that they were having a lift off a stripper who wanted some action, Stig got a lift in the other car and was a very lucky bastard on this day, as the girl decided to undo his trousers, lift up her denim mini skirt, and ride the be-Jesus out of him while in the car. Jeff sat there laughing like Sid James, while Stig had a face on him that looked as though he'd just won the lottery. Ka ching, ka ching. As for us, we sent in a white lad to do the talking at the village police station, because we realised that the only time these people round here had probably seen a black man, was when David Attenborough was doing a voice over on BBC2. The police generously gave us a lift to the nearest intercity train station, which turned out to be Leeds, so we knew the night was definitely not over.

As we got out of the Police van, Leeds juniors, the VYT were standing down the road from the station and instantly clocked us. We walked into the train station and sat down. By this time after rowing The Frontline and walking up the fucking motorway for hours, we were all knackered and just wanted to rest, but we are in Leeds City centre so that was simply not on the agenda.

From Birmingham humiliating Leeds at home on the 15th Dec 84, and winning 1–0, and also bringing a huge firm to Elland Road, we knew something was going to happen this evening.

The doors opened, and around eight Leeds young dressers came bowling into the station to check us out. They were actually sound lads and we ended up having a right good chat with them. Some of Blues even went to a local cafe with the Leeds lot and came back unscathed. Me, I stayed in the station because my instinct told me that Leeds is a racist city and the only reason they are talking to us, was to soften us up for something later. From my point of view I could not trust Leeds fans who I had just met, and are well known as one of the most fascist firms ever to be associated with professional football in Britain.

I was chatting to a guy from Leeds called Eddie Kelly who was proper clued up and a tidy little dresser, and a member of the VYT The Very Young Team. He was saying Blues had better be ready for last game of the season next week at our ground, because Leeds are bringing it. I laughed at Eddie and explained to him that the amount of firms that say this about Blues is ridiculous, but just remember that Birmingham City are no joke son, and just like Luv Injection sound system in the 80s. We nagh tek back no tark. Later that evening, one of the younger Leeds must have gone into town and told the older Service Crew there were Brummies on the station. Around 40 lads came bursting through the doors, hands behind their backs and veins up at the side of their necks. We got landed on; we were repeatedly kicked all over Leeds station. Every time I tried to get up, I was volleyed back to the floor. As I looked up through a swollen face, a guy was standing over me smiling, saying. "We're the real Leeds." They all walked out of the station and left us all over the floor. The stage was well and truly set for last game of the season at our ground now, and Leeds would feel what its like to come to Birmingham City where everything in your worst nightmares is waiting for you.

Sunderland vs Birmingham City FA cup 84

Birmingham met at the Roundabout pub and used Martins coaches from West Brom, which Blues lads used on a regular basis. Two coaches of lads went up to Sunderland and stopped off on the seafront near a huge hotel. One of the Blues lads took a huge piece of seaweed that was attached to two rocks, and placed it on the reception desk. It was shaped like a pair of huge balls and penis. The staff were screaming for it to be removed, but the Blues lads found it hilarious. Birmingham fans now enter the bar where Malcolm Allison, the Manchester City manager at the time, was with a young lady. At first, everyone was being very courteous to the Man City manager, and there were laughs and some jokes being shared. The atmosphere changed when one of the Birmingham lot swore, Mr Allison took offence. "Could you stop your swearing, I've got me girl here!" Somebody else swore, and then McCormick bounced a spoon of Mr Allison's head. Mouthfuls of spit now covered his round hat and over-coat that he wore. Mr Allison got up and made a quick sharp exit.

Some of the Birmingham lads were feeling peckish, so they went to the restaurant area of the hotel. A woman had collected her meal of roast beef and Yorkshire pudding with all the trimmings, and had just gone to pick up some condiments, when a few Birmingham lads relieved her of her meal, scoffing it down their necks in less than a minute. When the she came back, all that was left was some gravy and a few processed peas. A lad from Acocks green snuck under the counter and the till from the restaurant was also robbed.

Birmingham were now wandering round the hotel looking for something else to steal, when they come across a display cabinet. It was a black Lyle & Scott jumper, a pair of Levi jeans and various toiletries. They found the entrance to the cabinet through a janitor's cupboard, which had a false wall. After giving the false wall a bit of prising, it came away and all of the items from the cabinet were taken. The guy with the jeans called Chicken, wanted to swap the Lyle & Scott as the jeans were way to big for him, but it went down to stalemate. Chicken now puts the huge Levis over his own jeans and wears them to the game, but I was told that the jeans wore so big they wouldn't fit him to this day.

At the game, Birmingham won 2 – 1, with Kuhl and Harford on the score sheet but Birmingham were knocked out in the 6th round 3 – 1 by Watford.

Info on the clash with Borough away, one week before the Blues Leeds riot 84. The mighty few that stood and took on all comers in Middlesborough and the racialism shown to us by the local people up north.

Liverpool away 81 League cup

Liverpool is definitely the place in the UK that first set the trend for expensive designer clothing taken from stealing garments on their European travels from places such as Austria, France, Italy and Switzerland and wherever they played. Most of the well known names on the high street that are placed on youths backs were brand new to the young Scouse English man, and he robbed the hell out of them, starting a whole new youth culture that evolved and developed over the next two decades and onwards. Birmingham arrive in Liverpool in 81 when V-neck cashmere sweaters, wedge heads and Lois jeans and cords were well in fashion.

Birmingham at the time only had a handful of dressers as most of the crew were still favouring the green flying jacket and the Harrington with Levi jeans and Adidas Samba.

Birmingham takes a mob of around 100 lads on the train to Liverpool who knew each other very well. The likes of, The Yeoman, Woodies, The Friendly, The Roundhouse, The Southern Cross The Hiker and The Happy Trooper all came together from one area. A local lad used to work in a tool shop, and used to make rounders bats for the match especially for games that were extremely volatile. The bats were around 18inches long with a slim handle and a circular ball at the slim end to stop it from slipping out of your hand when in use. As the bat widened it moved up to its end and became thicker than a rounders bat, but very mobile and handy in close quarter battles. Birmingham arrive in Liverpool and march into town mob handed.

M. O'Burn, C. O'Burn, A. Barry, Coo-coo, Cockney Al, Aston, Clacka, Jeyes, Craffty, Troganite, Bobby F, Moggy, Deano, Cookie, Stan, Big Glyn, Trout, Zoffo, Smith, Pip, G. Delaney, S. Delaney, D. Sherlock, T. Sherlock ECT. The crew was heavy duty. The first words that were heard from Liverpool fans to Birmingham when they met in the centre was, "Get the darky"

"Get da fuckin darky" The lot goes up in the air outside a pub and Birmingham are being pelted with stools, bottles and beer glasses. One of the Birmingham lads has grabbed a bag out of a nearby bin, and started pelting the Liverpool fans with bottles. Birmingham rush Liverpool who are now trying to get back into the pub when the police arrive and the whole situation calms down. Birmingham now link up with another good mob of Blues fans and attempt to cross a huge dual carriageway now 300 handed. A few smaller mobs of scousers are on the other side of the dual carriageway calling it on, and Brummy Jimmy is so keen to get it on with the Liverpool lot that he gets run down crossing the road, and has to be taken to hospital by ambulance with a broken leg. It was a night match, but it wasn't quite dark and Birmingham had got to Anfield very early. Birmingham now marched around Anfields ground 300 handed and went into every pub around the ground taking the piss, and looking for Liverpool's mob, but they were nowhere to be seen.

As soon as the sun went down Liverpool's crews started to turn up, but they didn't realise Birmingham now had two mobs on either side of Anfield at least a 100 handed and were smacking the shit out of any wedge heads or lads wearing puffer jackets. Liverpool were walking round the ground in mobs of 20 – 30 looking to pick off any Brummies unlucky enough to be caught out, but what they didn't know was that Birmingham were doing exactly the same as them but in much larger numbers. Birmingham lost the game 3 – 1 with Bertchin scoring our only goal, but the Birmingham fans were evolving at the time into a different animal. The early 80's are when Birmingham lads were metamorphosing and trying to find a new direction. The football trendy was here to stay and had a lot of vocal words to say. Birmingham fans were becoming more confident and started to believe in themselves more than in the 70s era. Times were definitely changing for our Brummy fans.

Liverpool vs Birmingham 82

Around 12 Apex travel to Liverpool on the train from New Street, changing at Crewe. The Birmingham lads had been playing up on the train, robbing the refreshments bar and managed to be thrown off the train. A few who never got caught stealing stayed on the train and arrived in Lime Street. The 3 Brummies explained to the mob of Liverpool that there was a bigger mob of Brummies coming in on the next train. So not intentionally, the 3 Brummy lads had set the others up. As the Birmingham lot who changed trains got to Lime Street, they entered an amusement arcade and had a go on the fruit machines deciding what to do. As there were only 9 of them, they were extremely nervous about going to the game in such a small number. They knew it was going to be difficult to get to the ground because anyone will tell you Liverpool is not one of the most racially harmonious places in the country when linked to football fans, as only in Huyton in 2005 Anthony Walker, a young black lad was savagely attacked and killed on the street with a mountaineering ice axe by a lad who embedded it into his skull because he didn't like the fact he had a white girlfriend. Some areas of Liverpool are still rather backward in this respect. A mob of Scousers came into the arcade and started to threaten the Birmingham lot. They surrounded the 9 Apex lads when the Old Bill came into the arcade and immediately tried to throw all the youngsters out of the arcade thinking that they were Scousers. The Birmingham lot told the police officer that they were not with the mob of about 20 Scousers and were from Birmingham, and wanted to go to the game. The police officers took the Birmingham lot to the bus stop and told them what bus to get, and then left.

As the police leave, the inevitable happens, and the scousers now come back. The police are across the road watching and now come back across the road and put the Scousers on the bus and advise the Birmingham lot to get the next one.

The Scousers get on the bus and leave, then five minutes later the Brummies get on the next bus and only 500 yards round the corner, the Scousers get off their bus and now come onto the bus with the Brummies. The Birmingham lot are at the back of the bus trying to keep calm. One Brummy has a blade and a metal Afro comb, which he gives to another wearing an Adidas cagoule, Levis jeans and leg warmers. The metal comb falls on the floor of the bus, and all Scouse heads turn to see what was dropped. Everything was OK and nobody was cut up or lost teeth. The Liverpool lot started to give Birmingham some verbal but the Birmingham lads had nowhere to go except forward as they were all sitting at the back of the bus. As the bus arrive near the ground, they are confronted by a sea of Liverpool fans wearing red and white all walking towards the game. The Birmingham lads wait for the Liverpool lot to go down the stairs on the bus outside the ground. "Don't start anything, we wont do fuck all unless they start." As the Birmingham lads are now coming down the stairs, one of the Acocks Green lads decides on diving into the middle of the scousers and smashing people in the face downstairs on the bus. The Birmingham lads now kick the rest of the scousers off the bus and the doors shut. The bus driver turns and says, "Brummies?" They reply, "Yes!" The driver says, "Come on, I'll get you out of here." The bus driver drives down the road with the mob of Liverpool now chasing the bus. The driver now turns and says, "What I will do is flag down another bus going the other way, and you can go to the match lads, alright?" The Brummies couldn't believe how sound this Scouse bus driver was. The 9 Brummies now get on the bus going back to the ground and leave the scousers chasing an empty bus in the opposite direction. By the time they realised it was empty, and they had walked back to the ground, the Brummies were already standing outside the turnstiles of the away end smiles. The 20 Scousers have got back to the ground out of breath and knackered saying, "Where the fuck ave your lot bin?" The Brummies and the scousers ended up having a laugh together outside the game, with no trouble what so ever. The scousers were saying, "You lot, your fucking Barmy." Everybody was all smiles, and the two groups of supporters went and watched the game. Birmingham drew the game 2–2, with Evans and Ainscow on the score sheet for Blues.

Who left early at Liverpool

    To the faithful who travel home and away
    Started off come on admit it
    Listening to critics impending doom surely
    Destined to be relegated to
    Last game to be shown on match of the day
    Our opposition played well or gave a bad display
    The contemptible critics slaughter
    Under the bridge that passes no water
    Every good move or build up or through ball
    He was definitely offside the ref made a good call
    Our goofs and gaffs they share with the nation
    Do you see the game we play with passion?
    We march on with luck not usually on side
    Out singing the Anfield was never that hard
    Shall we sing a song for you we cried
    You fuckin mugging Scally retards

Liverpool Vs Birmingham City 83 Black Rejection
Morph

The biggest fear for most football fans back in the eighties was to be thrown out of the ground in a place home fans are milling around. In Liverpool you have the Scallies or the taxers who will without question, slice you to ribbons and kick your head in with no qualms at all. The reason I was thrown out of Anfield was that there was a big confrontation with the old bill, and the police were doing what they do. There was a lot of pushing and shoving.

    Missiles are thrown at the police; another officer is chinned and hits the floor.

    The police were pushing the fans around to cause a mini riot. An officer on a horse swings round on this huge beast and decides on one target, which unfortunately was me. The police now drag me to the gates and I am ejected from the ground. The Black Blues fans are pleading with the officer not to throw me out of the ground, as this is the same as signing my death sentence, and he knew it. The local police are aware that in 1983, Liverpool did not have any black fans, and if they did, they would not be dressers or casuals but just local Liverpudlians. You might as well say he hoped I am on the news later on in the evening for being slashed to pieces by a mob of Huyton or any other group of locals. As I'm standing outside, the police always tell you to get away from the ground knowing full well that the further you go away from the ground, the more chance you have of being attacked by a bunch of Scallies. Thrown out on my own wearing the football uniform that all of Liverpool's lads would know. The police told Morph that if he was going to go anywhere, to get down to Stanley Park, which is where Liverpool fans attack away fans. In-between Stanley Park and Anfield is a car park. I go and hang around in the car park and I would prefer to take my chances in there. There are two entrances to the car park. Morph has then picked stray bottles and large bricks found on the floor, and strategically placed them around himself and nearby just in case it becomes raving on top. I'm sitting down in the car park trying to do a low profile, as this was one of my biggest fears, to be caught by a group of Liverpool and slashed up big time. After around twenty-five minutes the gates have opened and another Brummie is thrown out of the ground. Morph hoped it was going to be another lad or a geezer who could have it when the time was necessary, and it was.

This guy was from Bordesley Green and has stood on for Blues on numerous occasions. They saw and greeted each other and then the important question was asked by the lad from Bordesley Green, "What's the score, have they been mooching around yet?" Morph replies, "I've seen one or two of them on the perimeters, but nothing significant, I've just kept my head down." The reply was, "Ok then." If you listen to this brief conversation, it could easily be taken from a well-known war movie. The two Brummie lads now walk into the car park and Morph shows the lad from Bordesley Green all of the bricks and bottles that he has accumulated to defend himself. Morph had even pissed in a bottle to give it a bit more weight when it flies.

Two Scousers have now walked trough the car park and the two blues lads have confronted them, "Come on then," there's two of you and two of us, what ya saying?" The Scousers saw that the two of us were not going to run, they have left through the alleyway. They have now come back with four lads, with two big lumps and two smaller lads. The two big lads have gone towards the lad from Bordesley Green and the two smaller lads have come for me. The two big lads walked towards the guy from Bordesley Green, when Morph steps forward and says to the guy from Liverpool. "Look lads" Morph points at one of the big Scousers and says, "I'll have you and him, so lets make it a bit more even" The lad from Bordesley Green bursts out laughing at Morphs comment, but this has sent a huge question mark through the Scouser's heads. The Scousers turn and run off having being bluffed by the psychology of Morph. As the scousers were about to run, you could here them saying, "Crazy, dees lads a fuckin crazy." The Scousers tried to intimidate us but realised that we were going nowhere. Near the end of the game the Scousers are now going to come back with heavy numbers and the final whistle has just been blown. This now firm of around fifteen scousers are now at the entrance to the car park about to make their move when low and behold, in the near distance was big Willy who was strolling towards us and behind this group of scousers. All I could see was this permed hair bouncing down the road. Morph has turned round to the group of Scousers with a smile on his face and says, "I'll give you ten seconds to run?" One of the Scouse lads says, "What you on about mate?" "Zulus are behind you mate." The roar goes up, ZULUUUUUUUUUUU! and the Scousers have done one as fast as they appeared.

Manchester United vs Birmingham City 82

Having a successful football team breeds arrogant football supporters who believe that because your team is clearly not on par with them, this means you are not entitled to give them hell. We at Birmingham City however believe wholeheartedly we will give any successful teams hell, because it is a tradition bestowed on Midlanders and supporters of not very good teams all across the country. Watch how Birmingham City plays football, and try to tell me they have an idea on how to actually win a fucking game. Yeah right! Believe it or not, I actually love Birmingham City down to the last molecule, but I also understand that in 2006 in the premiership, we do not have a bunch of players who are keen on putting in the effort to win games, but are happy they are getting paid in full.

Around 200 Manchester United lads were sitting in the paddock end at St Andrews, which is where Birmingham's home supporters sit. This mob of Manchester had come to Birmingham with the vowed intention of kicking it right off. Man Utd won the game 1 – 0, but left the game ten minutes from the end of play and took a walk round to the home supporters entrance. Around 15 Apex also left to see what was happening and to find out where Man Utd's mob was off to.

Man Utd had walked past the old Bingo Hall and were now heading up the road near the old bus depot. The 15 Apex spotted Man Utd and the Manks let out a huge roar and come bouncing up the road towards the 15 blues fans. Blues backed off up the road and were chased, but as this was taking place the final whistle had just been blown and the home crowd were now all spilling onto the same road that Man Utd's mob were chasing the Apex. Proud working class fathers with their sons by their side were all exiting St Andrews Kop stand, to see what was happening with the Apex and Man Utd. Hundreds of dads were now keen on helping the Apex against Man Utd, and many fathers were seen pointing at their sons to stay where they were while they went to help the 15 Blues lads. Man Utd got absolutely smashed to pieces by our mature section of Blues supporters who punched and kicked them all over the main road stopping all of the traffic. Combined with the 15 Apex lads, and mothers who took their shoes off to beat over the heads of the Manchester lot. Everybody turned on Manchester, and Birmingham fans now chase Man Utd down the Coventry Road, the dark of the bus depot was Man Utd's top lad at the time, Black Sam, standing up the wall with his sunglasses on hiding.

Bringing Them Round To My Way Of Thinking

ACT 1

As I swung the door closed behind,
And from a slide into a glide and a,

DAVID C GEORGE

The gate latch clicked first time.
An air of optimism about the day,
Fine as it was.
The Manchester United were to visit St Andrews
The weather even seemed pre booked for a photo shoot,
Casting light and shadow down red brick Digbeth facades.
Adjusting at Ye Old Crown we took Medicine at the Bar.
To a gathering at The Hen and Chickens.
Some came from over The Rainbow,
As we sunk in Open Moseley Arms,
You wouldn't Adam and Eve,
As the crowds outside toasted the skyline,
Smelt a fresher new air,
From our emerging new city,
Standing magnificent and ready.

As time grew near and glasses on the bar were ready for the wash,
Like birds to roost,
Supporters in the streets surround were ready,
Drawn.
We strolled and frequented,
Some laughed and lamented,
At tales of ruffling a feather or two.
Now it has been remarked and duly accepted,
That my attire like my opinion,
Are objective yet well presented,
Slightly nostalgic but not sepia tinted,
When it comes to the game,
And the art of supporting your team
Then definition behest on one truly blessed,
And an eloquent delivery indeed.
From a Mr Danny Blanchflower.
Rest In Peace.

'The great fallacy is that the game is first and foremost about winning!

APEX TO ZULU A2Z!

It is nothing of the sort
The game is about glory.
It is about doing things with style and with a flourish,
About going out and beating the lot,
And not waiting for them to die of boredom.'
On the way up the hill to the ground I skipped on the chance,
At the old Watering Hole as it was now corporately soured,
So I bought a tea from the van by the car park that was once Mecca,
The bingo that is!
St Andrews standing proud on its own hallowed ground,
A little further on,

And a pound was paid for my half time distraction,
The Zulu, our fanzine, the voice of the factions,
Where players caught aloof and salubrious the night before D-Day,
Or a Prima Donna behaving like he's bigger than the club,
Learn hell hath no fury come match day.
'Play for the shirt or fuck off!!'
The front page emblazed.
Just another idiosyncrasy of our amazing occasion,
As we assemble outside the ground,
Waiting,
Jostling,
To-in, fro in,
Listening to the turnstiles like a metronome
My dad lifted me over them there almost like home.

I sit in the Kop bottom left as you look at the pitch,
Adjacent the travelling support,
Our guests
Man U as always selling all there allocation,
The self assured nature and arrogance a mesmerising sight,
Watching three and half thousand spontaneous,
Chanting in unison with the timing of a church choir,
And although leaving me envious and infuriated,
Witnessing the nonchalance in following a champion side.

DAVID C GEORGE

I still felt a bond,
I still felt a pride,
Vilified at the sight,
To have the solidarity and camaraderie of my fellow supporters.

Was it fate our paths crossed or did it happen by chance,
As a result of an instance nearing the end of the game,
In a contest where we had not played dishonourably,
The seemingly inevitable transpired,
With Louis Saha putting the reds on course for a two one recovery,
The result a mere formality,
The verdict already,
The ruling of a Man-Chester zoo court,
And in there celebrations premature but probable,
They started the party and practised their wit.
Proclaiming their love for club over country,
Thus rattling the cage of a very patriotic Brit!

So adorned in my customary Bowler hat,
Three quarter length Macintosh,
Which cloaked my fine Crombie tweed,
I turned my trusty Alfred Sargeant boots,
Momentarily away from the path of decorum and sartorial elegance,
And placing them firmly on my seat,
I elevated Churchill's victory salute,
Thus drawing their attention,
Upon which I demanded an explanation or apology,
For if not a joke was damn near heresy.

Now the nations finest they may be,
But their appreciation for the bespoke and the man made upper
Was discouraging and duly noted by its absence,
One small faction even chanting that my pre war Lincoln Bennet lightweight bowler hat was the worst they had ever seen,
A fraudulent and unfounded claim,
Which was delivered without such detail,

APEX TO ZULU A2Z!

(Which in itself an admission along with the chance passed,
To poke fun and snigger at the unseasonable state of my attire,
As twas still classed as spring,
As a heavyweight hat,
Lined inside would be proper.)
So by seizing the opportunity I introduced the idea to them,
Also the guilty looking Brummies that by now were looking on,
My unfortunate friend in the seat next to me,
Who after being hired for the next fifteen minutes as my stooge,
Sacrificed his specimen so to help me elaborate my point,
Which many must share!
Can you hear me in the Olympic gallery!?!,,
Is there any one there?

'The wearing of the Burberry baseball cap,
Does not elevate your fantasy hooli-league status,
Nor are you soaring the heights in next seasons terrace couture,'
But for some all misty eyed in football like in life,
They show up thinking the parties just begun.

The baseball cap,
American sports apparel created to shade the eyes,
From the sun, floodlights, sun, floodlights, sun, floodlights,
Of an eternal,
Infernal preoccupation.
This protection appealed to the early strobe light trip heads,
Who unknowingly became the faces of Stoned Island council estate chic.

Draped in the trademark check of a reputable tailor,
First worn sport casually,
By early Johnny come lately,
After being given Carte blanch,
On the boulevards and in the boutiques of Europe's finest cities,
Scrumping the abundant fruits,
Thanks to the labours and endeavours of their club and countries

DAVID C GEORGE

torchbearers.
By requisitioning these quality garms,
From shops with doorbells,
Leaving card instead of plastic,
And parading them up and down intercity railway carriages,
Warehouse raves, and home and away terraces,
Instead of the catwalks at fashion week,
And all the "right places"

Even TV documentaries!
"We're like a family. Nice jeans nice top!"

Liberties taken the Nani Bon gone,
Pierre's Cardin and Sangen were both left hanging,
As the La Coste were lost and the Barbour went bye bye,
With only the sight of rainbow coloured Fred Perry's,
Hanging out of the Gore-Tex poachers pockets,
As the Timberlands ran away,
And came back!
You see they all came back.
Realised their mistakes,
When thanks to a marketing master stroke,
They had the last laugh.
I can still hear them now…
"Well out of order, they went mail order in the guise of your mums catalogue!!"

Pair of Rockport's, Ralph Lauren Harrington,
Burberry Baseball cap topped off with a nice Ben Sherman.

'Five pound sixty three for one hundred and fifty weeks,'
Delivered to the shark bait sign you put in the window,
As promised the real deal,
Not an inside leg measured or a cognac before the final fitting, no,
I see you chose the alternative colours though,
The ones in the smaller pictures or not at all,

APEX TO ZULU A2Z!

'Five pound sixty three for one hundred and fifty weeks?'
I do hope you like it youth,
You're going to be wearing it for the next three years,
And you may notice your mum having a few nights in from now on,
Oh silly me, you'll be out letting em get a load of you, eh?
In the laser beams!

To summarise 'You really ought to try to be an individual, or what's the use?
Are you a firm or a flock? Are you obtuse?'

Well.
Their response was inaudible,
And far, far from laudable,
When I held aloft my hat to thank them for our discourse,
There was a moment I'm sure the gust nearly parted my hair!

ACT 2
A large column in front of me,
Upstanding members of the West Midlands police farce,
They came inching along the row,
The advancing malnourished undersexed new recruit,
Was smugly rubbing his black leather Christmas presents together,
I couldn't help thinking after a close albeit brief inspection,
That it was a good job he was at the match having the pleasure of my company,
And not the miner's riots in the thick of it,
As the mock leather and sweat shop stitching I believe would of let him down.

'Right mate time to get you back to that fancy dress shop! Your nicked!!'

Well,
I've never been so insulted in my thirty years,
I'd have clipped the upstart if it wasn't for section eighteen,

DAVID C GEORGE

I supposed he was arresting me for being badly addressed in public,

It was bewildering to witness my audience animated,
Even the cantankerous old fucker, (and I rarely swear but words leave me,
This gentleman delivers a match day diatribe which is the reason the management don't let razorblades inside,
He tells me to sit down yet he stands in front of me,
And he gets on with my old man,)
Even he was protesting asking the man if he'd took leave of his senses,
When he revealed my charge was of inciting a riot,
The irony.

I implored with his judgement as we shuffled past friends to the steps,
And after the comedy of somebody else's tragedy had quelled,
Half the ground I'm sure were vocal in their dis-belief,
There was boo's and hisses,
Even the Man U were standing rallying to the cause,
And having a bloody good laugh about something,
This wasn't the time for japes.

As I grew nearer and made out the whites of their eyes and the width of their smiles,
I shimmied free from my captures grasp,
And acknowledged the appreciation with the universal football salute,
Two hands gently upheld gently applauding,
Dignified and respectful.

What happened next will never leave me!
As the sight of three and a half thousand away supporters,
Reciprocated the very same salute, all at the very same moment,
With the very same intent,
It brought a tear to ones glass eye.

APEX TO ZULU A2Z!

I have read the autobiography of a Mr Cass Pennant,
There at the ICF's inception and wise from these years,
Went on to lead a successful life,
Littered with many a colourful moment and the odd moral crusade,
A gentleman.
But the story I refer to goes back to his notorious days with West Ham,
When he and his pal Danny waded into the Shelf in full view,
Of the travelling claret and blue,
Bringing White Hart Lane to a standstill,
Even making into the nations front rooms,
As the Match Of The Day cameras momentarily glanced over in the pre match panoramic,
To witness West Ham giving Cass and co. a standing ovation,
When after satisfying his appetite with the Tottenham masses,
He then persuaded the police and stewards he was acting in self-defence,
And walked himself back to the away end.

Now a hooligan I am not,
I prefer to parade in the finer lines carved from a Sartor's blade,
Than explain the tares in my birthday suit that a rookie with a Stanley knife made,
But I could relate to the dumbstruck feeling, overwhelming,
The crowd, the size, as it dawns, a star is born,
If you've ever stood on a terrace, taken part in the chants,
Getting the odd gesture back when the ball goes out,
Bringing Gazza to tears when he's had his last chance.

Ok Cass had been pinging white and blue like he was the fairground hammer,
The notorious ICF, and he was on telly,
And he was anything he liked Mr Pennant sir!
But in my eyes I had triumphed,
I was knocking them dead, I didn't need telly,
It was music hall, Vaudeville,

DAVID C GEORGE

I was home and I brightened a great day,
And something to remember from three and a half thousand,
Manchester United away.
Louis Saha scored today, won them the game,
I apologise for stealing his spotlight,
Oh well better luck next time eh?

I paused and felt the warm glow.
A bonafide desert island moment,

Then I was lurched out of my moment by the two cuntstables,
Who were escorting me down the steps?
Obliviously oblivious to all around them,
My action, supporter's reactions and the way they used their powers to persuade,

In their defence they were young and cocksure,
It would be fair to say scared.
Our regular match day Bobbies appreciate what an uncomfortable position it is to be in,
Weeks on end,

Bad losers, boozers, crazies, and racists are all dealt with discretely,
Before our name and our game are brought into disrepute,
A respect and rapport built up over many different encounters,
But just as the hooligan drags down the fans name,
So the filth does the same to the force.

At the foot of the stairs, I managed a fleeting glance,
Cherishing the moment as it was so sweet, so surreal,
As I was lead away no encore or curtain call,
I felt the burn as my wrists turned,

'We want our Charlie back!
We want our Charlie back!
We want our Charlie back!'

APEX TO ZULU A2Z!

The echoing sounding off all around,
'Look what you did lads, you made me famous.'
Aaaaahh!!.
I was frog marched as they goose stepped out of the ground to my waiting containment,
As they swung the doors open and muscled me inside,
From an elegant mod leaving early to avoid the creases,
Their numbers were took and a verbal tirade,
About the disgrace he'd just seen and a complaint would be made,
The echoing sounding off all around,

'Look what I did lads, I made you famous!'
Slammmm…

ACT 3
I was walked into the holding cell,
I took the initiative and assumed the star shaped spread em against the wall,
Ready for the shake down.
The duty officer a mature gentlemen with a seasoned look on his face,
Calmly pointed out that I was in Birmingham City and not New York City,
And was in the safe charge of the West Midlands police force and not the N.Y.P.D!
But after enquiring if the cunstable who escorted me from the ground had attended the same public relations seminar,
Or merely mistook my thumbs for a computer joystick,
He changed his tune along with his face and preceded to cavity search me!

Well!
What he was about to get himself into I winced at the thought,
As in the ways to accessorise I have been exceptionally taught,
First off with my hat, then cravat,
Hipflask and solid silver cigarette case,
Handkerchiefs, cufflinks, and armbands,

DAVID C GEORGE

Oh the look on his face,
I daren't tell him in case.
As his windmill arms were festooning my lucky charms,
Which previously had so subtly accentuated my garms,
Now, strewn in haste,
He'd actually brightened up the place,,,
I thought,
He didn't.

There were beads of sweat rolling down both our faces,
Even though I hadn't moved a muscle I had never lost sight of his intent,
And I thought it was curtains when my waistcoat and fob watch went,
I stood there,
All alone,
In my all in one,
How humiliating,
The zipper jammed.

And so it was to come to pass,
That it was my poor quality long johns which saved my blushing faces,
Although the camels back was broken when he was baffled by my sock braces.

Joking was put aside as the charge sheet was read,
Inciting a riot, surely a more fitting discipline,
Like wearing the Kumar's Mark One kit,
The one with Evans Halshaw printed on the reverse, instead.
No?!

I was generally concerned for I knew of the gravity of the claim,
Banned for three years hold your head in shame,
An ordeal many of my fellow fans have been through,
Some justified others left mystified with all privileges denied,

APEX TO ZULU A2Z!

Another insolent tip of that damn cap from the Anglo-Saxon few.

But what's this?
Who should spring to my aid?
Than our regular W.P.C. from the stand,
The P.Y.T. had taken up the crusade,
All charges were dropped apart from my number and name,
'The way that gentleman was acting was in the best interests of the game!!!'

Well!
Another golden moment, how many that day?
And all those accessories piled up in that tray,
Took me a while to put them back in their rightful places,
Positioned with care,
Tweaked delicately, no rush,
No rush.

Finally I tied my bootlaces,
I felt I was two inches off the floor,
I thanked them for their time and stepped out into the bright lights,
With a slide into a glide,
And a,,,
The door swung gently closed behind.

Encore/Epilogue
As I walked back around to the other side of the ground,
Caught up in the full time sea of white and blue,
I couldn't help thinking maybe I should get back to that fancy dress shop,
I paused to see if he would appear, as if out of nowhere,
My head was swimming, had I made a scene,
Did it mean as much to them as it did to me,
Had I brought them round to my way of thinking,
Or was I just playing the jester or just acting the clown.
Maybe.

DAVID C GEORGE

A young boy pulling on an old mans coat tails,
'Look, look grandpa!'
A few pats on the back and some banter,
'Well done Charlie!'
My names actually Kingy but it was a pleasure none the less,
So I leave the last line to that good friend of mine,
Mr Charlie Chaplin,
Because he seems to sum it up the best.

'All I need to make a comedy is a park, a policeman, and a pretty girl'.
I am Blues.
Thank you.

Kingy.

First published Issue 155. The Zulu (The Mighty Blues vs. Manure United). 2004

Manchester Utd Vs Birmingham City 2003
Ry. Northfield

Birmingham young squad landed about 30 handed with many others travelling up in cars and vans. We met up with the older crew and went for a walk around the town. We've been rounded up by the old bill who took us up the Old Trafford. We had a firm of around 150 as we were walking along this dual carriageway. The Birmingham lads needed to take a leek, so 150 Birmingham fans are all standing in a line on the dual carriageway taking a leek. We clocked so many lads as we were walking up the road to the ground, and I mean loads. As we got to Old Trafford, the game had already started and everyone was pushing and shoving. As we near to the ground, the stewards just started bashing people as they were queuing to get in "Do you think we're stewards?" said one Manchester lad, "We're Salford Reds, we are." I ended up giving it one of the stewards when I was pulled behind a fence on my own and they were trying to shut the gates on me, with Barrington trying to pull me free. In the pulling that was going on, I've had a brand new Stone island ripped all the way down my back with the sleeve hanging off. £600 down the fucking drain. I was absolutely gutted, mate, believe me. As I'm walking up the road, my nose is all over my face, I don't even know how it happened, but I think it was when I was being pulled all over the place. I must have whacked into the fence or something. The way I was ejected from the ground had something to do with it, two had my feet and two had my arms and I think that's when my nose got done.

So I was outside the ground all game and I got talking to a local bobby. A local lad approached dressed head to foot in Lacoste with Armani jeans. He looked a bit of a dresser and he could see I was a lad. He approached me and asked what happened to my face, I explained and then we got down to brass tacks. The Manchester lad says, "Well if you can sort it out, our lads are up there right now." I've gone, "How many?" He says, "Two hundred, if you want it now, then get em out." I'm waiting till after the game because I ain't stupid enough to walk up there on my own, but I did have a little venture and there was a lot of lads outside the pub, so I just waited for our lot to come out. The first people to come out of Old Trafford's ground were some of Birmingham's elite. These were guys who had experience of taking on all sorts of foe all over the UK. An announcement went up in the ground that the rest the Birmingham fans will be kept in the ground for a least ten minutes, which meant the lads who had come out of Old Trafford early were only eight handed. The Blues lads all come round me and ask me what happened to my face, and I explain the situation to them regarding the 200 Manks around the corner who want a play up. One Birmingham lad says, "For a start, clean your face up straight away." I explain to Birmingham's few that there is a mob of Manks around the corner proper 200 handed who want to know. The Blues lads all looked at each other and said "Come on, let's go for a walk." This is what makes Birmingham different to Villa and many other teams in the country, as it has something to do with the hearts of men. As we're walking up the road, I say to the rest of the Birmingham lot how many there were of them, and I didn't want to be responsible for us all getting done.

235

DAVID C GEORGE

As we're walking up the road, a Birmingham lad starts banging random Manchester lads in the face. When we get to the crossroads at the top, the lads outside the pubs have clocked us fighting. More Manchester lads have come over to us, and the next thing you know in a split second, The Red Army had arrived. Now it wasn't that they were coming at us from the front, as they were coming from every angle and direction you could think of. Blues kept it tight and stood back-to-back fighting ridiculous numbers of Manchester's Red Army. As Blues fans were hitting the floor, someone else would pick them back up and they battled on. We stood back to back with our fists outstretched, punching Manchester lads in the face but also getting a few blows ourselves. Manchester's problem, believe it or not, was that they had far too many lads, and they couldn't really get at us. One of Birmingham's top boys was pinging Manchester lads right on the button every time they came close. That's what it's all about, the heart beating, the danger and being so outnumbered you really shouldn't be alive. This is what makes Birmingham's mob one of the best because I guarantee you that if eight of Manchester's finest tried that shit round St Andrews, I will put money on them not getting home with all their teeth. Even the old bill, who were fighting in the crowd to keep the Manks off us couldn't believe it, but we just kept on having with them in the middle of their firm up the main road. It doesn't matter if Manchester say this is lies, as I don't need to lie, and many other Manchester lads will remember that day when Eight Zulus went into the Red Army and went home with huge smiles on their faces.

APEX TO ZULU A2Z!

Oxford March 1985

Birmingham in Oxford taking on the blazer look – 1984/85

DAVID C GEORGE

Blues in Oxford – 1984/85

Blues in Oxford – 1984/85

APEX TO ZULU A2Z!

Blues in Oxford – 1984/85
Blues in Crewe on their way up north – 1984

DAVID C GEORGE

Highgate lads on the town – 1985

Highgate Style – summer 1984

APEX TO ZULU A2Z!

Blues 1983 still dancing

Birmingham lads in Boogies – 1985

DAVID C GEORGE

Birmingham chaps photo shoot – 1984

Jockey Move: Blues take up some dancing

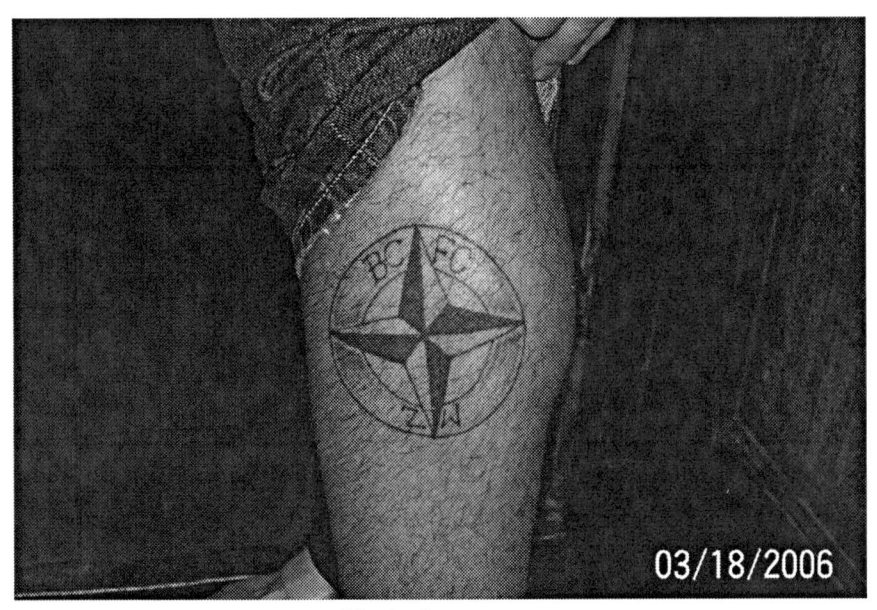

APEX TO ZULU A2Z!

Birmingham tattoo

Birmingham tattoo

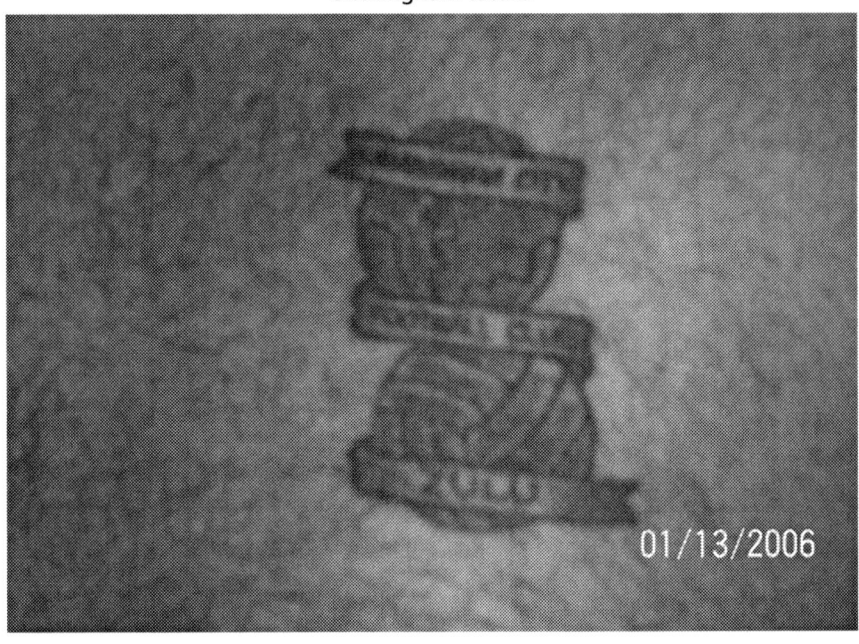

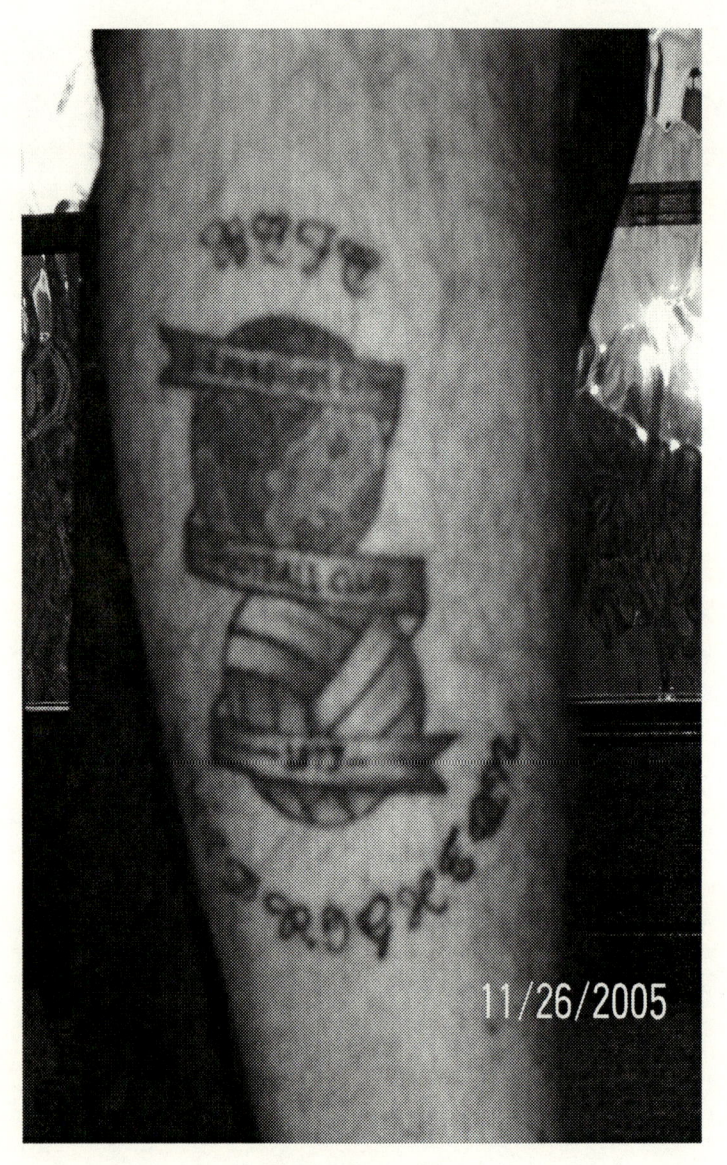

DAVID C GEORGE

Birmingham tattoo

CHAPTER 10

Yids are Kids

23RD NOV 1974–75 season two days after pub bombings. The Tottenham fans sang IRA songs to the Birmingham fans. Birmingham fans go mental and start climbing the fences to get at the Tottenham fans. A guy called Spike from Southend who used to support Blues was the one person who had a sense of organisation about him. The police didn't know what to do and tried to calm the emotional Birmingham fans. Nearly lost his life at Leicester by being stabbed in the neck in 75–76 season.

Yids are kids Birmingham City Vs Tottenham Hotspurs 22nd Oct 83

In 1983, Birmingham's average attendance at home games was 15,880 with Ferguson and Hartford on point for the Blues respectively. Tottenham at the time were a progressive strong team who had the swagger of a team on the up.

Tottenham's firm were very well organised and well dressed in 83 and came to Birmingham with the intent of causing as much mayhem and chaos as possible. I was fourteen when Tottenham came to Birmingham, and I have never seen anything like it in my born days at Birmingham since that day. Tottenham's firm was sitting in the lower tier of the railway end and they took up at least three sections in the seats of pure firm. Every one of their boys was so well dressed I felt sick to the pit of my stomach. They had got in the ground very early, which was a great tactic to completely baffle Blues, before they even got to the ground.

DAVID C GEORGE

Birmingham's firm, on the other hand, did not sit together in the ground at all, due to a lot of them complaining about the price of tickets in the seats when they could stand up and save a few quid. This was Birmingham's downfall on this particular day, as most paid to go into the Kop end of the ground, and stood underneath the clock in those days.

There were a number of Birmingham's girl dressers in the seats who were shitting themselves with the small contingent of Blues lads, as they were sitting right next to the Yids firms, and the only thing that separated Tottenham from Blues was a set of steps. Tottenham stood up in the seats and the small number of Blues fans realised they had bitten off more than they could chew, and jumped onto the pitch. Tottenham completely embarrassed blues in their own ground and it was a sad sight,

To this day, I know from speaking to many chaps over the years about this incident, that it was Tottenham Yids who woke Birmingham City's firm up, because they were not organised enough to deal with firms that used proper military tactics. Tottenham now got escorted out of the seats by the Birmingham police, and were bowling past the Kop end of the ground where most of Blues firm was standing, now wishing they had all paid that extra bit of cash to sit together in the railway. I was holding onto the fence and looking at the London's lads clobber with Eamon Delaney and Rankin, and I will be honest and say that for me personally, the Yids are the best-dressed firm I had ever seen. I thought that with my Fila tracksuit, Ellesse flat cap, Levis and a pair of Adidas centre court pro, I looked the part. Then I see the Yids bowling past me wearing Armani leathers, green Trim Trabb, Munchen, Burberry macks, Fila and Ellesse ski coats, Diamond Pringles and Lyle & Scott. Most of these lads were young and they didn't look like the heaviest firm I've seen at St Andrews, but what they had was organisation and front that we as Brummies didn't recognise until it was way too late.

The Zulu Warriors knew Tottenham Yids had taken them to school on this day, and what they now did was to study the methods used by Tottenham's firm and evolve and reinvent themselves so that a situation like that to never occur again. Birmingham now knew they needed to fight with tactics because using only pure aggression doesn't always work. When Birmingham fights as one whole not separately, they are organised, powerful and clever. One tribe/firm is like a single spear and can be broken, but with many spears, they have tremendous strength, accuracy and guile. This is the true Brummy meaning of Zulu, as Zulu means together.

Courtney's Recollection Birmingham vs Tottenham Oct 22nd 83

Birmingham were playing Tottenham at home in a league game, and the usual ritual of meeting up in town before the game with our mates from areas such as Rubery, Kings Norton and the likes. The Night Rider pub was derailed as the Yids had been into town early that morning and smashed it up by putting the windows through. After meeting up with several other lads, we bowled down to Navigation Street to rendezvous with the lads congregating in the boozers by Samwellers, when it went bang off with some Spurs Yids that were still in town. We managed to see them off, chasing a few down the subway where Pagoda Park used to be. I was particularly trying to get hold of one of their boys, who had a mint Armani jumper on his back.

Tottenham were by far the best-dressed firm in the country at this point, and if anything, these were probably the best days in fashion at the football matches, with lads regularly seen in Aquascutum, Armani, Farah's, Kickers, Burberry & Daks. At the time, a trip to Birmingham to the Cockneys was seen as a walk in the park, so we felt good having got the better of small mobs of Yids with the same numbers of us in our own personal skirmishes that afternoon. Thinking back, Tottenham must have landed at about 11–12 o'clock. They had obviously done their homework to know where our main boozer was, and this should have acted as a wake up call for what was to follow later that day.

There were other incidents of note until we reached the ground, and Birmingham was wondering where all the Yids were drinking as we scoured the town looking for them. It soon becomes evident that they had moved onto the ground to take up good strategic positions. They had obviously heard what had happened to West Ham on the pitch, and were making sure this was not going to happen to them. Our entire firm was outside the railway end with the intention of taking up our usual positions behind the goal as one firm, but some decided on going into the Kop underneath the clock because they could save a few extra quid.

The plan itself was cancelled as Spurs had beaten us to it, and were now occupying approximately 3 blocks of seating, leaving the last section for us. This was the section nearest the Kop. Tottenham also had another firm in the seats next the away end on the other side of the ground. At this point, I don't believe the police realised we were not the same firm, and probably confused us with Spurs due to some of the garments being worn, and the firms being of mixed nationalities on both sides. Although Birmingham was outnumbered, we didn't want to lose face so we tried to front it out. Verbal exchanges were taking place, and before long we were on our feet squaring up to each other in a real hooligan manner. Eyebrows dropped, and heads are bouncing with many displaying rituals that would be better suited to wild birds on the Continent. Designer clobbered lads foaming at the mouth to confront like-minded lads from another tribe. From my position, it appeared that Blues definitely took it to the Yids but we were not able to maintain the initiative once they started spraying ammonia into our eyes. The Spurs in the seated area on the other side of the ground saw their lot having it big style and invaded the pitch to get at the Blues who had jumped onto the pitch half blind, to get away from the ammonia assault. Trying to jockey for a good position to attack or defend yourself in tight seating is not easy, and it also makes it worse when panic has set in.

Determined not to give up our place in the seats, a few of us retreated under pursuit from their mob until our backs were against the wall next to the Kop stand. We tried to put up a last stand, but this was to no avail as Tottenham pressed home their advantage. I clearly remember thinking afterwards, how the hell did we get out of that? Now on the pitch by the corner flag and completely sandwiched between their two firms, my pal called Tim grabs hold of the corner flag and starts swinging it round as wildly as he could in order to keep the Tottenham hordes at bay. At the time, it saved us from getting a right hiding but now we laugh about it so much as it must have been comical to watch. Tim is now a well-respected sales director and has plants all over the country, one of which is run by a Tottenham lad who was present on that day. Needless to say, they became friends and Tim was invited to a Villa game with him. At the game with their lads, the Spurs lad rang the geezers Tim had tried to hit with the corner flag and said Tim was there to have a straightener with him. The phone was given to Tim for him to play along and wind this geezer up. Tim had the Tottenham lads in stitches as he played along with the blag. This was a funny incident but it should not be forgotten how well the Yids executed their objectives that day. It was done with military tactics of the highest order and gains respect as the best tactics employed by any team at St Andrews inside the ground.

Tottenham Hotspurs Vs Watford at Villa Park semi finals 87.

987 30 Birmingham were drinking in the Crown near New Street and were told Tottenham wanted to come and have it with them, even though we didn't have a football match on this day and most of Birmingham's lads were not in town. I had seen the Yids come in earlier in the morning as I had met them on New Street and walked up Queenway with them and had a drink in a pub offside.

One of the Blues lads knew Tottenham's firm very well and was talking with the Yids about past incidents between the two rival firms. They had at least 400 good lads for this trip to Birmingham, but they were not interested in Watford at all, as it was just The Zulu Warriors they wanted it with.

Three of us left the Yids in two pubs offside near Queensway and walked down to the Crown to give Blues the info. A few phone calls were made and Blues could only get another ten or so lads who were on the town on this day, as most people were not aware of the Yids wanting to have with us. The now 40-handed Blues were very anxious on this day, as they knew the Yids firm was huge. Myself and three other Blues fans jumped into a mini and drove up to Tottenham who were getting ready to leave and walk down to the Crown. They were standing outside the two pubs finishing their drinks when we pulled up. Tottenham surrounded the car and started shaking it and taking the piss out of us squashed in the mini. We left them at the pub and drove back down to the Crown to get ready for their arrival.

One Blues fan stayed with Tottenham to show them where the

Crown pub was situated, and was also trying to explain to the Yids that it was not going to be a walk over as they thought it might be. One of Tottenham's older heads agreed, and said they should be ready for a proper battle, because Birmingham were not the same Birmingham they met in 83. Most of the Yids didn't think Blues were any threat on this day, and were drinking and singing about beating Watford at Villa Park. If you watch the video filmed by the police from a high-rise office block across the road, you will see the meagre numbers Blues had on this day.

Tottenham march down Hill Street and Blues line up in the road.

Blues go straight in to the Yids and back them off in the main road. The JBB and The Zulu family kept it tight as fuck and smashed Tottenham up the road. A guy who was drinking in the Crown who wasn't even a Blues fan had heard everybody speaking about the row with Tottenham, and had joined in and stabbed a guy from London who ended up recovering at The Birmingham Accident Hospital, where my mother used to work as a nurse. She looked after him on her shift. If it wasn't for a doctor who was driving down Hill Street this day, the lad from Tottenham would have probably died as he was losing a shit load of blood.

There were a handful of heads that ventured into the railway end, but they did not know how many Tottenham were in the seats at the time.

Clashes with Yids in the early eighties and the continued clashes whenever Yids & Zulus meet. Thoughts and opinions on Tottenham as dressers and of the firm.

Birmingham City vs Arsenal 1982

Another incident where the police were confused by our appearance happened in London outside Arsenal tube station. Around 100 lads all in our teens made the trip down to London on the Inter City train for a game against the Gooners. None of the usual well-known faces were there that day whilst we waited at New Street for the firm to grow. Realising this gathering was not going to get any bigger, we left rather reluctantly on the next train to Euston. We must have left late as we got to Arsenal tube station at around 2.45pm. Once outside the tube station we were met by approx 15 –20 Gooners, both black and white. I was at the back of the firm exchanging obscenities with their lads when the police showed up and ushered us together. We were taken to the ground and put in the Arsenal section of the South Bank. It was clear the police thought we were Arsenal as we're identical to them. Black and white, and wearing casual clothes. We went into the clock end, keeping our mouths shut. Now walking from the top of the clock end terraces to the bottom was the most daunting experience I had witnessed in the whole of my hooligan career. We knew we didn't have the numbers to do much and we certainly didn't have the audacity to take it to them, being as young as we were. So we decided to firm up at the bottom so we could see them coming if they attacked.

I was sitting on the advertising boards facing looking up at their lads when suddenly, led by a big fat geezer, they steamed into our lot. Wanting to remain cool, I waited remembering (T-cup) Total Control Under Pressure. I didn't run or panic but still ended up on the pitch as a Blues lad is trying to get away in the melee, has dived head first onto the pitch knocking me over as he flew past me. There it was, I had ended up on the pitch, not by choice but by force. Only not by the force I was expecting. The police soon gained control and we were put with the rest of the Blues lads on the other side of the fencing. One of my old school mates (Martin) was there with some black and white lads I had met earlier at the Tube and he said they gave me rating for fronting them at the station. Incidentally, Martin was a Blues fan and responsible for taking me to my first game. For Birmingham going to Highbury was one of the highlights of the calendar year, as you know there is a higher probability of it going back up in the air at any given moment.

Arsenal Gooners are another London firm who have a proper decent crew, but never seem to be consistent with regards to being naughty, but they are so unpredictable. Birmingham has had many run-ins with Arsenal both home and away around Highbury and Kings Cross train station, but this one takes place at Birmingham when Arsenal took notice of one of the most respected and game geezers at Birmingham City, Cuds. Birmingham has a small mob of lads walking down Garrison Lane towards the park near the island. They have walked across the park and noticed a firm on the other side with plenty of black faces, faces people didn't recognise. Big lumps are at the front of Arsenal, with half a dozen Blues lads now walking towards the other side of the park to catch up with rest of blues firm, but in their way were the Arsenal Gooners, it was a proper tidy mob. The Gooners have come onto the park, and this is Denton and Miller's firm, the proper firm. Blues have carried on walking down towards the far end of the park near the island, and there is a bit of a confrontation. Cuds has gone down low near the floor into a martial arts stance, his hands held out in front of him. He then starts to bounce on the spot, ready for anyone who came anywhere near him. The Gooners circled him but nobody came near for some reason. Cuds kept on bouncing round in the circle of Gooners, laughing at them, then the Gooners chased the six Blues fans a distance up the road. When meeting the same 50–60 Gooners at New Street a while later, they got smashed to pieces near the glass doors by a firm around the same size in numbers who were waiting for them to get into town.

Birmingham City vs Arsenal March 15th 1983

Arsenal Gooners had brought a good mob to Birmingham on several occasions, and this was to be no exception. On this day the weather was mild and the feeling around St Andrews was very optimistic with regards to getting a result. Even though the crowd was only 11,276 we managed to win 2 –1 with Van Den Hauwe and Dillon on the scoresheet for Blues. Around ten minutes from the end of the game, 100 Arsenal came round to the side seating area in the car park where the players park before coming into St Andrews. I was standing at the top of the stairs near the exit watching the game, but also wanting to find out if the Gooners were here at the game, and lo and behold they came bowling through the car park whacking any Blues dressers they saw leaving the game early.

A loud voiced Brummy comes running back into the seats to inform Blues firm of around 300 that the Gooners wanna know outside right now. It was like a fucking stampede, as Blues firm literally sprinted out of the seated area to have it with the Gooners mob. As I have come out of the seats and into the car park, the Gooners are trying to hold back the amount of snarling Brummies taking swings at any Cockney in sight. The Gooners try to have but are well and truly dealt with by Blues in the car park, and most of them run off up back to the away end. Londoners at this time must have thought that Birmingham was easy pickings, as West Ham had tried it on around the same time. Around 30 Gooners were caught in the car park and got a right hiding, and were only saved by the police. Arsenal's ET was among them, the brother of the mouthy Tottenham lad I had the pleasure of meeting in his gaff in Camden on the Mayford Estate. I wasn't in a good mood at the time anyway because somebody had trod on my Fila trainers and smudged the sign which really pissed me off. At the time, that was the equivalent of watching your girlfriend in a porn film with your Dad. I was proper upset, believe me.

Back at New Street, Arsenal were standing behind the barriers waiting for their train home and a number of the Junior Business Boys were talking to a few Londoners on the station. They had that confident cocky spoon player attitude which makes anyone from out of London want to stove their heads in quick time.

It must be said though that the Gooners have got a very good mob, but could never bring it to West Ham in the 80s. Their dress sense was top drawer with many Gooners dropping some serious clobber of the highest calibre at the time. Smurf calls over one of the Gooners who is wearing a velvet suede type Fila that looked the absolute bollocks. He had the Trim Trabb and the Levis and was a proper tidy dresser. Smurf, "Mate, where did you get your Fila from, it's fucking proper quality, that is?" The London lad steps forward and cannot wait to explain where he got his garments. "Oh this, I got it from, Wallop..!! A McDonalds strawberry milkshake is thrown all over the Gooner at the barriers, and he is covered from head to foot in thick milkshake. Me, Smurf, Stig and a number of other Juniors are standing at the barriers pissing ourselves laughing at the London lad who is speechless for a change, and then he goes absolutely mental and comes for us at the barriers but is collared by his mates and dragged away.

We still stood at the barriers taking the piss and telling the Gooners that if they wanted it again, to walk down onto platform twelve and you can get out of the station for free and come back up to New Street round the back. We are still at the barriers area oblivious to a mob of around 100 Gooners who have done exactly that and are now at the glass doors behind us. A loud roar is heard as the Gooners are now coming for us near the barriers. We fuck off quickly because there were only about seven Juniors who would have been annihilated. What a good day that was for everybody. In fact it still makes me smile.

Swansea away 81 – Can You surf?

In 1981, Birmingham's Evans, Frank Worthington and Mick Hartford were keeping the fire burning for the Blues. Birmingham's team were still looking for an out and out goal scorer, and the quest went on.

Around 300 Birmingham fans break down a fence to get into the away end at Swansea, and the rest of the Birmingham fans who are already in the ground, rush the 300 who have just broken into the game. "We're Blues, we're Blues," said a number of lads before they got a punch in the mouth off other Blues fans.

Birmingham lost to Swansea 1–0 and left the game and as they did, Swansea had brought over the lads from the Welsh valleys for a bit of knuckle. A few scuffles occurred around the ground but nothing major, but rather than going straight home, Birmingham took two coach loads of lads and a minibus for a drink in a place called Neath. Birmingham at the time of the early 80s would travel with crap coach companies to destinations around the country, as it was a lot easier to consume ridiculous amounts of alcohol and soft drugs without anybody being on your case, or trying to arrest you for smoking a bit of black or double zero. If you travelled with crap coach companies, you had more opportunity to stop wherever you wanted for a drink, or even just to pull up on a back street to bash mobs of away supporters. On the way to Neath, the Chelmsley lads decided to have a competition on who could stay on the top of the van while flying down country lanes. It was called, the van surfing game. With a lunatic driving the van and a bunch of the Barmy Trooper Army crazy enough to attempt this kind of madness, the game begins. Coo-coo is on top of the roof rack and holding on for dear life, with the driver doing 40 mph. They pull up and Jeyes has a go, with the van now doing 50 mph with no lights on the small country lanes. How they are all alive I don't know, but Jeyes had leaned over the windscreen of the van with one arm, and was now banging on the window saying, "I've had enough now, stop the fucking van" Birmingham reach Neath and manage a few cheeky drinks before closing time, and we're then off for a curry. Two big hungry chaps from the Trooper called Glyn and Cookie, couldn't be arsed with waiting for everybody else, so they went in search of a Chinese takeaway while the rest of Birmingham's lads had another drink. More Birmingham went and got a few take-aways and were on their way back to the coach, when two local couples who had the mouthiest women with them, didn't know when to keep their traps shut. Welsh accents "Look, it's those fucking English bastards who have been causing trouble in our village all evening." The Birmingham lads told the two lads to shut their girlfriends up or they will smack the two lads' heads in. The two lads didn't say a word, but the women carried on until the two lads got bashed and one of the girls gets a curry thrown over her head for good measure. While this is happening, big Glyn and Cookie are strolling back down to the pub eating their take-aways, when a Welsh lad stops them. He says to the two Brummies, Welsh accent, "I wouldn't go down there, lads, there's a fucking riot." Birmingham have now crossed over the road to another pub mob handed, and chin a number of Welsh blokes sitting at the bar who happened to be the local CID- Police. All hell breaks loose, with Birmingham throwing fists and bottles at the police and locals as a number of Brummies are arrested and taken to a local police station, which is just a small house on the high street. The Chelmsley mob took one of the coaches down to the police station and walked in demanding they let Jeyes go, or they would smash the place up and kill every copper in the station. The local police shit themselves and let Jeyes go but still had a couple of lads locked up. The Birmingham lot got back onto the coaches and drove home with Jeyes in tow all singing about the eventful day they have just had.

Swansea Vs Birmingham City 1981

Pontoon Pat used to run coaches to a few away matches back in the day, and there was a Rugby match taking place in the afternoon in Swansea, so this was a night match. The Apex has taken a coach into

DAVID C GEORGE

Tewksbury, where we've gone for an afternoon tipple. A few of the light-fingered lads have decided to rob an Army and Naval store. As the police gathered everyone together, they were asking for the person who stole some items of clothing from the store. The police wanted to arrest everybody if we didn't give up the person who was busy in the store, so fair play to the lad from Castle Brom, he put his hands in the air and was arrested and taken away. Around 50 Apex stopped off after the game in Newport for a drink and six of us have decided on going for a mooch around the town. We walk past about eight local skinheads when the verbal started to fly. Airy gets chased up the road, so we now get the rest of the lads out of the pub and chase these skinheads up the main road. A few bottles were exchanged but it all calmed down pretty quickly. All 50 of us are now standing outside the pub when we get a message off a local lad telling us there are some bikers up the road who want to have a go. Birmingham walk round to the bikers pub and there are a row of motorcycles outside looking like mechanical dominoes. A lad from Highgate kicks one bike and all the rest hit the floor, one after another. The bikers come steaming out of the doors, obviously not very happy and they get a right slap in the main road. 16–17 year old lads fighting 30 year old bikers and they come off the best. The police arrive and escort the Birmingham coach out of Newport, but as the coach is leaving the centre of the town there are a few people throwing cans at the police who are following the coach on motorcycles. The police drive off and leave the coach to go on its way and were happy that the Birmingham lot had left the centre of Newport. Most of the Birmingham lot were wearing Kios strapovers, flying jackets, leg warmers and second image, as they were in a crossover stage of fashion. On the way home on the coach, Pontoon Pat is having a bit of a kip when Brains decides to stick newspaper up the front of his glasses. Pat has woken up and because he has had a few shandies and is disorientated, he says in an Irish accent, "Oh be Jesus, I'm feckin blind." Pat then realises it was just newspaper under his glasses, pulls the paper out and falls back to sleep. Everyone is laughing on the coach. Brains now stuffs newspaper into his leg warmers and decides on setting him on fire while he's sleeping.

After dousing Pats legs and pissing themselves laughing till they

APEX TO ZULU A2Z!

were crying, the Birmingham Apex head off up the motorway back to the Midlands enjoying another eventful day with a few tears and laughter all rolled into one.

CHAPTER 11

The Cardiff Stronghold

WHILE AMERICA WAS SPENDING hundreds of millions on the Vietnam War, Britain was hit with oil shortages. The 70s era was filled with protest, oil crisis and much lower economic growth rates than previous decades. Social movements such as Feminism, Gay rights and Environmentalism were gaining strength throughout this decade and would become even more mainstream during the 80s. With super groups such as Genesis and Pink Floyd taking centre stage, the experimental nature of progressive rock was beginning to gather pace. The first wave of Kung-fu movies also hit the cinemas from far East Asia, introducing the world to great action heroes such as Bruce Lee and Jackie Chan. Young lads at the time would come out of cinemas across the country making funny noises and attempting martial arts moves on the street which they had just seen in the movies. It was an epidemic that has stayed with many who enjoy this genre to this day.

Cardiff City Vs Birmingham City 1970

Birmingham and Cardiff have a long history of serious knuckle dating back to the early 70s and there is certainly no love lost between them. When Cardiff want to play, everybody comes out from the city and the valleys to take your head clean off. Going way back to the English taking the piss in Wales's years gone by, this feeling of hatred is still strong within the Welsh population. Even though most of us as Brummies do not know why the hell they are holding a grudge, it is well and truly apparent that the Welsh hate the Englishman's guts and will do everything in their power, to send you to the hospital or the cemetery.

Birmingham took a whole special full of skinheads to Cardiff and got off at the station, walked into the centre of Cardiff and smashed shop windows causing thousands of pounds worth of damage. Absolute mayhem was taking place in Cardiff central everywhere they went. A Birmingham lad from Ladywood who wasn't into football at all used to follow the Birmingham hordes around town, and as soon as it went up in the air, he would smash a jewellers' windows and rob trays of gold on his own and head off home. It's a decent walk from Cardiff centre to the ground, and Birmingham had a great big fucking firm of boneheads. The irony here was that recently in the same season, Cardiff had won the John White best behaved supporters' award. There was a massive portakabin near the away end that Birmingham fans were going into, and the police were telling everybody you couldn't get into the ground with Doc Martins on. Most of the Birmingham skinheads left, but a number took their laces out of their boots and went into the ground to watch their team play.

Johnny H has gone into the ground with bare feet to watch his team play, and as soon as Cardiff scored, Cardiff Greabows attacked the Birmingham fans in the ground. "I will never forget this guy as long as I live, peg leg with long ginger hair with a peak cap on called Frankie. "So their first goal, they've attacked us and this guy has come at me with a fucking iron bar, and a knife. I fucking crapped it," said Johnny," and swear on my life, the police had got to him and took the stuff off him." "Birmingham fans were climbing over barbwire fences to get out of the ground, and with only a handful of Birmingham fans left." "The ginger haired guy has stalked me all over the ground everywhere I went, but I'm not leaving, I'm fucking not leaving the ground." "We lost the game 2–0 by the way, but who has made his debut on this day?" "A young raw kid, Trevor Francis, made his debut that day, and I was there to see it, fucking fantastic." "Got outside and never even put me boots on, I had to fucking run like hell." "By the time I had put them on, the fucking mayhem that went off at Cardiff Central was incredible." " The Blues who hadn't gone into the game were at Cardiff central and had a fantastic fucking battle against

Cardiff." "I fought me way through the station and onto the platform, and who do you think is coming down the platform after me?" "Peg leg." "He says, "You ya cunt." "I've just trapped on the train I have, I thought, I cant have any more of him." "You know when you've had enough, I can't have any of him again." "But I got my revenge a year later though," "but I swore I'd never go there again, I've been there five times since."

The Soul Crew thingy – Saturday 12th March 2005.

Phone rings at 10.00am, I'm half in a coma from a night of debauchery ending with me back at home in the wee hours. I pick up my phone and it's a guy from the Cardiff Soul Crew. My head was banging like an AC-DC concert and it felt as though I had a dead cat on my tongue. Cardiff were travelling to Coventry today and had a coach full of lads going for a drink offside in Hockley Heath, Solihull. I was meeting a brother of a Welsh lad who now lives in Birmingham to ask him a few questions about his thoughts on meeting The Zulu Warriors in the eighties and nineties. My friend Martin and I walk into the Wharf Tavern at 12.15pm with my tripod and camera case, and there they were. As I get near to the back of the pub, I scan the room to try to find Andy. Andy was standing to my right, and waved. We shook hands. He introduced me to his brother, who was a real gentleman and we got talking. As I'm chatting, a number of Cardiff lads started to try to intimidate me by walking round me, and saying in a broad Welsh accent. "Zulus is it?" "You Zulu then?"

Andy's brother was keen to talk to me but not on camera and it turned out none of them would talk on camera, but they would answer questions I had written. I showed Andy's brother the list of questions and they were passed round the pub like a virus. As the questions were passed further down the bar, I could see people leaning forward over the bar and pointing at me. Things didn't look too good, to be honest, and it was understandable because they didn't know me from Adam, so some of them started to get paranoid. More people from the bar started to gather round Martin and myself and a lot of uneasiness was in the room. Andy's brother walks over to a guy sitting with his back to me and whispers in his ear. The guy half turns his head and says "Zulus in here?" He jumps up off his chair to face me; I smile and shake his hand. The Welsh lad had a face that had seen a million public houses and he was dressed very scruffily. He seemed to be the one person in the room who could make this journey over to Hockley Heath a fucking nightmare, or absolute top drawer quality. The Welsh guy looks at me and says with a bitter look on his face. "Fucking Zulus, fucking animals, man."

He then proceeds to lifting up his jacket and shirt to reveal a Birmingham City fans handy work with a Stanley blade, his multiple scars each over a foot long. Martin was sitting near me with a group of Soul Crew lads standing over him. He looked a bit paler than he normally does and was chatting with a couple of them.

This Welsh guy says, "Fucking Zulus man, they fucking got me, man."

For a moment the room went quiet, and I could feel everybody in the bar looking at Martin and me. I looked the guy in the face and simply said. "Fucking mad ennit?" But what else could I say really? I could have gone straight into a well-known Shaggy song and said. "It Wasn't Me," but would this really have made any difference to him? Andy's brother directed the conversation back to the interview and twenty or so minutes later, the Cardiff lads started to relax a bit more in our presence.

I gave Andy's brother a handful of Birmingham City Zulu fanzines, and in return, he gave me a Soul Crew T shirt, which said on the back, "Terrifying The English Since 1982" I folded the T shirt and thanked Andy's brother, but to be honest, the Soul Crew have never terrified the Zulu Warriors throughout the 80s or 90s, but we had had some splendid clashes against the Welsh army. We have had some good clashes with Cardiff, but to my knowledge they never gave it to Blues full firm in the 80s.

Cardiff City Away 1st Dec 84 away.

Robert Hopkins was one of the most likeable characters playing at Birmingham city in the mid 80s, and was very passionate when it came to standing up for Birmingham city. He was always seen in Solihull in pubs, clubs and bars and would cause many Birmingham city supporters to sing his name every time they saw him out and about. It must have been slightly embarrassing for him hearing his name when all he wanted to do was use the cash machine, but I suppose it goes with the territory when you're a local hero.

Mozza; Into The Vallies

A couple of Kings Norton Juniors used to work the flower stalls pitches for extra cash to pay for football days and the clothes that went with it. Sometimes on a Saturday, they worked New Street Station concourse and as Juniors, this was a favourite hangout. Birmingham is a major crossover point on the rail network, and on Saturday evenings during the 80s it became a war zone, mainly due to the flower stall boys who would inform us who had passed through earlier in the day. As a result, we would lie in wait for their return later that evening. One Saturday in October 84, I was chatting with the flower lads in the afternoon when the British Transport Police came charging onto the station. This could mean only one thing, a football firm was landing right now. Sure enough a few minutes later, hundreds of dressed geezers started milling around on the other side of the barriers. We clocked a small firm of Junior lads with them and called them over. "Who the fuck are you lot then?" Faye asked. "Cardiff Soul Crew" came the reply. We started to chat with them near the barriers and they must have had a firm of around 400 out on that day. They were very impressive, make no mistake. After a couple of minutes, the old bill moved them on for their connecting train and they left. This was the first time I had clocked sight of the proper Cardiff Soul Crew and they are a proper tasty mob.

A few weeks later on the 1st December 84, thinking I looked the bollocks wearing 18inch bell bottomed Levis cords (believe me, everyone was wearing them for a period) Fila Polo neck and Burberry golfing jacket. I left home at 7.30am to head to New Street Station destination Cardiff. Normally on away days you couldn't get onto New Street concourse due to the amount of lads that Birmingham's firm commanded. A lot of our chaps were driving down in vans, lorries and cars.

There were still a good 70–80 older lads and 30 Juniors who now got onto the train heading for Bristol where we could change to get to

Cardiff. As the train arrived at Gloucester, the old bill was waiting and as was the norm in those days, everyone was jibbing the train. A few of us got off the train to avoid paying and met up with another Junior lad called Coaly. Coaly said he had found another train going straight to Cardiff, so five minutes later 30 Junior lads were now pulling out of Gloucester on a different train while the rest of the firm were digging deep to pay for their fares. We got to Cardiff and passed the ticket collectors on the barriers when a local lad comes to front me. "Where are your boys then?" he asks, and looking around the station I noticed that they had lads spread all over the place in tens and fifteens. I started to splutter, "They're coming down later" when Coaly has leant over my shoulder and drilled the geezer straight on the nose. From then on it went bang off all over the station, and we actually backed them off out of the doors onto the station forecourt. That is when the full firm hit us. We were school kids trying to fight blokes and they treated us like ragdolls, throwing us around. The old bill finally landed and rounded us up to be escorted to the game. We had heard where Blues firm were meeting, so me, Anthony .H and another Junior lad jumped the escort and headed into town. We were walking down one of the main shopping streets when suddenly "Whack," a golfing brolly was smacked off my head. I spun round to be confronted by 10 – 15 Cardiff boys, snarling and charging at us. We had no time to react and they literally lifted us off our feet and whacked us down the road. We managed to scramble into a shoe shop for sanctuary and the Cardiff lot just steamed into the store with displays going all over the shop with boots and sandals flying everywhere. I managed to grab hold of a stiletto shoe and hit out blindly as my other hand was protecting my head from the blows being rained on us. Finally, the store manager came to our rescue by shouting that he had called the police. The Cardiff lads dispersed as swiftly as they had appeared, and we legged it out of the shop and down the road. We headed towards the ground with one eye on our backs. We met up with another Junior firm who'd also jumped the escort and had all had similar fates.

Georgie

Around fifteen Junior Business Boys were in Cardiff bright and early

DAVID C GEORGE

wandering around near Cardiff's ground. We walked past a pub called the Ninian and then went under a bridge where we saw a cafe, so we all went in and ordered some breakfast. As we finished eating, a large local man came into the cafe and stood at the door. We looked up at him, but paid him no mind, then he walked over to the counter and I couldn't believe what he said as loud as you like. "What the fuck are you serving these English bastards in here for?" Now being a person of colour, I was used to being called this name and that name in particular circumstances, but this was the first time I had ever been called an English bastard.

We decided to leave the cafe at that moment, because the local man didn't look as if he had all of the tokens for a pop up toaster. As we are near the door, the man decided on hurling chairs across the cafe at us screaming, "Get out" We left the cafe and walked up towards the ground now but we are still early, and we bump into two Juniors from Kings Norton and Westheath.

Blue from Westheath was complaining he had just been taxed of his Burberry jacket by a group of Cardiff lads, so we thought we would go and sort it out because, to be perfectly honest, we didn't think, or didn't know much of Cardiff at all in 1984. The average age of our group was 15, but we had courage a lot of people at the time would have classed as insane, but we were far from that, though we did have our fair share of over eager youngsters in our group. We now bowled straight to the Ninian pub under the bridge. As we get near the pub, a group of Cardiff lads are looking out of the window and calling everybody else in the pub to the entrance. Cardiff now come out of the pub and Coaly and myself were talking to them trying to negotiate the release of our friends Burberry. We knew there wasn't any chance of getting the jacket back, but we really wanted to see if these guys were the firm or just a bunch of tramps. As we are talking, more Cardiff are spilling out of the pub with numbers up to about 60 –70 lads. We are outnumbered big time and the situation is not looking good, but a handful of juniors are still talking to Cardiff who have still not made a move. As this is taking place, Blues Zulus around 60 handed are enroute from Cardiff city centre after robbing the Burberry shop. They now catch a bus to the Cardiff's ground, which takes them past the ground. As they are coming near to the Ninian, there was a good mob of Cardiff standing about on the corner who noticed the Birmingham lot coming past on the bus. Cardiff's mob started to come together at the time, while Blues got off the bus one stop further down the road. A few of the nineteen year old lads walked up the road to bait the Cardiff lads into coming down the road, as Cardiff didn't know how many Blues had got off the bus. Cardiff have now clocked the few Brummies and are running down the road towards them, around 100 handed, while the rest of Blues are waiting round the corner. When Cardiff get about twenty yards away from the handful of Blues, the Midlands lads turn and pretend to run away round the corner where the rest of Blues small firm is. Cardiff come steaming round the corner when Blues go straight into them. A full-on battle ensues in the main road where people are getting brollies wrapped round their heads and bodies are hitting the floor on both sides, but mainly Cardiff. They got the shock of their lives. In the early 80s, you have to understand that people didn't bring a mob to Cardiff, rob a designer store, catch a local bus and drive past their firm then ambush them in their own town, it was unheard of. The small Birmingham contingent now appear at the end of the same street we are on. This was not planned at all and a complete coincidence. The Cardiff lads outside the Ninian pub, see another section of Blues older lads now walking towards the pub. It looked as though the carnival was in town, and it was. Birmingham City had stolen Burberry umbrellas that were open and all sorts of accessories from scarves and hats and were now bowling towards the pub. As we had nearly had it on top with Cardiff, it was interesting to see how they reacted when the tables were turned. Cardiff backed off towards the entrance of the pub and Blues let out a mighty roar. "ZULUUUUUUUUUU" The brollies were wrapped around Cardiff lads heads and Birmingham scared the hell out of Cardiff who had never seen a multi racial firm of this calibre before in their born days. They had a little bit of a go outside their pub, but were outgunned by Birmingham's firm. Most of them got back into the pub and Blues sang Zulu, Zulu Warriors to them while being pushed up the road by police.

The main areas that the Cardiff Soul Crew come from are varied, but most the firm are, Blackwood, Neath, Rhondda boys, Aberdare boys, Merthyr boys, Trowbridge Firm handed, Ely, Grange town, Canton and the Llanrunmey boys.

Blues are now escorted to Cardiff's ground around the corner. In the ground Birmingham City scored first and I jumped on the fence in the away end of the ground and shook the fence. The police saw this as violent behaviour and I was kicked out of the ground. The day will be here soon when you won't even be able to celebrate your team scoring at all, so as not to offend the middle classes who are in control of the prices, and making the beautiful game so PC that real working class supporters will be priced out of the game completely. Social issues surrounding the building of all seater football stadiums have led to facilities being aimed at those whose earning potential is traditionally considered to fall within the middle classes. If working class supporters cannot even celebrate a goal, what will it soon be replaced by? Bravo, Bravo, Jolly good show? Birmingham won the game 2–1 and seventy of blues firm hung around Cardiff for some knuckle as they had hired an eighteen-wheel long vehicle lorry that was parked on the outskirts of the town after being escorted out of the town a while earlier. Blues knew Cardiff had had a right good turnout and were probably a bit depressed about what happened in the morning, so Birmingham went to find them again. Birmingham are now around 70 handed, walking the streets of Cardiff trying to find the Soul Crew. A few Cardiff lads are mouthing off to one of Blues' main heads who has managed to find a mob of about 150 Soul Crew. Cuds has fronted Cardiff's firm and been chased down the main road by all 150 Cardiff. The rest of Birmingham are on the same road, but around 250 yards further down. Cardiff chase Cuds about fifty yards, when he doubles back and runs straight into the lot of Cardiff. The rest of Birmingham are running up the road trying to get to where the one Birmingham lad was fighting Cardiff on his own. The adrenalin rush to get up the road had people's chests burning. Birmingham are now having it with Cardiff again and a number of Cardiff get bashed so Cardiff have it on their toes again. Cuds has held his own and was absolutely fine, with only a few bangs but nothing major at all.

APEX TO ZULU A2Z!

Birmingham City Vs Cardiff City 4th May 85

Cardiff's firm come out of New Street 200 handed and are met by the Junior Business Boys. From the looks on their faces, they are nervous as hell and are looking left and right constantly. We explain to them they should get off the streets as soon as possible, so we walk with them down the spiral steps and past the bus depot up to the Bull Ring. As they are walking, I could see they were nervous and didn't trust us an inch, and they were right not to. We were trying to get them to walk up to the Crown pub where there are four pubs full of Blues firm all on the same road, but they were not listening to us at all. As we are walking through the Bullring, I notice a guy walking at the side of us clocking the Soul Crew but I didn't have a clue who he was. He called me over and asked who we were, and I gave him a calling card, and said, "We're the Junior Business Boys, Pride Of The Midlands," "Who are you?" He looked at me then the calling card, smiled and walked off with the card in his hand chuckling to himself. I found out later that this guy was very well known on the town and was one of Birmingham's older firm connected to Bordesley Green.

Faye says to me his memories of meeting the Soul Crew are painful. In 85, we heard the Soul Crew had just landed at New Street, so 8 – 10 of us had gone to wander by the station. Faye was with some respected heads who were a few years older than himself. Ward End Fat Gary, Kingsheath Baz, to name a few. Ten Blues were outside The Toreador pub, when a firm of Soul Crew came into view at the top of the road.

Faye thought it was time to boogie himself, but the lads he was with were having none of it. "The spirit in those days was tremendous, the cry went up, "Make a line," all ten of us fronted this mob of Soul Crew outnumbered ten to one.

As Cardiff saw how few of us there were they really started to bowl towards us in a confident manner. What happened next still makes me smile to this day. Fat Gary has just led the charge and we actually ran into them with fists flying everywhere. It wasn't long before I ended up on the deck being filled in by this mob of Soul Crew with the usual kicking and stamping. After a few dozen kicks to the body, I thought, "Fuck this," and grabbed hold of this sheep shagger's leg and thought I'm not going to let this guy keep kicking me. This all happened on a busy street on a Saturday morning, and it wasn't long before the dibble arrived on the scene. Faye still had hold of the Welsh guy's leg and wasn't letting go, so when the police got there, this Welsh guy was the first to be nicked. Faye gets up off the floor, dusts himself off and walks towards one of Blues' main pubs. Tales of the incident had already reached the pub and he was welcomed back like a hero. Battle scars were inspected, and he was congratulated on standing and had gained some respect from the older Blues lads. That's what it was like in those days. And to be honest, I've never had a buzz like it since.

Cardiff didn't want to stay around the Bullring and headed off towards Digbeth and to the game. After Birmingham won 2–0, Birmingham's Zulus came round to the away end of the ground and went straight into the Soul Crew. Cardiff were run a number of times back to New Street, which is two miles of being on your toes. A Birmingham police officer even joked with the Soul Crew, "Can't you run any faster?"

Birmingham vs Cardiff 95

Seats ripped out and thrown at Cardiff, coach load of Soul Crew are driving round the island and towards the Watering Hole public house, as they start goading the Blues lads as they are walking up the hill towards St Andrews. Being match day the traffic is heavy and the Cardiff lads get caught at the lights. As this happens, two blues fans run towards the coach and press the emergency exit for the coach door, then spray the front of the coach with CS gas, and jump back off. The coach moves a little way up the road in traffic then pulls over as everybody piles off the coach, having major difficulties breathing and seeing.

Birmingham has met up with Cardiff on numerous occasions including the night before the Worthington Cup final at the Millennium Stadium against Liverpool. Birmingham were walking round town the night before the game and smashing up any pubs with Cardiff in for most of the evening. Birmingham do rate Cardiff as one of the best in the country, but on this night, they let themselves down a bit.

APEX TO ZULU A2Z!

Blues in Cardiff – 1984/85

Blues in Cardiff – 1984/85

DAVID C GEORGE

Blues in Cardiff – 1984/85

Blues in Cardiff – 1984/85

CHAPTER 12

The Pompey Estate

Birmingham City Vs Portsmouth 18th Sept 84

WE HAD HEARD A lot about Portsmouth since the seventies being a rough part of town and that it was a crew that had a lot of big burly dockers who would smash your face in at the drop of a hat. Pompey had brought a nice firm up to Birmingham for this clash, but when I read what they had put in their book about their exploits in Birmingham, I realised the days binging at Glastonbury must have warped their fucking minds. If you've never heard a Portsmouth accent before, I will try to explain it to you.

Put Arthur Daly, the character from the TV show Minder, and Pam Ayres the poet's accents together, and you will be very close. Here is the truth from the get go, Pompey have never done blues proper firm at all. Full stop.

When the 6.57 crew came to Birmingham City, I was standing outside the game near the side seats with four Juniors as we didn't have the cash to pay in. We had heard that their had been a minor skirmish in the lower tier seats, but Pompey didn't have enough of a firm in there to do much at all. I know some people who drink in their local boozers and rant out victories all over the place and some may be true, but it is a shame when Rob Silvester, himself well known in Birmingham, can write that sort of tosh about Blues and think he's telling it how it was.

It was more shouting and swearing than rowing, and they were escorted into the away end very quickly. A Pompey lad was thrown out of the ground and we spoke to him. He was a confident, cocky bastard wearing some tidy garments. He stood there with his arms folded wearing a navy blue Guernsey jumper, Armani jeans, and a pair of dockstep shoes. The Pompey lad never said a word about any fighting in the seats, as he was thrown out for using bad language at the time. A Blues fan walked past and the Pompey lad joked, "Fack me, a Brummie wearing Armani."

Blues had a firm of girl dressers who used to go to a number of big home and away games and they were now approaching in the distance. Five girls turned up wearing kickers, Farah slacks and double-breasted Burberry macks, with umbrellas and G2 sweaters. They stopped and had a quick chat with us, but would normally take the piss out of our clothes, and then leave. This was a Brummy greeting at the time, and we were used to their sharp tongues on a number of meetings.

Portsmouth Vs Birmingham City 13th April 84 away.

6.00am, I arrive in Birmingham New Street bright and early to catch the train to Portsmouth. Birmingham City's numbers are not up to full strength, but the 350 that had turned out were most of the boys you would want when going to somewhere like Pompey. Everyone looked tidy today as per usual on all big occasions, Birmingham City Zulu's will dress to impress. Style was something that meant a lot to Blues fans, and even to this day, proper heads still have an eye for a nice bit of clobber when shopping on the town. The main garments being worn by Birmingham's firm in 84 were varied, but the most popular were Nino Cerutti, Matinique, CP Company, Pooh, Hugo Boss, Pringle, Gianfranco Guffantti, Nicole Farhi, Benetton, Giorgio Armani, Best Company, Jaeger, Marco Polo, Angelo Santini, Horns, Christian Dior, Arnold Palmer, Ball, Browns, Munsing Wear, Aquascutum, Allegri, Pop 84, C-17, Nani Bonn, Emporio Armani, Nazrino Gabrielle, Burberry, Ricardo Bini, Chippie, New Man, Daniel Hector and Chemise.

On the way down to Portsmouth the atmosphere on the train was incredible, everyone was in a good frame of mind and the piss taking had started early. Big Stig had found his way into a room where he had access to the intercom used to inform passengers of the next train station, and proceeded slating people on the train who he thought had not made an effort with regards to their attire. One of the blues lads had bought a large portable stereo with him, and was playing some serious dubs while the rest were sitting down grinning their faces off nodding their heads to the vibe. Artist – Wayne Smith – "Under Me Sleng Teng Me Under Me Sleng Teng – Under Me Sleng Teng Me Under Me," He he he.

A heavy-duty game of cards was taking place along with the occasional waft of cannabis in the air throughout the journey. A few lads were even dropping lyrics over the dubs while we were on the train, and making up rhymes about the journey and the day. Birmingham City had turned the Inter City train into a fucking casino.

The train pulled up two stops from Portsmouth and the Police told us, there had been disturbances with Birmingham City fans and Pompey throughout the morning. As we were waiting for the train to move, Gizmo and myself ran across the bridge to use the toilets on the other platform. As we were coming out of the toilets the Birmingham train had decided to carry on without us and we were forced to wait for the next train into Pompey. It turned up five minutes later and guess who was on it? The train was full of Portsmouth fans, but there were only a few 6.57 lads on there. A few people were looking at us, but nobody approached us in the slightest, even though it was obvious we were not from this neck of the woods. It's not very often you would see a black lad supporting Pompey wearing Kappa jeans, Baggy hooded leather and a Cerutti scarf with Matinique shoes, is it? As we arrive at the station, Gizmo is making me nervous by telling me people are looking at us, which to me was the understatement of the century. We bowl straight out of the station and there are around thirty 6.57 standing outside who clock us instantly. We clock them and they clock us, but before they even get a chance to approach us, we turn right and walk straight into the centre. As we turn the first left corner, Blues are standing in the road singing their hearts out, taking photographs. You can still hear the dubs in the background from the stereo, and everybody was buzzing and full of energy. Now I realised why the Pompey lads had stayed where they were because they must have seen what was around the corner already. As the Birmingham had joined

273

up with another mob of Blues who were already in Portsmouth and enjoying themselves outside the pub, a guy comes out and whispers into Cud's ear, and he then goes into the pub.

Pompey have just phoned the pub and asked for a meeting up by the Guildhall Square, which was five minutes' walk away. Blues were up for this big time, with numbers swelling to 450 as they proceeded over to the library in an orderly fashion. As we're walking round through the centre, there were a number of Pompey's juniors walking with Blues showing us where to find the library. This guy had some Pompey calling cards on him, and I swapped him one of our Junior Business Boys calling cards for a 6.57 one. This was a very strange situation because from my knowledge, the only time these cards were usually seen was when you had a mouth full of blood and a swollen eye, or worse.

Blues are now on the steps outside the library and decide to take pictures of their firm sitting outside this building, when all of a sudden there is a mighty roar. Blues stand up on the steps and walk towards the sound.

This was Pompey 6.57's proper firm about three hundred yards away.

As Pompey come into view, they let off a flare gun at Blues, which screams up into the air. Blues made no noise, as we saw no reason to until Pompey are right in front of us, so we bowled towards Pompey who were now calling it on. The local police had now arrived at the scene, but Birmingham advanced in silence towards Pompey because the way the local lads had come around the corner; we knew the police couldn't stop a mass onslaught by rival fans. Blues were now right in front of Pompey at the beginning of their housing estate, then they let out the roar. "ZULUUUUUUUUUU" and it went bang off. Pompey had some geezer standing right at the front of their firm wearing dungarees with shoulder length hair. He was standing toe to toe with Blues lads and made a good account of himself. This was Rob Silvester, Pompey's top boy, but Blues kept on moving forward. The police were with us, but it was still going off up and down the road. The guy with the portable stereo was kneeling down in the middle of the road, as someone had thrown a brick at one of his speakers, which had now come unattached. The police held Blues on the street for about a minute to get us under control again, then walked us through Pompey's estate. Pompey are walking in front of us and are still trying to kick it off with Blues, and Blues are doing exactly the same. As we get to a crossroads, Pompey are on both sides of the street waiting for us to cross, and the police are telling all of Blues firm that if there is any more fighting, there will be arrests straight away. Pompey now bounce into the road and Blues run straight into them again. It's one thing telling Blues fans to be pacifists, but it's another thing altogether for the police to think that Blues are going to back down to Pompey's invitation to knuckle. A full-scale brawl broke out at the crossroads ending with nobody getting the better of each other, and I have to tip my hat to Pompey 6.57, because they were game enough to have it with us rather than throw a few bricks and then run like so many other firms did in the eighties. Birmingham won the game 3 – 1 with Geddis scoring a memorable hat trick.

Pompey Vs Birmingham Round 2 – The Mighty Few

The second occasion Birmingham travelled to Portsmouth, they took a firm that were ready for anything the 6.57 had for them. Blues had marched into the Pompey estate after the game to wait for them before they got there, and decided on ripping down pieces of fencing to use against Pompey. 36 Zulus now sat on a grass verge in Somers town, with planks of wood sitting next to them while having a chat. 15 long minutes later, Pompey turn up with numbers of around 300 strong, and begin hurling house bricks and bottles at Blues for at least two whole minutes. As soon as the aerial attack is over, Blues get straight into them with the trademark, ZUUUUUUUUULUU! bashing the shit out of Pompey's firm in the main road. Birmingham cleaned the streets of Portsmouth's famous 6.57, and had them on their toes until Blues stopped chasing them and decided on walking through Somers town instead. The police were now with Blues as they carried on up the road after Pompey. The crew of 36 Blues fans had travelled there in vans and cars, and were concerned that where they had parked their vehicles was right where all the Pompey were now standing. The police told the Blues crew that if they wanted to stop their transport from being written off, they could go ahead at their own risk. This is just the same as offering a red rag to a Bull, as Blues now go into Pompey again and give them a right hiding. Pompey ran again and Blues had truly shown the difference between the mentality of a mixed race mob, with regards to one race. Black faces, combined with a lot of red headed Celtic people, with a splash of Asian, puts Blues firm in a different category to Pompey. The United Colours of Birmingham.

I don't know how this is supposed to work, but Pompey were dangerous as hell in London in the early and mid eighties, but have never given Blues a hiding.

We will always look back on those days in Portsmouth and smile, because Pompey get respect from Birmingham's firms because they were game enough to have it with us even though they must have wondered what the hell was going on, when they were being run off their own manor by 36 Brummies.

Getting out of the escort is one thing but walking through Pompy's estate with small numbers is a different kettle of fish altogether. Better when outnumbered.

APEX TO ZULU A2Z!

Give me the music, blues. Take a boom-box to Pompey – 1984/85

Blues just arrived in Portsmouth – 1984/85

DAVID C GEORGE

Blues outside Pompey's main boozer – 1984/85

CHAPTER 13

The ICF situation

ALL YOU NEED TO KNOW about what happened when the Zulu's met with the ICF home and away, plus why they know Blues can have it proper.

Johnny H – The 70–71 season, I was seeing a girl from Bristol. Bristol Rovers fan I had met the previous season with the most lovely name I've heard in me life at the time, Lucy Hurrell, I reckon she's some fucking writer now like Pam Ayres or something. And I never had the ride, so every time Blues were playing away, I used to go down to Bristol. Aug 7th 1971, I'm waiting to go back to Brum, when all the West Ham have got off the train and it was a proper crew. A couple of the West Ham recognised Johnny and approached him, "Birminum ennit? Johnny thought to himself, here we go. "We remember you from last season." I'm around 15stone now, but bearing in mind that at the time, I must have been about 10stone easy. This black guy has walked out the front of them; to me he looked like Frank Bruno, the stature of the man at the time, well built, proper solid looking. He had on white stay press, black Doc Martins, and all down the back of this guy's Docs written in gold paint it said, Natt. West Ham football club with the hammers crossed. I know now it was Natt Lesley, obviously one of the fucking main main men at West Ham. So I've changed me mind on going home, and instead marched all the way around Bristol with these West Ham lads, fighting Hells Angels on the way coming out of all these cafes. We got to Bristol Rovers, I don't even know what the score was, there were coppers on horses on the terraces, I'd never seen that before until Blues Leeds 85, oh and Sheffield away. Fantastic battle, we all shook hands when I got back to Temple Meads, fantastic day out, no mobile phones as you say, and I couldn't wait to tell all the boys. And Bristol Rovers are a tasty bunch of cunts, I tell ya. The battle lasted for the full ninety minutes throughout the game, mate, no joke.

Later in the same season, Johnny had arranged to meet Natt and the West Ham boys in London. Birmingham were playing Fulham at the time, and Birmingham were just arriving at Euston. Jayo had got there before me, and fucking Natt had done him on the station, so I never saw Natt again. So we head over to Fulham and were outside this lovely pub, with the parasol things above ya, when this geezer has approached us standing outside this pub. And you know heads, I had never seen a head on a geezer like this in me life. He had a burst football under his arm, black geezer, and he says, "Do you wanna game of football?" We all thought, "Who's this cunt here?" Later on, he became my best pal for three years; he was a main head at Tottenham. O'Neil Whitely, known as Brixton, but the sad thing about it is that he and some other geezers were in the paper for allegedly raping a bird on the Tube. On some of the websites, Blues slag Tottenham for having a nonce on the firm.

The late 70s saw Archie Gemmill and Keith Bertschin and Lynex as the present days heroes at St Andrews. Birmingham's average attendance at the end of the 70s for home games was 20,427.

Cona and Dex met the ICF at New Street Station when big sheepskin coats, tank tops, mullet haircuts, skinheads and Doc Martin boots were in fashion. Around fifty ICF walked towards the escalators bumping into Dex & Cona. West Ham were wearing what must have been the earliest ICF cross hammers badges that looked as though they were very cheaply made. One ICF guy says to Dex, "Who the fack are you then?" Dex says, "Birmingham." The London guy says, " Well, whatya doin eya?" Cona says, "We've come to meet you lot" .The London guy looks the two Brummies up and down and says, "Wot, two of ya, you're avin a fackin laugh aintya, cam an av a drink?" The ICF walk towards the ramp and then turn left down the steps at the top of the ramp towards the bus depot. Cona says to the ICF they will see them in the ground, as they were planning on going into the away end at St Andrews.

A number of Blues caught up with West Ham near St Martin's church near the bus depot, where someone was hit with a shovel.

At the ground, six Trooper now walk into the away end at St Andrew's, and straight away are clocked by a lookout that runs into the Tilton end of the ground. The six Chelmsley walk through West Ham and down towards the corner flag and as soon as they arrive there, the same fifty or so West Ham lads who they met at New Street are now standing right behind them smiling. The one ICF guy is rubbing his hands and says, "Alright boys, what happening nen?" "What, is this fackin it ey?" Cona starts laughing. The one West Ham guy kept saying to Troganite that his mate has a sword for him, and he wants to cut his ears off. West Ham knew that with only six blues in their end they were certainly no threat to them, but what you can also say is that how game must those lads be, to walk into the away end six handed when West Ham were mainly skinheads and boot boys. The Chelmsley Wood lads had some backbone that some would call insane, but this mentality was something that spread through Birmingham's mobs in the early eighties onwards and came from a feeling in Birmingham that they as a crew had to become more on the ball when it comes to fighting fans from up and down the country, because everybody knows that the best firms are the ones that use different kinds of tactics to lure you into traps using ambushes and wrong directions for a meet, then showing up on two different sides of the street at the same time, pinning the other firm in, hitting them from both sides. These firms have been consistent over a considerable amount of time, but the list is changing. The list is short when it comes to consistency but here are my choices in no particular order.

Birmingham
Cardiff
Millwall
Leeds
Man Utd

All these firms throughout the last 20 years have been consistent and have also taken a few falls along the way, but on the whole, these are the teams that have had people's gums flapping the most.

DAVID C GEORGE

West Ham United vs Birmingham City 81

16 Blues Apex lads catch a National Express coach from Digbeth in Birmingham to London Victoria. Yardley Wood, Acocks Green, Chelmsley Wood, Warstock, Kingsheath, Billesley and Highgate. Reven, Smithy, Morph, Pete, Winston, Dock, Billy, Cuds, Cozie, Fizza, Duds etc. Birmingham caught the tube train to Upton Park with hundreds of West Ham fans all getting on the train at each stop on the journey. One of the Birmingham lads turns round and says to the rest of the Birmingham lot, "Here's an idea, what we will do is tuck our trousers into our socks." Why? The reply was, "So they don't see it when we shit ourselves." Blues come out of Upton Park station and walk down the hill towards the ground. As you turn left to go to the away end, there was a huge black geezer standing on the corner on his own. Reven went over to confront him, and he backed off. At the same time, at least 30 West Ham were running up the road towards Blues and this was the under 5's. Blues went into the under 5's and it was bang off all over the main road. A Brummy lad gets put on his arse and the rest of Blues drag him out so he doesn't get a hiding. The police now arrive and split it all up and take Blues down to the turnstiles. West Ham are giving all the bravado outside and Blues pay into the away end. In 81 at Upton Park it was a regular occurrence for the home supporters to pay into the away end with the police doing nothing about it. Winston bangs a West Ham lad and gets grabbed by two police officers, and as he is being led out there are a number of West Ham mouthing off to him, so he pushes the police off his arms and head butts another West Ham lad. He was arrested and had to appear in court but decided not to go, so two months later, the London police travel to Birmingham and arrest Winston and take him all the way down to London to face a court appearance. Earlier in the same year, one of West Ham's top boys at the time called Taffy was on New Street when a number of Blues fans wanted to open him up. A Brummy lad called Pete stopped this from happening and Taffy thanked him. Pete is now standing in the away end at Upton Park with mobs of West Ham in the Blues end watching the game. Winston has just been arrested when a group of West Hams proper ICF come towards him. Right at the front was Taffy with a huge smile on his

face, the same guy who Pete had helped earlier in the year on New Street Station. People say that what goes around comes around, and on this occasion it was true.

Birmingham vs West Ham United Oct 3rd 1981
Courtney

My first experience of West Hams notorious firm came in the 1981-1982 season back in Division 1 under Jim Smith. We had the likes of Colin Todd, Dave Langan, Jim Gallagher, Alan Curbishley and Keith Bertschin in the team so dreams of staying in the First Division in the big league. I must admit that still being at school I wasn't aware of West Hams awesome reputation. This day would prove an emphatic introduction. It's absence in the Zulu book beggars belief. To me, this was a milestone in Birmingham's history as a firm. This was the game where several West Ham invaded the pitch led by a black geezer. It appeared that West Ham were getting attacked in the Kop and provoked the anger. The ICF were at-it so much I don't even remember the score until somebody told me after. We drew 2-2 with Langan and Dillon netting them for Birmingham City. After the game, we went into the car park where there was lot of pushing, charging backwards and forwards in the main road, with the police trying to protect the route for away fans to walk through. After about twenty minutes, we decided on walking back into town via Digbeth. What my fragmented brain does recall was the stampede of Blues fans were running away from their ferocious mob. I have never in my life of travelling to Blues from Redditch had to run back to the city centre. We used to catch the bus from the old Midland Red station near the rag market. West Ham came through looking for Blues, and we had to hide in amongst shoppers in the bus stops. This day is often referred to as a turning point for Blues, as it meant we had to get a proper firm together and more importantly more organized. As in any stampede, everyone has to run to avoid being trampled. There's nothing more frustrating when running from some-thing you can't see. Everyone there that day has their own story to tell on how they survived a good kicking. To be fair, we were young kids compared to the grown men we faced then toed it from, but within the year, the Apex was up and running.

DAVID C GEORGE

Before the match several Redditch, Rubery, Northfield, and Kings Norton lads tried to ambush West Ham drinking in the Old Crown. Despite our numbers being low, we set off with real intent. We were not the firm that had been trounced in the early 80s, we were more mature and organised than back in those days.

West Ham United Vs Birmingham City Aug 23rd 1983

It has been said on numerous occasions from some of Birmingham's top boys that by far the best firm to come out of London in the early eighties was West Ham United. Not only looking the part, they were the part. No hiding place, these lads had a proper firm. Unlike Millwall who in the 80s tended to enjoy burning pubs and throwing bricks, West Ham's ICF would stand and trade, which is what a lot of firms don't do anymore. In 1983 Birmingham City played West Ham away and took a firm of around 350 lads to Euston Station. Birmingham City already had a firm of around a hundred that had landed in London earlier at 10 o clock in the morning and had been fighting with other factions on Euston station before the main bulk of the Birmingham crew had arrived.

As they arrived at the station, they were met by a sea of police who tried to contain Blues in the station but couldn't do so due to the tenacity and numbers of Birmingham fans. Birmingham bowled out of Euston and split into 3 firms, each at least 100 handed. More police were now called as Blues started to march up the main road and towards the shopping area on Oxford Street. The police though had other ideas and decided to round up most of the Blues fans and around 250 of Blues firm had been arrested and had up on jumped up charges. It was a boiling hot day when the police decided on making the biggest arrest in one go relating to football. Blues fans were put into small cubicles in vans not big enough to turn around in. Birmingham had brought a hell of a lot of big lads to this game, as they know full well the capability of the ICF home or away. Birmingham fans were taken to Bow Street police station to be locked up, and the first twelve people to be arrested were from Chelmsley Wood. The desk sergeant throws his pen down on the desk and says to the thirteenth person from Birmingham to come through. "Don't tell me that you're from

APEX TO ZULU A2Z!

Chelmsley fakin Wood an all?" The Sergeant stands up and looks down the line of a hundred Brummies and says, "I tell you what, is there anyone here who is not from Chelmsley Wood?" Big Glyn was the first person to be put into the cells, and ended up being in a cell with an Arsenal fan who had been arrested for fighting and had a bandaged hand. Big Glyn walks into the cell, all 6ft 3, and 18 stone of a man, sits down on the bench, across the room from the Arsenal fan. Nobody says a word, and the room is silent. The Arsenal fan now gets up, and repeatedly bangs on the door for assistance. An officer arrives and the Arsenal fan says, "I don't wanna stop in here with him!"

Glyn never said a word to the Arsenal fan, but just through his sheer presence, he had given this lad nightmares of what this person could be capable of doing to him if he was left on his own. This, however is not true, as Glyn is a gentleman, and would only punch your lights out if you deserved it, and would be more interested in beating you at a quick game of poker and taking all of your possessions. If this tragedy hadn't happened, I am sure that Birmingham's firm would have shown the archetypal London lads a thing or to about what Brummies can do. A small firm of around a hundred still went to the game and made a good account of themselves, but it could have been so different if that Blues fan on Euston had not got carried away and smashed some glass bringing more Old Bill to the station. As Cass states in his book, the real Zulus he had to give respect to, because they are the real deal.

Groups like the Cockney Rejects were forming in the East End in 1979 and clearly stating their intentions to sing about being from London and supporting West Ham United, to get up everybody else's noses. With tracks like "We Can Do Anything" and "We Are The Firm" and, of course the West Ham-inspired anthem "I'm Forever Blowing Bubbles." Gives you an idea of what Londoners thought about themselves and their capabilities, which is why most people hate their fucking guts, but admire them at the same time.

West Ham was the firm that came into New Street station wearing bleached Lois jeans, frayed at the bottom with Nike Wimbledon. Kios and Adidas Gazelle and specials with Farah action slacks. Fila Bubble coats and Ellesse ski coats in abundance. Flying jackets and diamond Pringles, also Lyle & Scott. The year was 1982 and they looked the fucking bollocks. West Ham have a long history of being the number one firm in London throughout the 80s with lads who were four or five years older than the majority of Blues crew. The Under Fives, who were the younger version of the ICF, are around the same age as the new firm Birmingham were putting together as most of the Under Fives are now 39–40 years old. Big Bill Gardener & Cass Pennant must be knocking late 40s easy; while Blues top lads from the 80s are now age 39–45. Birmingham did have a number of old guard from the late 70s, but with the introduction of the new fashion, the younger generation took the helm and began to establish themselves as the new crew, combined with a few old guard who still have a lot of respect in Birmingham City.

Birmingham City Vs West Ham United Jan 14th 84

This was a big day for Birmingham Citys firm, as the ICF had a huge reputation with regards to catching the opposition out and banging it right off, good and proper. Birmingham's firm met in town near Gino's and The Knightrider pub, and walked to the ground. In 83, a lot of Blues firm used to stand in the Tilton end of the ground near the front behind the goal, with another firm at the other end of the ground in the lower tier seats. Blues firm at the time was made up of skinheads and trendies who were the new movement coming through in Birmingham, and getting larger all the time. Some of the older lads at Birmingham didn't like the trendy look and used to take the piss out of the new trendies, and call them the Scouse look-alikes. West Ham's ICF brought a firm into the lower tier at the far end of the ground sitting right next to Blues fans, and also had a mob of around twelve big ugly monsters standing in the Kop end of the ground under the clock. The Brummies behind the goal in the Tilton, made a move towards the clock end of the ground and were marching through the crowd to get over to the ICF. Some of the Blues lads were so small they could fit through the bars in the Spion Kop end, while the rest had to walk all the way to the top near the toilets, and walk down to get to West Ham. The younger Blues lads who were around seventeen got to the ICF before the older lads and just stood there looking at them, as they were too big and ugly to run into. They were all big fucking lads who looked very handy indeed. The younger Blues lot waited for the older Blues to come through the crowd, and come they did. Blues rushed the ICF and there is a bit of a knuckle as fists are thrown until the police step in and shield the twelve ICF who where game as anything I had seen. As this is happening, Swallow has brought the rest of West Ham's firm onto the pitch and they came all the way across to Birmingham and kicked it off in the corner behind the goal. Blues firm are now jumping over the fence in the Kop end and onto the pitch to back up the rest of Blues firm behind the goal. I have to hand it to the ICF for having a great plan in being in the Kop, also in our seats in the lower tier and also bringing a firm across the pitch all at the same time. More and more Blues fans were jumping over the fence onto the pitch to fight West Ham including Chelmsley Wood Brownie, who was just thirteen years of age who twatted a Cockney lad and put him straight on his arse. Fats was throwing ICF lads against the fence of the Kop, and then dishing out some serious body shots. Blues now all spill onto the pitch from behind the goal and run West Ham across the pitch, then get chased off the pitch by the police. Around 80 ICF stayed behind the goal in the seats next to Blues, and Blues wanted to get at them again, so ten minutes from the end of the game, Blues firm leaves the ground and at the same time, the ICF do exactly the same. It goes right off at the blue doors with a bit of to and froing, bottles and bricks are exchanged at close quarter. Birmingham's Ginger Jamie fronted the 80 West Ham at the gates in his Kung Fu slippers, and starts throwing kicks and punches at the ICF. There were a lot of stand offs and bravado, but the police managed to shut the doors and calm the situation down. Birmingham won the game 3–0 with Hartford, Ferguson and Gayle scoring. We had a right good day, but since reading West Ham's book I realise they must be suffering from selective memory loss, as 10,334 Blues fans will tell you this is how it went down.

Birmingham City vs Westham Jan 14 1984
Courtney

That morning, I left Redditch by train into New Street as this gave me access to the station after games, which was handy for obvious reasons.

DAVID C GEORGE

That particular morning I bumped into some of their ICF lads behind the barriers outside the cafe on New Street station. I instantly get the distinct impression these West Ham fancied a bit of knuckle. I can remember saying, "Not here, because that black glass bubble thing that is sitting on the ceiling has got cameras in it. There were five or six of them, they glance back at the dome-like thing on the ceiling and see my reasoning. Eventually we get talking and they were asking if we had a firm ect, we had the usual banter about what was going to happen that day. After the game, I met these lads again back at the station. The West Ham lad said to me that their day of having it with Blues at the match was 50/50 on the pitch.

That was the ICF giving us their respect, they didn't claim the result and knew we were game and had numbers. I saw it differently, of course, as more 60/40 to the Zulus. All the same, that day gave us kudos. It was our first major victory in confrontation with West Ham's top firm. We have had West ham on their toes at New Street, but it was only after years of learning and creating the Zulu family unit that it came together. It gave us the confidence to tackle other firms away from home, using tactics that on some occasions are taught to you by many different firms you get to meet throughout the years of travelling with Blues, West Ham was the benchmark.

Swindon Vs Birmingham City 87
Mozza

By the time the 87 season started most of the Juniors were 18 and legally adult. We also had access to motorised transport, which made a hell of a difference with regards to getting about. Early on in the season we played Swindon away, and a group of 30 Kings Norton Juniors and Harborne Juniors met up at Frankly service station on the M5 for the journey south. The journey down was uneventful, except for 3 of our cars missing the motorway exit and having to reverse up the hard shoulder while the rest of us tried to stop traffic to allow them up the exit road. We arrived in Swindon and parked in the town centre and went for a mooch. Bray, Spud and M.S. were some way in front of the others when we came across a side road. Down this side road was a pub with around 30 lads standing outside. Spud & Bray started to walk down towards the pub while I called the others on. The lads calmly walked down the road and banged it straight off outside the pub. I ran down the road and flew into the Swindon lot with the rest of our lads. Because of being spread out, it was touch and go for half a minute, but eventually the organisation and determination to succeed came through. Birmingham now ran them back into the pub and Swindon managed to lock the pub doors. A few of the windows went through when sirens could be heard in the distance. We went up an alley towards the shopping precinct when the pub now emptied and around 80 lads now came after us all tooled up with furniture, bottles and ashtrays from the pub.

It was Saturday dinnertime and the precinct was full of shoppers when Swindon attacked us with a hail of bottles and glasses. At one point, I was leaning over a pram in order to stop any glass from hitting a local child. We were not interested in harming the local shoppers, as that is not what we were about. Finally Mossy and a few others got into them and gained a foothold in the alley. We charged right through them and smashed them up. They ran back into the pub and this time, we finished the job, doing them over until the police arrived. Birmingham now disappeared in the shopping precinct and met in a pub further down the road. A few lads had cuts and bruises, with one Harborne chap having a badly cut arm. I took off my Hugo Boss jogging top and used it to dress the lads wound.

When the old bill arrived, they took us all outside and placed us into vans. We thought we were being arrested but instead, they drove us to the ground and dropped us off. Months later I found out the Boss-jogging top was being used as a dog blanket. How's that for gratitude?

Birmingham City Vs Northampton town 89
Sooty

This was not a high profile game against Northampton town, even though Birmingham City are aware of the N.A.T./Northampton Affray Team. I decided to go to work in the morning until midday and then get into town. I didn't even feel like going to the game on this day, so I was making my way home on a bus when I saw about thirty

DAVID C GEORGE

lads bowling around the Industrial estate as if they were the business. They were certainly not from off our manor as a number of them had dungarees on, and dungarees were not fashionable in Birmingham anyhow. So as the bus was coming up to St Andrews I got off near the ground and bumped into a few of the boys and mentioned what I had just seen. Nothing happened during the game, except that we beat Northampton 4–0, with both Gleghorn and Bailey on the score sheet for Blues. A small firm of Blues were on Digbeth high street after the game when we see the same lot of dungaree wearing lads again all bowling up the road. I've walked across the road next to them to find out where they from, and were definitely not from Birmingham, as the accents were proper crunchy. Birmingham now followed this group of Northampton into town making sure they kept a fair distance away as not to be spotted. Northampton were bowling about as bold a brass and had walked from St Andrews there and back, and in those days there were only a few firms that would attempt this, as Birmingham is a fucking scary place. Around fifty Birmingham decided on a plan of action as the 30 or so Northampton Affray Team, stood at the bottom of the ramp in central Birmingham just hanging about without a care in the world.

Birmingham split into two firms and decided on hitting them from both sides as to have them in a pincer movement to catch as many as we could when they took them out of the game. Northampton are totally unaware of what was being planned and chatted away nonchalantly, when all of a sudden, "Bang, bang, bang, bang! The N.A.T. are hit from both sides by Birmingham's firm, sending people on their arses backwards. We chased loads of them though town, caught them and absolutely mullard them. There were a few Asian geezers in their firm and one in particular was saying, "I'm a Brummie, I'm a Brummie." The only problem was he was still talking with a crunchy accent. A Birmingham lad was going for the height of humiliation and asking one of the Northampton lads, "Who's the best firm in the country?" The Northampton lad was saying, "The Zulus are the best, I'll be a Zulu." It's funny what some stupid things people will say not to get a hiding, but people must understand Birmingham is a city of over two million population, so when you want the rough crowd, then it's very rough.

Birmingham now went through the lads' pockets and found their train tickets home and ripped them up in front of them. They left the Northampton lads on the floor dazzled and went for a nearby drink

Bristol City Vs Birmingham City 26th Aug 89

300 Birmingham Zulus had tickets for the game today and were escorted to the game straight from the station. A handful of Birmingham fans hung around and were clocked by a few local Bristols girls who informed the BBC who are one of the local firms, The Bristol Business Crew.

30 Blues fans who didn't have tickets are being told to move on outside the ground and are contemplating where to go, when a group of only a small Bristol firm rushes down the hill at the 30 Birmingham. Birmingham are looking at the 5–6 Bristol lads who are running straight into Birmingham with no fear whatsoever. As they are right in front of the Birmingham lot, the picture unravels in front of everybody's eyes. The Bristol lads all put hands in their jackets and produce cans of CS gas. The 30 Blues fans are overwhelmed by the gas, and retreat up the road running blind. Some Birmingham stayed in a local pub and didn't know what was going on. The Birmingham fans that had no tickets outside the ground had an absolute nightmare being chased by Bristol fans all around the ground. Bristol took advantage no excuses. It was Birmingham's 1st away game of season in Bristol and we lost 1–0.

The Blues fans were disorientated, leaving one poor Brummy being caught by the Bristol firm, beaten up and then thrown through a shop window. Birmingham tried to have a go outside the ground throwing huge chunks of tarmac at the Bristol firm while the game is still on. One Birmingham lad had a Batman shaved in back of head as he came running down the road being chased by a mob of Bristol. Some Birmingham who couldn't run any more hid in bushes. One lad was caught on a doorstep by the Bristol firm, knocked the door of the house he was outside. As the door opened, he ran straight through the house while a tea party was taking place. He pleads with the guy in his house while the bloke is having a tea party for his daughter. As strange as this may seem, the guy who lives in Bristol turns out to be from

Birmingham originally and drives the half-blind panting Brummy back to the nearest train station.

On this day, Blues got caught out no excuses, it just happens. Birmingham are aware Bristol have long established firms and on this day, they turned up and said hello to a group of our supporters.

Bolton Vs Birmingham City 91
Sooty

It's a 12.00pm game for blues, and Birmingham catch the train up north the day before and head into to Manchester for a drink. We book into a hotel then have a couple of drinks in some local pubs and then we notice this rave club called

The House. This was when the rave scene was really in full swing and twenty of us decide on going into the club. We are all enjoying ourselves and having a good time, when another mob now enters the club. Lo and behold, it's another mob of Birmingham who just happened to be in booked into the same hotel as us down the road. The Birmingham lot now had about fifty lads in this small club who were all enjoying the evening and singing Birmingham songs and having a laugh. The Manchester girls were enjoying our company and we were having a good evening. As the night rolls on, another lot of Birmingham enter the club with a number of well-known black faces. Birmingham now had a mob of about eighty lads in this club and everyone was shaking hands and dancing, it was a proper good night. The Birmingham lot were standing on one side of the club singing Zulu, Zulu Warrior, Zulu, Zulu Warrior. The thing was the Manchester girls loved us, but the local lads were wandering what the hell was going on.

They were looking at us and checking our numbers but they didn't really want to know to be fair. As we get back to the hotel all of us stayed in just two rooms with myself sleeping in the fucking bath. The floor is covered in bodies and the smell of farts in the one room was unreal. In the morning a few Birmingham have left early and had run up a bill of over £250 on the phone, they had also ordered heaps of food and the bill needed paying. We left the hotel and made our way to the station at 9.00am. Were getting into Bolton now around fifty handed, with the other room dodgers leaving much earlier. I'm looking out of the window as we are slowing down at Bolton station when I see a huge firm standing on the platform, "What the fuck is that?"

"Everybody look out the windows now." There's about a hundred lads standing on the platform. The last time Birmingham went to Bolton, they only took a small firm up there and got a bit a slap. We thought to ourselves that we had better be prepared as we had half the numbers that were standing on the platform.

We ripped up the seats and grabbed everything we could use when we come off the train for this firm. As we get closer we noticed, "Hang on, they've got a lot of black lads on their firm haven't they?" This other firm turned out to be a lot of Birmingham's top lads. I spotted a lad well known to Birmingham's firm who stands at least 6ft 7inches. Relief went through the crew on the train, as the size of a lot of the firm standing on the station would have made most people question what the hell they are doing there. Birmingham are now 150 handed and bowling round the streets of Bolton at 9.30am in the morning. There was nowhere to go that early in the morning and we were rounded up by the old bill and taken to the ground.

We drew the game 1–1 with Rogerson scoring for Birmingham, but to be fair the game was a bag of pants. As we left the game, Birmingham went in search of Bolton and marched past a few of their pubs that were full to the rafters. A few scuffles broke out but nothing major occurred as there were too many old bill around us but it was a really good weekend a lot of lads will remember.

Keep Right On!

DAVID C GEORGE

Private warehouse party in London – 2001. Jarvis was the DJ

Meeting Mathew Upson at the end of season bash

APEX TO ZULU A2Z!

Birmingham hero, Frank Worthington, at end of season do

Meeting Dugarry at end of season do

DAVID C GEORGE

Meeting the Horse at end of season do

Meeting Damion Johnson at end of season do

APEX TO ZULU A2Z!

The Marvin Hagler in London

He wasn't happy

DAVID C GEORGE

Writer of The Firm, Al Hunter Ashton, Kingy, and myself

Myself, Danny Dyer, Mozza – 2006

APEX TO ZULU A2Z!

UB40's Jim Brown and myself

Jade with Steve Bruce at the end of season do

DAVID C GEORGE

Caroline and myself at 1st Zulu book launch

Myself meeting Cass Pennant at 1st Zulu book

CHAPTER 14

World Cup France 98

Brains

I TRAVELLED TO NICE by plane on my own and then jumped on a train to Marseille. It was around a two an a half hour journey on the train and I had a bit of bother from a few Everton lads because I had my Birmingham badge on. They were generally slagging Birmingham off, so I've fronted the one Everton geezer, but they were fucking idiots. So what's happened now is that I've walked up to the buffet car with my little rucksack on carrying my four tins of Heinekan, and as I've got to the buffet carriage there must have been about 8 lads, good lads from Oxford.

Good lads older lads, some of Oxford's old tops boys. I have a lot of respect for them. I'm in this buffet car now and the one has started giving it loads of verbal about Birmingham. One of his own mates has told this guy to shut his mouth, as he had already been told to shut it earlier in the day for being a nuisance.

One of the Oxford lads has turned round and said, "What ya drinking Brum?"

I've got my cans with me, but they had a number of bottles of this and that to drink for the journey. We had a drink and started talking, and they've asked me to come and stay at their hotel as I had nowhere to stay as of yet. We've got to Marseille airport and jumped into taxi's to their hotel, and the biggest coincidence was that when we got there was that Smiler, Mackie and a few other Blues lads are all stopping at the same hotel. So I've put my bag in the Brummies' room because obviously I know them a lot better than the Oxford lot. Don't get me wrong, as these Oxford lads were all right, but still I just preferred it that way. We are about three four miles from the town of Marseille, so we had to get a taxi back into the centre. As soon as we've got into the town, a few of the Oxford lads were up for a bit, but the rest declined. We went into a few bars in town and they were pretty quiet really. A couple of England fans have come up to us and said, "Don't go going up there lads, it's going right off." So me and these two Oxfords lads have looked at each other and said, "Well what the fuck we waiting for, let's get down there?" It was mid evening just getting dark when we made our way down to this bar were you could see that a load of tables and chairs were all over the place. England fans had locked themselves in the boozer shutting all the doors. There must have been around fifty/sixty of them in there, but they weren't all lads and were mainly made up of people who thought that they were, but clearly were not. There were a few Portsmouth in there but nobody was budging from the boozer. So as I've got there now, the lads who had chased them in there were not actual football lads, but local North Africans who absolutely hated the English.

So what me and Dave from Oxford did was try getting all these England lot out of the boozer, but they didn't really want to come out, and kept all the doors shut and just looked out of the window.

A North African geezer comes over to me jumping up and down in front of me, so I've just walloped him. He's now run off, and with that, I'm now calling all of the rest of the scared England fans out of the boozer, and a few of them started coming out realising that I was proper up for it. With that, when these North Africans have come back again to make another attack, and we've had them right on their toes and this was the first time all evening that these England had run em as they were now all stirred up. England were now chasing these local lads up and down the side streets for around ten minutes, when the old bill have landed. I could see this idiot with the police pointing me out. I've been jumped on by the police, and it turns out the local person who was performing in front of me who I chinned, was now pointing me out to the old bill. So I've lasted around half hour in Marseille and I was locked up for at least 48 hours and then I got deported but was never charged with anything.

The second game I had a ticket for, the police took my ticket off me and basically told me to fuck off. The third game for England, and I was back in Brum, Blues were turning the firm out for this one. England were playing in Lens, but everyone was meeting in Lille. So what I've done after all the aggravation in Marseille, I wanted to see a game at the World Cup. I got in Al's car and we drove down to the Blues shop in Birmingham where I bought a football shirt. We have now driven to Lille from Birmingham and I've got my Birmingham football shirt on, and while were here today, I will calm it down a watch the game without getting into any bother, but it didn't turn out like that at all. A few Birmingham are having a drink in this bar when I've overheard this Derby lad called Tomo slagging Birmingham off, saying, "Birmingham have only come and done it once at Derby." So I've turned round and said to this Tomo guy, "Well, once is better than nothing at all," even though we have done Derby more than once anyway. This Tomo guy has looked at me and said, "Well what do you know anyway, you're only a shirt." So this guy and i have ended up arguing, and this Tomo guy has asked for a straightener, and I've said to Tomo, "Have you ever been banged out by a shirt?" There's about thirty Derby in this boozer, with a few other smaller Midlands firms having a drink in this bar. What Derby didn't realise was that across the road was another firm of Blues around 150 handed just seconds away from these Derby. So I've gone for a straightener with this guy and we're walking out of the pub now, when this Tomo has punched me from behind and we hadn't even reached the square where we were heading, but instead we've just had it right off where we were which was still in the bar. As I'm giving him a good few digs, one of Tomo's Derby's lots has come and glassed me. With that, a number of Birmingham have now seen what was going on, and have made a bee-line for the Derby D.L.F. Birmingham have now gone straight into Derby, and just scattered them everywhere. Derby, and whoever else was there.

The funny thing about it was, these couple of Oxford lads who had turned up in Lille for a drink with me had now got it put on em by

DAVID C GEORGE

Birmingham who had now turned on everyone there who wanted to know. I had to go to hospital to get some stitches put in my face and I still hadn't seen a game at the World Cup.

By the time I had got my face stitched up, the last train had gone to Lens, so I ended up staying in Lille and getting absolutely paralytic with Nappa and few other chaps with one of our lads being able to speak fluent French from his days in the Foreign Legion. So we've ended up having a good drink and getting bang on it, but we moved to the outskirts of town to find a few more venues for a good drink.

Obviously most of England had gone to the game with a few who were with myself who didn't. I had a ticket for the third game, but because of all the carry on with the Derby lot and me getting Judased and stitched up at the hospital, I've missed another bloody game at the World Cup. I'm wearing a pair of shorts on this day with a tattoo on my leg saying Zulu Warriors B.C.F.C. Some foreign lad who I had never seen before has come up to me and we've got talking. This guy has seen the tattoo on my leg Zulu Warriors B.C.F.C. and this guy was from Red Star Belgrade.

He was an absolute fanatic on English football violence, needless to say, we've spent the next few hours drinking and discussing football violence. His name was Nikola from Yugoslavia and he was a nice geezer. Nikola started talking about the firms in Yugoslavia, and he told me they have a firm over there called the Zulu Warriors, so we got on like a house on fire. Nikola told me Red Star have three different firms in Yugoslavia who all have it bang off. He mentioned the political scene regarding the Serbs who do not like the Yugoslavs and what was going on over there. The Red Star lads are absolutely fanatical not only following the football, but also the Volleyball, basketball and handball. They go to everything they can go to. This Nikola has asked me for my address in order to send me some paraphernalia in the post, but to be honest, I thought it was just talk, when around a month later, he has sent me pictures of Red Star Belgrade's Zulu Warriors having it bang off in the main road at a few football matches. I was contemplating writing back, but within a few weeks, the war had kicked off big time over there between the Serbs and the Croatians, so I never bothered. He's probably fucking dead now, but I hope not as he was a bang on geezer.

APEX TO ZULU A2Z!

So The Fat White Leary One's The Brains of The Bunch

We got ourselves a luverley gaff,
Three bed detached turn it up not in,
Out in January so we better begin,
Line em up get the boys round,
Most casuals are compatible,
Sociable and happy to attend,
Which is sound,
Set the scene swept the stage,
Scripted slightly about the early days,
Action the cameras running,
The tales start flowing,
With a sense of pride about the untouchables,
Like the Ready Brek man they'd stride,
Glowing!

Time moves on there's no stopping evolution,
From Teddy boy to Rudies to Skins and Mods,
Punks Soul boys from Casual to Hooligan,
Late seventies on the Tilton it was knees up mother brown,
A hundred bananas in the back of the nets,
To the black faces down the match it brought a monobrow frown,
The Apex was born out of these events,
Heads fed up with the ritual humiliation,
Grouped together with the others to serve retribution,
Stamped out the hobnail boots and the nazi bulldog invasion.
The tigers of wrath are wiser,
Than the horses of instruction!

Villa's C crew were well dressed first,
It was strange to hear,
In Europe first and the trophy shelf full,
Didn't stop the Blues who were very mindful,
About the ways to make a raise,
They embarked to Europe on their rival's coat tails,
Exported the imports acquired from the rails,

DAVID C GEORGE

Made sterling from funny money,
Back before the postcards,
Draped in Fila and Tachinni,
Jimmy ConAr-tists,
Venture capitalists,
Thatcher's rapists,
I bet the Vile didn't know this,
Took the piss,
Like watching the backs of their trainers,
Disappearing on the realization,
The Zulus gorillas were in their midst.

They were good at their work,
Very talented,
But we were like nothing else,
Well dressed in numbers different colours,
No mobiles yet organized,
Every week it was contested,
On the pitch every team gives there all against Man U,
At the time on the terraces down the dark lanes or New Street,
It was our team that would always meet you.

Home and away we had the Arsenal,
First the aerial assault with brick and bottle,
Then the frontal assault of a roundhouse and Wing Chun,
Close combative arts from boxers and nutters,
The Millwall The Pompei The Boro would all run,
As the boozers were burnt and the shops closed their shutters,

What do you know about the Zulu Juniors?
The Junior Business Boys what was your thinking?
Fagin less little fuckers occasionally started the party,
By the time we'd finished drinking,
Arrived at the station or at the ground,
To scenes from Platoon bodies strewn all around,
And after the whistle in the escort back home,

APEX TO ZULU A2Z!

They'd get tripped up and sparked,
Relieved of the natty clobber,
Which they intended to own,
Nerves of steel for youth half stoned!

The man used to saunter with the seniors,
Yes that's right if you don't know it,
Lemon and gentlemen,
The Zulu warriors,
What a firm!

When we asked him to draw,
From a goldfish bowl memory he tried to recall,
A fond battle story whether in defeat or glory,
Which we could impress upon the outsider,
That would go down in history,
This was when it dawned as I sat jaw on floor,
At the many tour of duties and regime changes he saw,
Only the maddest of the few are in Terrace Legends,
For part two 'Top Boys' Mr. Pennant gave him a call.

Pompei was a funny day the MP's had battled all night,
Against the 657 who had led them a merry dance,
'They stepped aside and allowed us to fight,
They thought we didn't have a chance,'
Protected the motors which assured our safe passage,
The impending threat of damage to your carriage,
Would turn the calmest of men into a savage,
But we managed even made it look good,
After we'd finished the militaries old bill understood,

Come if you dare!
Try and test as Portsmouth often did,
Lot of respect for there boys,
Got a right firm they have kid,
But the rainbow warrior firm destroys.

DAVID C GEORGE

Take Huddersfield away for instance,
A who dey are?
Are you ready to dance?
Three times in thirty minutes,
It's good to know the feeling you're the best,
The theatre of battle science,
Exercised with defiance,
Belligerent young men,
Incensed but well dressed.

Then back to the safety of the social,
Open the doors the crowd roars,
The old the young,
The songs we stood by each other and sung,
Fathers become immortal son,
We will journey on,
And on,
No matter what manor or end you came from!

Kingy..!

Anglo Italian Cup Perugia Vs Birmingham City
Brains

Cockney Al, Gibson, Russell and The General set out to go to Perugia in the Anglo Italian Cup. So we've made about a week out of our trip and flown into Rimini on the coast. We had a day there and enjoyed ourselves on the town, and a day before Birmingham were playing their first game in Perugia, we flew to Pisa which was absolutely shit. We are having a drink in a local bar when some verbal has been exchanged between some locals and ourselves. The one Italian lad has gone for something in his pocket, and we thought that he was going for a tool in his jacket, but it turned out to be his asthma inhaler, so it's all calmed down.

We've had a night in Pisa, and made our way to Florence on the train. Whilst there, an Italian guy who was selling pop had left hid bum bag on his bikes seat with all his money in, so that's gone missing straight away. So we're in Florence spending this guy's lira and then we travelled over to Rimini on the coast and it was pretty quiet, to be honest. They did have some lovely Sergio Tachini's over there that we noticed which we hadn't seen before in the UK, so the five fingered discount was well and truly on the cards. We've now made our way to Perugia and booked into a hotel, then bumped into a few more Birmingham lads with us now having a decent little mob of around forty lads, mainly from Chelmsley Wood. We booked into a separate hotel, as we didn't know where everybody else was staying at the time. We've got freshened up in our hotel and then went and met up with everyone else in a local bar. We then all made our way to Perugia's ground and we all split up and did our own thing. The word has filtered back to us that there are a number of local Italian fans who were riding past on Vespas with a passenger on the back carrying a baseball bat while smacking it at Birmingham lads heads as they are riding past. Nothing has happened during the game, but as soon as the whistle had gone, Birmingham have now come out of the game and gone straight round to the home fans end forty handed. As we've come round to their end their firm has appeared and it's gone off in the main road. Blues have gone into Perugia and scattered them, but they had one big lad at the front that was proper game as fuck. The next thing you know, Sherry has now rushed the guy from the side, and has smashed a dustbin right off this guy's kisser and finished him.

Perugia have run away into a fairground called the Lunar Park, and the next thing you know is that all these gypo geezers have now joined up with the Perugia lot combined with the local police and we are getting backed off up the road by not just the local football fans, but the whole town including the police. Everyone was against us and a couple of our lads were now being arrested and handcuffed to these fences and being left behind as were are still being backed off up the road.

As the Birmingham lads were left behind totally defenceless, the Perugia lads were now surrounding them and kicking them unconscious while we're still having it further up the road. Blues have gone fucking mad, and now steamed into Perugia growling and battling the locals who, to be honest, were a bunch of cowards, but had loads of numbers.

The situation altered again when the police now draw their guns to bring the order back from chaos. Most Birmingham lads had not experienced trouble abroad with foreign firms and were certainly not prepared for the local police pulling guns on them. More police have now landed and have dispersed the local Perugia and Gypo characters and now escorted the small contingency of Birmingham back to their hotel. Because we were stopping in another hotel on the other side of town, five of us have been escorted back to our hotel with the police holding their guns out of their holsters in order to protect us from the local firm that was still milling about. Outside the other hotel where the majority of other blues lads were stopping, had a mob standing outside the hotel all night without even a bit of shuteye. The next day there were a few Birmingham casualties, with Sherry receiving a broken arm by the police continually beating him with batons.

The fact of the matter is that if you cannot look after yourself abroad, you will end up in a whole heap of shit, as most foreign fans hate the English. Because of the legacy left from Thatcher's hungry hooligan Britain, most European firms were not ready for England fans taking the piss but have now after a considerable number of years, got together and give out a lot of what they used to receive.

Anconnia Vs Birmingham City
Brains

There must be something in the water in Italy as at this particular game, the Anconnia players were very unruly indeed. The attendance was only 1,000 or so home supporters who threw bricks at us throughout the entire game but we didn't have a firm there at all and there were only four or five of us who were well pissed off having to duck from stones being thrown at the away end for 90 minutes.

Near the end of the game, players like Liam Daish did Birmingham proud by steaming into a load of their players as it went bang off when the players were going back to their dressing rooms. One of the Anconnia players refused to shake hands with one of our players. The Anconnia coach ended up getting stretcherd off the pitch after being nutted by one of the Birmingham players. It was a strange day to be fair and the Italian fans were not scary really, but just loud and mouthy.

Scotland Vs England 1999

It must be very strange supporting England as a black casual because if anyone wants to be honest, you have got more chance of being attacked by a group of right wing northerners from Barnsley or Blackburn, or some southerners who have supported Chelsea, Millwall or Glasgow Rangers all their lives. Racism is still very potent at England games especially if you follow a football team that has a reputation a lot of the rest of the firms could only dream of. A lot of football firms across the country enjoy beating up rival fans especially if they are from a well-known firm. This has being going on for over two decades and does not seem to be changing what so ever. Even though on the professional side of things, The Kick Racism Out Of Football seems to be a successes, but in reality as a person of colour who watches the game, nothing has changed much in peoples views on ethnic minorities what so ever.

Birmingham left the White Lion pub in Birmingham City via coach at midnight heading for Glasgow with cars also en route following the coach. They arrived at 6am in the morning around 100 handed. There were a few small firms roaming around in the morning when Birmingham's lads got into a pub in the Barrow Lands and had a few drinks. Throughout the day, more Birmingham lads kept on arriving with the numbers swelled to around 160. Birmingham were getting phone calls from some of Villa's lads in the morning, trying to arrange a link up with ourselves for a bit of knuckle. Birmingham met Newcastle lads and also Reading firms on the same day, but there was no trouble what so ever with these two crews. Some of the Birmingham lot had found out where the Villa were drinking in town and informed the rest of the Birmingham firm what the script was. Birmingham now enter the pub where the Villa are drinking, and McCormick, who was standing on the door of the pub, enters and locks the door behind him. With some of Birmingham's top lads all present, Birmingham decides on putting it on the Villa.

Tables are now picked up from the middle of the room and placed at the sides of the bar so that the Villa have got nowhere to run. A

DAVID C GEORGE

Villa lad from Castle Vale with a name well known to be similar to a famous local chocolate brand, tries to calm the situation, which makes everything worse. He gets chinned and ends up backwards over a nearby table when the lot goes up in the air. From a firm that has so many negative things to say about Birmingham City, it's no surprise that when it is all put on the table, the usual thing happens. I agree this is hard for a lot of Villa fans to swallow, but if you speak to Villa's proper lads, they will honestly tell you how it really is. Bottles, glasses and chairs are all flying at the Villa lot, with them all now looking for a way out of the pub. The Villa lot ran upstairs in the pub and out of the emergency exit to get away. They were very lucky on this day, because the Birmingham lot let them go really. Birmingham now left the pub with a few Brummies being arrested. Some of the Birmingham's mob now walk towards Hamden Park for the game and bumped into a huge firm of England who were having it bang off with pockets of jocks off all of the side streets around Hamden Park. After the game, trouble started with English and Scottish fans all the way back into the centre.

When Birmingham arrived back into town, it was going off with the Jocks and the local police. Kilmarnock turned up to have a go at Birmingham before they left Scotland and ran straight through a line of police to get at the Brummies, a minor scuffle occurred but it's all in a day of being a blue nose. Fair play to Kilmarnock though, as they were some of the gamest Jocks Birmingham had met all day.

Shep from Birmingham was arrested and beaten up by the police, and spent two nights in the cells before heading off home. When the Birmingham lot were in court two days later, half of the coach was also in court, which meant the coach must have gone home half-empty.

England Vs Wales – In Manchester
Ry. Northfield

We've gone up to Manchester to meet up with a number of other Birmingham lads who were also going to the game. The first pub we went into was full of Stoke and moody as hell, as everybody knows Stoke would put it on an old man in a wheelchair who was blind if they got the chance. We've left that place and gone in search of a better venue to drink in the town. We met up with a few Newcastle lads we knew, and they took us to a bar where

Sooty was having a drink with a few Sheffield Wednesday lads. As we left this next pub, I've recognised two lads standing across the road, one wearing Stone Island and the other wearing C.P. The one guy kept on looking at me and I was sure I remembered his face from somewhere. It was a guy I had put it on In Portugal at the Euro 2000 tournament who was part of the Voile firm. As we were coming out of the pub on the left hand side of the road, a few of his mates have flanked us from behind, I turned round and went straight over to him. He was looking in my eyes and I was looking straight back at him without blinking. I thought, "I've gotta whack him." We end up having a scuffle on the floor and give him one good shot and his hood has come of his jacket in my hands. The rest of Blues have come charging up the road, and Villa have had it on their toes. Deakin and Mear with the rest of the Voile have been run down the road and I've still got this guy's hood in my hand. Every time we would get close to them, they would run that little bit further to get away. They were absolutely knackered from running, and so were we. Carl kept on asking me for his hood for his jacket back and my reply was, "If he wants his hood back, then he can have it if he comes with me for a quiet little drink. "By the way, I've still got the hood."

DAVID C GEORGE

Ry. Northfield in Holland

APEX TO ZULU A2Z!

Red Star Zulu's using an aerial assault

Red Star Belgrade vs. Partizan

DAVID C GEORGE

Red Star vs. The Police

Red Star Belgrade UF begin to run away

APEX TO ZULU A2Z!

Red Star Belgrade at home

Red Star Belgrade Zulu Warriors in Yugoslavia

DAVID C GEORGE

Scotland vs. England

Blues in Glasgow: Scotland vs. England

APEX TO ZULU A2Z!

Blues in Holland

Junior style

CHAPTER 15

Leeds United Madness

Leeds United vs Birmingham City Dec 16th 1972

JOHNNY H – "If I remember rightly it was like walking down Station Street where The Crown is in Birmingham, the road looked very similar. A special full of Birmingham have walked past this pub in Leeds, and I've never seen so many people come out of a pub in my born days." There must have been at least five fucking hundred coming out of this pub, and we got fucking legged and it's fucking miles to the ground." "Bashed everywhere along the way." Coo – coo – We had skinners on then, which are huge flare denim trousers, a lot of Blues who got chinned didn't go to the game and went straight back home to the station because it was one of the scariest moments Brummies have ever experienced at the time" Johnny H. – So every fucking where were running, and all these areas of Leeds were being built up at the time in the 70's so the area was a bomb pecked, basically a building site. And I will always remember that the sky went fucking black with bricks, bottles, debris, it was like fucking Armageddon. About twelve of us have ended up in a cul de sac absolutely fucked. Ribbs who was with us, and was one of the most unlikely hooligans you would ever meet. He had bifocals, long hair, public school educated, and a long yellow jumper down to his knees. So when all of these Leeds have come for us, I will never forget this about, them they were all men as apposed to us just bloody kids.

They are all in jean jacket suits; they had the back of the Levi trouser pockets on the front of their jackets. They were all fucking men, no boys at all, just a sea of men. So we are standing near this phone box, and they've all come down the road and you could see the crowd swelling up of people in front of us. "What are we gonna do now? The question asked by the small contingent of Blues fans near the phone box. Ribbs has pulled out an axe from his jacket and shouted at the mob of Leeds through gritted teeth who all stopped in the main road, "Right, the first fucker that comes is gonna get it." Leeds have started running, so twelve of us are now on our toes chasing hundreds of Leeds fans up the road, and you know what they did, they grassed us up to the old bill. So we've had to ditch the axe on the way to the game haven't we. You used to be able to buy them 50p in the Birmingham market at the time, with a stall close by. I thought there must have been football fans who went into the market that felt a little peckish before making a purchase. "Bag of chips off the one stall, and an axe off the next." Just an average day for a young teenager who was proud to stand up for his City, and was proud to see the Blue boys run out and give it what they'd got for 90 minutes.

They searched every single Blues fan, but they did fuck us up on that day, we didn't have a firm and most of Blues lads went straight back home on the train. At the ground, Birmingham fans were treated to taunts by the Leeds, which went, "You're going home like Sandy Richardson," who was the cripple in the Birmingham soap Crossroads. Birmingham lost the game 4 bloody nil, and it is a day Birmingham fans will never forget. Birmingham fans have memories like elephants so we never forget fans who are known to give it loads.

Leeds United vs. Blues 15th Dec 84 away. No Show From The Hitler Crew

15th Dec 1984, Birmingham City Zulu Warriors landed in Leeds station. We knew we were in hostile territory and the natives were definitely not friendly due to being from Yorkshire. It is true that racism in this part of the country is rife and that C-18 and the BNP have a stronghold in this city. Blues get off the train and walk up to the barriers in the station and notice around 20 Leeds fans on the station. With no Old Bill accompanying them, Blues chased the

DAVID C GEORGE

Leeds group out of the station and were now bowling into the city centre. Around 20 Leeds were chased out of the station and slapped outside Jack & Malley's bar. Eddie told me this was the first time that he had seen a firm come straight out of Leeds train station with no escort. Birmingham's numbers were up to around 400 for this trip and were thoroughly up for getting hold of The Leeds Service Crew to show them what the firm from the Midlands can do to a bunch of racist northerners. Blues are now on the Service Crew's manner and made their presence known by rushing into the first pub they saw to give it to Leeds, but it turned out to be full of coffin dodgers. The police land on us and we get a heavy escort to the football ground, but we are told the game may be called off due to the weather being so foggy. A few Leeds boys walk past us to check our numbers and vanish round the corner. The gates are now open and Blues are in the top tier in the corner facing the Service Crew behind the goal. Leeds firm stands up and show their true colours by every one behind the goal lifting up one arm and screaming out loud Adolf Hitler's favourite anthem. Seik Heil, Seik Heil, Seik Heil.

Blues response was immediate, and a flare gun was shot from our seats into the Leeds part of the ground. Leeds fans are now clambering to get away from the flare, which is now spinning and flying all over the floor at high speed. Blues now notice that in the Service Crew end behind the goal, there is one black guy supporting Leeds and fascism. Seeing this, all Blues lads black and white stood up in the top tier and pointed in unison at this deluded black guy and sang a song to embarrass the hell out of him. "Who's the nigger in the seats? "Who's the nigger in the seats? If your from Yorkshire and you happen to be black that's absolutely fine with me, but if you seriously think you should be sitting in the Leeds part of the ground while the whole end of Leeds fans are passionately in favour of a one bollocked Austrian looney, then whoever that was, needs to go home and ask himself some serious questions.

Birmingham won the game 1–0, with Clarke scoring. Blues now walked back to the train station with a strong police presence. Leeds were nowhere to be seen and to be honest, apart from us winning the game 1–0 there wasn't much else to shout about. As we got back to the station there were a few Leeds juniors milling about and they said they didn't realise Birmingham City had such a firm which, if you look at it makes sense because, they must have thought there would only be a handful of us to bash all the way to the ground.

Birmingham City Vs. Leeds United 11th May 85. They Brought It – We Had It

1st Aug 05. Since researching this topic and speaking to people from around the country, I was fortunate enough to get the telephone number of the guy I met on Leeds station in 85. Eddie Kelly and myself burst out laughing on the phone when I called him, and started reminiscing on our teenage years on the football casual scene.

I arranged to go and see Eddie in Leeds to talk about what the hell happened on that day in 85 when all hell broke loose at St Andrews. Myself, Adrian and Tommy, drove up to Leeds and met Eddie and his friend Chalky. We pulled up in our motor near a bus stop by the Pontefract turn off, and nodded to each other, and then we followed his car into Leeds. To be honest, we were taking a huge risk in doing this, as this could easily have been a set up, so we're keeping our eyes open and staying on the ball so not to get caught out.

We drove up to The Angel pub and pulled onto the car park. Eddie gets out of his motor, and instantly I recognise him. His mullet had completely gone and he had a face that had acquired a lived in look. We sat in the pub and had a good chat about back in the day, and Eddie and Chalky were both gentlemen. After a couple of drinks we went offside to one of Eddies friends gaff and sat down. Eddie phoned a good friend of his from way back in the day called China who also popped in to have a chat with us. Eddie started to tell me about the beginning of the 84–85 season when Birmingham had just been relegated. The consensus in Leeds was that when the fixtures come out, they hope to get Birmingham City either first or last game of the season. When the Leeds lads looked at the fixtures they were chuffed to bits as the last game of the season was exactly who they wanted.

Leeds took a handy mob of around 450 on the train to Birmingham made up of the younger chaps called the VYT and a good mob of older heads. Another mob of older Service Crew travelled in coaches and vans to Birmingham, and had landed a lot earlier than the firm on the train.

Last game of the season is here, and Birmingham city's firms are on the streets early. Leeds Service Crew is one of the most respected firms in the country and we knew they would be coming in their numbers. The Highgate & Kings Norton firms had been having some joy with vanloads of Leeds that got into Birmingham about 9.30am and were thoroughly dealt with. As for the Juniors, they congregated around Navigation, which is an area near New Street station where you can buy an assortment of fast food. It was very busy with people eating sandwiches and talking about how they thought the game would turn out today. A number of the Juniors were on the phone to each other the night before, talking about what clobber they were going to wear, because for Birmingham's firm, looking the part was nearly as important as doing the business. The size of Birmingham's numbers on that day was hard to predict, because there were five different firms around the town waiting for Leeds to arrive, each with numbers of around 120 in each team.

A lad comes running up to Navigation and tells everybody that a pub full of Leeds are drinking in Chinatown and everybody starts munching on their food and gulping down cans of fizzy pop, smiling and burping at the same time. The Junior Business Boys were up to full strength today, with a hundred good lads, some from off the town. We took a mooch down to Chinatown to check out the situation. As we walked past the Kaleidoscope and the Grapes, more lads started to walk down towards Chinatown with us and the numbers had now swelled to around 200. We walked past The Crown pub, which was also full of blues lads, but most of them stayed where they were with a few exceptions. I looked at Cuds, and smiled, and said to him. "We'll show you what the Juniors can do" Leeds were drinking in the Australian Bar at the time, which is now the gay quarter in Birmingham.

Blues are now outside the Australian Bar and instantly it goes bang off.

Blues rush the doors and fists are thrown from both parties. House bricks are flying through the windows and at same time, Leeds fans are throwing what ever goes through the windows back out of the windows.

APEX TO ZULU A2Z!

Leeds wouldn't come out of the pub, and were more concerned in lobbing ashtrays and pint glasses out of the already broken windows. Inside the pub, some of the Leeds had taken it upon themselves to make a bit of change while the place was in total chaos. Leeds fans robbed the tills from behind the counter when the bricks were coming through the windows on both sides of the pub. The staff had run away and hidden from the carnage and Leeds profited.

Police sirens are heard in the background, and Leeds boys haven't really shown us yet what they are all about. As the sirens get louder, and there are no windows left in the pub, blues take foot down by the ice skating rink and now walk back round to the Crown pub. Everybody is buzzing and in a real good mood, even though the clash with a small amount of Leeds was minor, we knew the full firm hadn't yet arrived.

People were talking about The Australian Bar and how they had to dodge ashtrays outside the pub. Blues were still wandering when the full firm of Leeds would be arriving, as time was ticking. The Crown public house is about a minute away from New Street station along with Boogies, The Grapes and the Kaleidoscope, which were all full to the rafters.

The Leeds train was in, and blues marched up Hill Street with all firms coming together to welcome our racist fascists from up north. Blues numbers were around 600 standing outside the station and everybody was ready for action.

There was as you could imagine a heavy police presence as they led Leeds out of a side door and out of New Street. This was the firm; The Leeds Service Crew had arrived. As Leeds were led out of the side doors, Birmingham let out a huge ZULUUUUUUUUUUUU! just to make Leeds feel at home. When speaking to Yorkshire China, he told me when he heard the ZULU! cry before Leeds had all come out of the station, he said it sounded well intimidating, as most of the Leeds had not seen what was waiting for them outside New Street. I can safely say this was the biggest firm that had come to Birmingham in my born days. I've seen all of the London firms and most of the northern crews, but Leeds was definitely one of the largest and heaviest to come out of New Street station. The National Front must have passed out information about this particular game, as I had not seen so many racists, since watching early footage of a speech by Adolf Hitler. Leeds were separated from us by 6 lines of police frowning at us and pushing Blues back down the hill where we had just come from. Leeds stood and watched the Birmingham police take control of the situation and Leeds were now being escorted to the ground with the heaviest police presence I had ever seen at a home game.

Blues now walked with Leeds to St Andrews hopefully to get some knuckle before the game starts, but it was very difficult to get a sniff due to the sheer amount of old bill protecting them. I wondered if the police would do the same for Mussolini! At the ground the Leeds firm that had arrived on the train had now bumped into the Service Crew, who had travelled on coaches. Everyone from Yorkshire was buzzing, as they knew this was going to be a day to remember.

Leeds now took a firm up to the turnstyles to have it with Blues but only got a minor scuffle with around 15 blues fans round by the Cattell Rd entrance. Duffy tells me, "We made a line and tried to have with them, but the numbers were far more than we could deal with." Duffy nearly gets dragged into the middle of Leeds firm while swinging lefts and rights and is helped out by another Brummy who pulls him out of the abyse. A number of black and white Birmingham fans were slashed up outside St Andrews by Leeds, who were not actually firm, but were into dressing in the designer clothes.

Outside St Andrews, Eddie spots Elvis from Birmingham who was also one of the most respected Juniors that got slapped with me on Leeds station a week before. Eddie walked round to the home end with Elvis and stood chatting to Blues firm. As Eddie got back round to the away end, the police were trying to get a huge mob of Leeds to actually go into the ground, but the Leeds firm refused. With the Birmingham police not really having much of a choice, they let over 350 Leeds into the ground without paying to get them off the streets and under their watchful eye.

When Leeds escort was walking to St Andrews a handful of us went back down to the Crown for another quick tot, and were contemplating today's events and how the game would go.

As I lift my glass to my lips, I see a group of around 10 lads further up Hill Street walking down towards the pub. These lads were not from Brum. Another 20 were now walking down to the Crown and we all looked at each other and flew through the list of other teams that were playing in Birmingham today. West Brom were also playing at home and sometimes this is a real treat as you can get other rival firms in Birmingham at the same time. This was the fucking Gooners. Arsenal had now brought a little firm down to one of blues main boozers and was looking for a showdown. Most of the London lot were wearing extremely long bright coloured shirts that we thought looked like nighties and they also had on the trademark red & white bobble hats to boot. The only problem was that blues proper firms had already gone to the ground and we were left with the Birmingham beer monsters to defend the Crown. The Gooners now lined up in the road, then they started to march straight towards the pub door. The pub now erupted and everyone from the pub came outside holding bar stools and still drinking pints of beer. The Birmingham beer monsters were now mobbing up in front of the Crown and rushed at the Gooners who stood their ground. Pint glasses were hurled at the Gooners who sidestepped the broken glass and just stood there. A few of the Gooners decision makers had a quick chat in the road while the Birmingham beer monsters also stood their ground and were now calling it on. The Arsenal looked at what faced them in the road, turned and walked back up the hill and went about their business. To this day, I am sure the reason Arsenal didn't want to fight the beer monsters was 1. They wanted to row the real Zulus. 2. They would all have got kicked to pieces by alcoholic Brummies. How embarrassing that situation could have been for them. There simply weren't enough of them to do anything except walk away, and to be honest, they were right to do so. Blues still had around 100 monsters standing outside the Crown at the time, and even though these guys were not interested in Armani, they still had the capability, to push your fucking face in, quick time.

Beer monsters can't run, and are extremely prone to getting very pissed off if they have to leave their drinks anywhere. Therefore, they were angry as sin.

At St Andrews the atmosphere was electric, Leeds Service Crew had turned up with huge numbers and were looking to crush Birmingham for two reasons. 1. Embarrassed them in their own town. 2. They simply hate black people and Brummies in general. If the local police had any sense at all, they should realise that on the two occasions when away fans have been killed at our ground were when the most racist fans came to our City. Chelsea & Leeds.

The first song the Leeds fans sang to Birmingham was in the category of most of the songs that made Leeds fans very happy. Belting out from the away end of St Andrews was "You're just a bunch of Niggers," "You're just a bunch of Niggers."

On this day Birmingham's firm was enormous and filled the whole of the bottom tier of the railway end, and was also in the Kop end under the clock. Leeds were singing their hearts out but it didn't help their team at all. Blues score and the home fans celebrate which annoys the Service Crew to the point that they are shaking the refreshments bar near enough to the ground in the away end. Kuhl scores for Birmingham City and all hell breaks loose.

3,000 Blues fans stand up behind the goal and move forward towards the advertising boards and are told to sit back down on the grounds intercom system.

Blues start to kick the advertising boards away until there are absolutely none left at the railway end of the ground, and they now have a clear run straight onto the pitch. It was the Zulus intent to get to Leeds Service Crew as quickly as possible and take on the full firm, but the police had other ideas. The police had now started fighting with Blues fans who were walking onto the pitch while the game was still in progress. More Blues started walking onto the pitch and were being beaten back by the local police who were trying their best to stop over three thousand fans getting onto the pitch. It was futile. If 3,000 fans decide on getting onto the pitch, it is near impossible for stewards or police to stop them, it just happens. The teams now leave the pitch and the police send for reinforcements in the shape of coppers on horses, who trot down the line of Blues fans smacking as many fans in the face and head with extra long white batons.

This was probably not the best way of dealing with this situation as Blues now start to stamp on seats, rip them out, and throw them at the police on horses. As a working class person, it is very rare that you will ever get the opportunity to give it the old bill, and what happenes is a frenzy of activity of people who are not prone to violence getting carried away and going mental for the day, combined with the harcore firm who end up having a tear-up. If you have ever seen the whole end of a football ground throwing seats at the same time, then if I was a police officer, I would have backed off also. When the police decided to retreat, Blues let out a mighty roar, ZUUUUUUUUUUULU! And charged onto the pitch, some carrying a seat in each hand throwing them at the police who were now running scared. Blues had advanced all the way to the half way line still hurling seats, when Leeds Service Crew started to climb the fences. Leeds fans must have been worried because if I had seen that many fans running towards the away end, with the police in no position to take control, I would have had my reservations about staying in the ground. Some blues fans had got all the way to the away end and started kicking it off with the Service Crew, and were chased back to the centre of the pitch. Leeds now started climbing the fences and jumping into the side seats stamping on plastic seats and hurling them at the police at the other end of the ground. Some of Leeds lads had faked injuries so that they could get from the stands into the seats without being arrested. As they got to the first aid room, they were fighting again with injured Birmingham fans were already there. This chaos went on for around forty minutes of tit for tat with the police, until Blues now ran across the pitch again and sat in the side seats in the same end as Leeds but near the half way line. This was the best opportunity for The Zulus to get at The Service Crew now because they were in the same-seated area with nothing to stop it from going bang off with The Service Crew. In the middle of the pitch talking to match officials was the guy who I had had a chat with in Leeds station a week earlier. It was Eddie Kelly, I shouted him while I was in the middle of the Birmingham fans and beckoned him over. I then realised I had more chance of French kissing Halle Berry than having another chat with Eddie, but it was a buzz to see him. I waved at and he smiled and waved back. We both told the truth the week before, but it looks as though the day isn't over for Leeds just yet.

The Police were trying to control the situation by using more violence than any of the rival firms. It was utter chaos all over the ground, as fighting in small numbers were taking place for what seemed like forever. Inside the away end at St Andrews, the Leeds fans were being beaten back by the local police who opened the gates from the pitch, and started randomly bashing any Leeds fans in the stand.

Leeds are now being forced back against the walls of the away end, and at the same time Blues had taken a mob outside the ground and bowled over to the away end, throwing slabs and half house bricks over the wall. Leeds fans were being forced back by the Police and were also having house bricks thrown at them from outside the ground by Birmingham fans keen on kicking it off with The Service Crew. With the sheer pressure being put onto the wall by the congested away end, the wall collapses and a young lad from Leeds is killed by the crumbling debris falling on top of him.

Mozza

In the side seats, a stocky skinheaded geezer came bowling along the seats from the Leeds end of the ground. He said he was Chelsea and do we want it outside. "Outside – Outside now. A couple of lads went for him and he backed off. Birmingham now took a mob outside in order to see what the score was and it was total mayhem. Emergency services and the public were charging about all over the place, as the scene resembled a war zone. A few seconds later we clocked Leeds coming through the crowd about 100 handed and we started to get tooled up.

Smashing up a fence nearby that backed onto the flats behind the main stand.

We formed a line across the road by the old ticket offices and everyone kept on repeating, "No one run, stand. Leeds come for it, and the lot and us goes up in the air. Birmingham at this stage did not have the numbers as wave after wave of Leeds kept on coming at Birmingham. To be fair, Leeds should have slaughtered us at this stage, but Blues stood firm. Birmingham's line now broke and we backed off and regrouped further down the road. Birmingham went into Leeds this time and it was utter chaos with bodies falling all over the main road on both sides. As there were only around 30 proper Blues heads at the time, Blues line was stretched so every now and then, Bobby would bring the group back together and charge into Leeds yet again. This happened two or three times until we reached the school.

Across from the school was the old park and it was full of the rest of Blues firm who were having it with the old bill. We called them on and in seconds, a massive firm of Birmingham went into Leeds escort smacking as many Yorkshire lads a possible. Several of their lads took a right kicking as a number of old bill now tried to restore some sort of order to this madness. As the front of Leeds escort backed off and scattered, one of their lads was in a bad way with about 30 Leeds standing around him. He was stretched across the front of a car bonnet about a hundred yards up the road. A Birmingham lad stole a cone full of money from the Evening Mail guy outside the ground and then belted it off a Leeds fans head.

After the match, while hundreds were still rioting against the Old Bill, Faye was walking behind a firm of around 30 Leeds who were up for a bit of action. At the bottom of the road there was a cross roads with some of Blues lads on the other side of it. A stand off ensued with only a handful of police in the middle. The usual gesturing and "Lets have it" were screaming from Yorkshire mouths and Brummies alike. Faye is now right behind the mob and his adrenalin is pumping, he then picks up a police road cone, which was a 2.5ft with bags of sand inside. He runs through the middle of the Leeds mob and wraps the cone around the Yorkshire bastard's head that was giving it the big one at the front. He went down like Bruno against Tyson, while Faye bowls across the road to join up with the other Blues lads on the other side of the road. When Blues main firm left the ground, they walked across the then waste ground at the back of the railway end with the police wanting to beat a few people up again. The police pull out their batons and charge the Birmingham fans who turn on the police and chase a huge mob of them back up to the ground. With at least 4,000 fans chasing the police they all jumped back into a huge line of police vans and thought they were safe. Birmingham fans now tip over at least 15 police vans, with the police in them and start rocking them on their roofs. The police tried keep the main contingent of Leeds near the ground for what seemed like forever, while Birmingham were in town waiting for Leeds to try to get home. After standing around for a good while, myself Rankin, Wilf, Brownie, Eamon, Hopkins were walking down New Street, and just before we get to the corner, Rankin says, "Wouldn't it be mad if we just bumped into Leeds full firm now?" So as we reach the corner, we nearly walked straight into Leeds Service Crew who were being heavily escorted by the police. We freeze for a second, turn and run, because the idea of standing in front of a massive Service Crew firm 6 handed, when one of their fans has just died would not have been the cleverest choice to make on this day. We would have all been killed and strung up, as the police would not have been able to stop them, as their way of dealing with violence does not really work a lot of the time.

Leeds United Vs Charlton Athletic 87 – St Andrews Playoffs.

The playoffs were taking place at St Andrews in Birmingham City between Charlton Athletic & Leeds Untied. Leeds fans had been in and around the centre of Birmingham for most of the day. Around 30 Service Crew came into east Birmingham to the Medway pub to have a drink. The Medway was at the time one of Blues strong holds and from this pub, a firm could be rounded up in a matter of minutes to deal with any football firms that decide to stray out of Birmingham city centre when having a drink. Next to the Medway is an area called Lea Hall where another firm of Blues used to use The Tavern On The Green. This was another Birmingham pub with a huge reputation for being staunch Blues fans. Kluvert was playing a card game called Crash, where he needed just one hole to win.

The phone has rang at The Tavern On The Green, and the lads there have just been informed there's a firm of around 30 Leeds Service Crew, asking for the Zulu's, and wanting to know where they are. Here is some information for all fans across the country. From the city centre all the way to the NEC and as far as the Lickey Hills is Blues manor, and where these Leeds fans had decided to ask for any sign of Zulus, was in the top five of areas in Birmingham at the time that could pull a handy firm in one click of the fingers. Leeds had a mini bus and two or three carloads of lads as Blues pulled up outside the pub in a mark one Escort estate, and in the back of the car were a number of large pieces of fencing and gardening equipment. It's already bang off with more Blues landing fives minutes earlier. Everybody gets out of the van with tools and a car load of Leeds has just driven off at high speed and left their mates, and there is also another car full who were not so lucky that ended up being smashed to pieces on the car park, dragged out of their vehicles, and kicked all over the place. There is only the mini van left, and this was full of Leeds who were trying to block house bricks in a stationary van, with no windows, while Blues surround the van, and start rocking it from side to side as the driver was trying to start the engine that doesn't seem to want to help the Yorkshire lads out. Everywhere the Leeds fans moved in the van, they were being bashed or stabbed. It was like shooting fish in a barrel.

A Blues fan is lying on the bonnet of the van on his back, and kicking the driver in the face due to the mini bus now also having no windows. The Leeds fans are crawling all over the van, trying to stay away from the open windows where a Brummy lad was running round the van, and stabbing the Leeds in the back and the arse with a blunt garden fork, as they were trying to avoid being bashed, stabbed, and stamped on. Unfortunately for Leeds, they had chosen one of the worst pubs to land at and start giving it the I am nonsense, as in those days, Blues firm was all over east Birmingham and still is today. On the same evening, another group of Leeds fans were unfortunate enough to pick the Yew Tree pub to have a drink. Back in the day, the Yew Tree was another pub that was staunch Blues through and through, and definitely not the type of place you should go looking for trouble. Numerous Leeds lads were cut to ribbons that night, and Elvis has done his time for it. The reason why Elvis had got such a huge sentence, was that he threatened the Judge, and also said in court that he had enjoyed carving Leeds up in Yardley on that night.

DAVID C GEORGE

APEX TO ZULU A2Z!

Blues vs. Leeds. The 1st lot of Blues find Leeds – 1985

Leeds are not having a good day – 1985

DAVID C GEORGE

Police confront the Leeds fans

Blues in Leeds 1985 walking towards the ground

APEX TO ZULU A2Z!

Leeds are hearded off the pitch – St Andrews 1985

Leeds fans on the pitch at St Andrews – 1985

DAVID C GEORGE

Birmingham have kicked away the advertising boards. Blues vs. Leeds – 1985

Blues vs. Leeds Kn and Lawless – 1985

APEX TO ZULU A2Z!

Australian Bar. Birmingham make a move. Blues vs. Leeds – 1985
Horns of the Bull technique surround the pub. Blues vs. Leeds – 1985

DAVID C GEORGE

Birmingham vs. Leeds United 1985. Leeds perform with the old bill
Blues vs. Leeds. Zulu's moving along the streets to get closer to Leeds – 1985

APEX TO ZULU A2Z!

The lot went and so did the bin. Blues vs. Leeds – 1985
Blues vs. Leeds. Birmingham's firm are moving along seats towards Leeds – 1985

DAVID C GEORGE

Behind the goal. Blues vs. Leeds – 1985
Blues firm attempting to engage the enemy. Blues vs. Leeds – 1985

CHAPTER 16

Different Grade

Why the rest of the midlands firms were no way in the same category as The Zulu Warriors – Junior Business Boys

Notts County 20th Oct 84

NOTTS COUNTY IS NOT a place that is renowned for having a firm of casuals that like a bit of knuckle in the main road, but Forrest on the other hand are a different kettle of fish. On this day Birmingham only took a small mob of around 200 to County just to get a bit of fresh air and watch our boys in royal blue. As per usual, the Juniors have gone for a mooch around the centre. Little Ears and me have clocked a tall well dressed casual in the shopping centre wearing a gorgeous Armani jumper and jeans. We ask him where we can find the nice clothes shops in town and he gives us the run down of local boutiques. While the Nottingham lad is pointing in the direction of the clothes stores, Ears pulls a tool on him and asks him to take his jumper off. The guy looks at the 4ft 1inch lad standing in front of him and says, "You mad?" Ears then jumps onto his back with his arm around the guy's neck and the other arm punching him in the face. The Nottingham guy is now running through the shopping centre, with Ears on his back punching him in the head, he looked like a human rucksack. I was supposed to be giving chase, but the scene was so funny I ended up holding myself up on a shop window, and trying to stop myself from laughing till I cried with tears streaming down my face.

DAVID C GEORGE

Ears and I met up with the Birmingham firm and went walkabout around Nottingham centre. A designer clothes shop is attacked, with Armani leather's and jumpers going missing, also Hugo Boss sweaters and anything else people could get hold of. Birmingham now make their way to the ground and all decide to sit in the seats. Only ten minutes into the game, The police arrive at the top of the stairs with an assistant from the robbed clothes store looking across the seats at the Brummy lads who were all now sliding down in their seats and trying not to look conspicuous. A few people were pointed out and arrested who were stupid enough to have the new garments on show straight away. Birmingham won the game 3–1, with Clarke scoring two and Harford one. As for the Soul Crew incident at the train station, most of the Blues lads ran them off the platform as soon as we saw them and then got back on our train. They just scarpered but wanted to meet up after the game for a bit of knuckle dancing. Nothing happened.

Coventry City?

Sitting in a pub on New Street having a quiet drink with Caroline who is also writing a book on Birmingham Cities exploits throughout the years. We are having a private chat about what other firms in the Midlands were handy over the last two decades, and I explain to Caroline that Coventry were really shit. An Asian guy who is sitting at the table away from me interjects and says to me, "Woe woe, I'm from Coventry mate." I looked at this poor misguided soul, and to be honest with you, he didn't know what the conversation was on about in the first place. The guy's name is Manni and he begins to tell me there are people in Coventry are in their forties who wouldn't be happy with what I have just said. I asked Manni, "What's his point? and if he had ever had it bang off down the football, and he replies, "No." I smile and explain to this misguided individual that he shouldn't jump into conversations he has no real knowledge of. For instance, if I was talking about nuclear science, I'm sure he wouldn't have a comment to make, but because it's football violence, then he felt that he had a relevant point, which he still has not made. I explain to Manni he is in a Birmingham pub and talking nonsense about a firm he has only heard about from newspaper reports and Sky News. Manni then tells me violence is not as potent as it used to be in the eighties, which was an obvious thing to say, but to try and tell two Brummies in the centre of Birmingham that the Zulu Warriors don't exist anymore is beyond the realms of stupidity. I turn to Manni and said, "Remember when you were a lot younger and you've just noticed a few hairs round your bollocks and you think that you know, but really, you haven't got a clue?" He said, "Yes." I reply, "This is one of those moments for you my son." "Do you remember an old reggae song from the seventies that went, "No tek it up if you cyant manage it?" Manni was talking as though he thought Birmingham Cities Zulu Warriors do not exist anymore, which made me laugh. I said to Manni that, if he knew anything from confrontations between Coventry and Birmingham casuals in the last two decades, he wouldn't have jumped into the conversation in the first place. When referring to Coventry being shit, I do not mean the whole of Coventry, but the casual firm who used to get turned over on the regular by Blues. If there are anymore intelligent people from Coventry who recon that Cov had a proper firm in the 80s, I would love to meet you for a chat. I asked Manni how many times that Coventry had turned over Millwall, Chelsea, Cardiff, Leeds, Portsmouth and also Man City, Boro which was the only one he had said they had done, but couldn't remember the date. I also offered the guy to take my number and give it to the Coventry heads in order for them to get their point of view across about who they think were the top firm in the Midlands. He refused. I told Manni this conversation was null and void and is a waste of time, and with that, he finished his pint and scuttled off out of the pub with a bright green waistcoat on his back. I am not sure, but I think Manni worked as a refuse collector on the bins.

Nottingham Forrest Away 97/98
Mozza

Forrest had been relegated the season before from the Premiership and had come down with a reputation of being the boys. I knew a few of the Forrest lads from England games, and quite a bit of banter had been going on throughout the summer before the season started.

Around 30 Birmingham lads met in a pub in Beeston, just outside Nottingham at opening time for the pubs. We had a quick drink and started phoning around to see who else was about. At around midday, we drove into Nottingham and plotted up in another boozer just off the ring road, far enough away from the centre so the plod didn't bother us until we wanted to make a move. There were about a hundred of us waiting here, and we knew of another hundred who were in another pub opposite Nottingham train station. The old bill were with them and had locked them in so they were going nowhere. A few lads went down into the cellar and escaped in order to join up with us. By now we had good numbers of people to do what we came to do. A couple of Forrest spotters clocked us as we made our move towards the centre of town, and within minutes a small firm of Forrest fronted us and had it quickly on their toes when we went for them but the damage had been done when the old bill had appeared and now started rounding everybody up.

I slipped away with a couple of other chaps and headed back to the pub we had left earlier. About 40 of us regrouped and decided town was a no no, so we headed towards the ground. We bowled down the road towards the ground and could see the floodlights in the distance. We crossed a school playing field and had to climb over a fence, which left us on a pathway leading to a subway and shopping precinct. As we got closer to the subway, we could see a pub in the distance with Forrest's lads milling about outside. They saw us coming towards their pub coming towards them as we grouped up and kept the 40 in a tight formation as we descended into the subway. We calmly walked out of the subway and were hit by a hail of bricks and bottles. We never let out the roar or charged at Forrest, but instead calmly walked towards them. There must have been around 100 Forrest but it was hard to judge in the confines of the centre. We got to within 5 yards of their front line, and the roar went up. ZULUUUUUUUUUUUU! Birmingham waded into Forrest. After no more than a minute of fierce fighting right across Forrest front line, they broke and ran. We chased them back into the pub where the fighting continued in the doorway as the pub was trashed. By now, more and more Forrest lads were turning up on the side streets and the battle continued for a good few minutes before the old bill arrived. When the old bill had rounded us up, Forrest made a show of trying to attack our escort but the result was never in doubt. We'd come onto their manor and taken the piss and they know it. That was that for the day and nothing much happened, but the fuse paper was well and truly lighted for the game at our place later in the season.

Birmingham Vs Nottingham Forrest 97/ 98
Mozza

After the events at Forrest earlier in the season, the phone lines between Brum and Notts were working overtime. It was well known that Forrest were coming firm handed looking for revenge and we'd arranged for a bar in the centre of town to open up early so we could be plotted up and ready before the old bill were even out of bed. A couple of lads then drove up to Nottingham to scout around. It wasn't long before we found a group of likely looking lads having breakfast in a café just outside the centre of Notts. Birmingham knew they had found Forrest when a couple of cars and mini vans filled with lads turned up and joined their friends. It was around nine in the morning and we already had a hundred good lads gathered together, and all we had to do was wait. Eventually the call came that this group was on the move closely followed by our boys who were in Nottingham bright and early. While we waited for confirmation of where they were, our numbers in Birmingham were swelling all the time. Around 200 lads were waiting to welcome Forrest to Brum, with some of our lads following Noting hams convoy of vehicles all the way into Brum but managed to lose them in traffic on the far side of St Andrews. This meant only one thing, they weren't planning on coming into town at all, but were meeting in Small Heath away from prying eyes. The decision was made and a now 300 handed firm of Blues left the streets heading to a place we've used occasionally on the far side of the ground. The first few cars with Birmingham lads in, parked up in the area, and went from pub to pub checking them out. Forrest were in pub called The Marlboro down a side street opposite Small Heath train station. The first lads to find Forrest were no more than 10 handed, but steamed straight into them. By the time I had got there, we had about 25 blues trying to hold the street against 250 Forrest. It was going off big style all over the shop with people getting hurt and messed up badly. Every minute that passed, our number were swelling, but from the first car load that arrived, we were now about 50 handed and had lost about 20 metres of road. Now it was our turn to show what we could do. The roar went up, ZULUUUUUUUUUUUU! And Birmingham now ran straight into Forrest's front line. Forrest buckled and then broke, and with more and more of our boys turning up all the time, it was over for Forrest who had now been spanked everywhere, there cars and vans got totalled with the Forrest lot having a very draughty journey home in cars and vans with no windows and dents all over. A few of their lads got nicked that day and some Forrest boys even made statements to the old bill concerning the goings on, but in the cold light of day, most retracted them. One Nottingham lad did turn up and gave evidence in Crown court, which helped put three Birmingham lads away for a holiday, and with this he broke the golden rule. You don't grass, no matter what. To be fair, Forrest have got a decent firm and it has to be said, but what they met in Birmingham on this day was a different class altogether.

Keep Right On!

Leicester City Vs Birmingham City 4th Feb 84 away

Leicester is another place that could pull a decent firm back in the early eighties, but yet again would only deliver when at home. I'm not sure what it was about other Midland firms in general, but a lot seemed to act like a drunken fat man on a ship, as they never travelled very well at all. Birmingham knew Leicester Baby Squad had good numbers at home games, and back in the day used to give Blues a few good scuffles. This was a midweek night game and Birmingham had taken around 150 good lads over to the east Midlands to watch the match.

They sat in a pub near the ground having a drink when the Baby Squad came outside the pub. Blues steam out of the pub and run Leicester up the road, but they kept coming back. I'm not sure that they had any strategy at all, or they just enjoyed running up and down the road.

Blues won the game 3–2 and after the match went looking for the Baby Squad. Everyone was up for this, as they wanted to teach Leicester a lesson in manners.

Birmingham are now on a main road with shops on both sides, with doorways that were edged back off the street. A blues lad tells a few scouts to go and front the Leicester firm, and get them to run them back down the road where we will all give them a hearty welcome.

Everybody is buzzing and eager to kick it right off, and the more responsible people were telling everyone to get back off the street in the shop doorways, so nobody can see them. Wait, wait, not yet could be heard through the Brummy crowd and shhhhhhhhh.!

A minute later, the Blues lads come steaming straight down the road being chased by around 70 Baby Squad. Birmingham waited for Leicester to get right in the middle of them, and then they came from both sides of the street from the doorways and had the Baby Squad in a pincer movement.

ZUUUUUUUUUUULU!

Leicester didn't know what had hit them, as Blues steamed into them from the front and back. The Baby Squad were ambushed and mullard in their own shopping centre, and to this day are probably still wandering what the hell happened. When you are attacked from front and back at the same time, you don't have enough know-how to make your next move, except to get the hell out of there. I can safely say that Leicester in the mid 80's have never even brought a firm to Birmingham and I'm not sure why.

I know that they have took a little crew to Villa a few times, but have never called it on with Blues in our fair city.

Leicester City Vs Birmingham City Seconds out – Round Two

Blues were in a neutral area in the Leicester with at least 150 blues in the upper tier at Leicester. At the end of the game we stayed in the ground. The plan was to come out of the ground behind Leicester. We have down toward the fire exit that is open, but for some reason they have not yet come past. Leicester have come full hammer and it's gone right off on the stairs. Leicester was trying to come up the stairs but we were holding the fort. This has happpend a number of times on the stairwell, when we have noticed Fat Errol had been caught down stairs by the Baby Squad. He has taken a bashing by Leicester who had been stabbed a number of times. The Birmingham elite now went back down the stairs and straight into Leicester retrieving Fat Errol who was in a bad way. This I believe had an effect on Errol's persona, as this changed Errol who has not been the same person since a little time after this incident. I can't speak for anyone else, but this is an opinion I have had which was shared by Morph.

Birmingham City Vs Leicester City 2004
Ry. Northfield

I get phone call early telling me Leicester are in a bar called OC's around fifty handed. We get together about thirty good young lads and we thought this was enough to take them on. We now went down the road towards Digbeth high street towards the pub. We jumped over one of the barriers in the road when Leicester have come out of the pub and we've just went steaming into em.

Leicester end up running past the Audi garage on Digbeth towards the Dubliner.

Leicester never even put up a fight, but were instead running towards the Dubliner to call on more lads. The Dubliner has now emptied with Leicester now coming out of the front entrance and the side. It's now raining bottles and Leicester's firm is standing outside singing, BS, BS, BS. It's gone bang off outside the Dubliner with the Baby Squad with a few Blues getting caught on the other side of the barriers in the main road. They took a bit of a wack to be fair, but we were only 30 handed and Leicester wouldn't fight us when there was fifty of us until they got around another 100 lads from the Dubliner. Blues are now on one side of the barriers with the Baby squad on the other and as a number of them were trying to jump over and have with us, we were just banging em. A Leicester lad was chased up the road and as he was running he was pushed into a bus stop knocking himself out. A car has pulled up at the side of me and I've jumped in, and this was when I noticed I had been slashed through my black Stone island jeans. I've had some quick stitches at the hospital and went back down to OC's to wait for them to come back. It was more fighting the old bill than with Leicester though this time and not much happened, but I can definitely say that if Leicester cannot do thirty of Birmingham's finest youngsters with a mob of 150, they have got some serious problems when it comes to bottle. I mean the best things to come out of Leicester over the years are Walkers crisps, Mark Morrison and Showadywady, do I need to say more?

Wolverhampton Wanderers – Bridge Street who? Selective Memory Loss

Reputation has always been something that has made a lot of the other Midland firms jealous of Birmingham's exploits up and down the country, and this is definitely the case with the Wolverhampton Wanderers firm. Throughout the 80s, Wolverhampton Wanderers as a firm were useless, and their idea of having a fight was to get a handful of away fans, out number them five to one, and give them a kicking near the subways before you get into Molineux. If you were to list the major victories that are put under the Subway Army & the Wolves firms belt against proper firms, you would only need a piece of paper the size of a credit card. Wrecking seaside towns in Division 3 are not major results, and the idea back in the day used to be taking on the heavy-duty crews and standing with your boys. I cannot remember in the last twenty-five years Wolves Subway Army or Wolves firm, caining any proper firms in London or up north, but I suppose someone from Wolverhampton would tell me different. The Subway Army disbanded in 1982 and were responsible for kicking away fans in when they enter the underpass on the way to Molineux. They were quite handy back in the day, but didn't really make a mark on the 80s or 90s onwards. There is a network of communication throughout the length and breath of the country and I have never heard any information regarding much at all about the Subway Army or Wolves firm if they are not at home.

The Lafayette Incident 78

Birmingham and Wolverhampton had had many run-ins with each other through the Mod Skin and Punk era, ending with casualties on both sides. The Angelic Upstarts were playing live in a club called The Lafayette in Wolverhampton, where 10 of the Chelmsley Wood skins were watching the band play. When watching live bands at the time, the crowd would generally jump around nutting each other, while spitting in each other's faces. A number of the Chelmsley lot had stopped jumping up and down, and were now thinking the punches they had received in their backs while po going, were a bit heavy handed. At the time, nobody had noticed the Wolverhampton lot of skins were stabbing the Chelmsley lot while they were jumping up and down in the middle of the floor.

The police had to be called, as the huge group of local skins were now attacking the Birmingham Skinheads. A few Brummies got well and truly bashed, while the Wolves lads were very proud of their handy work. It was literally ten to one in favour of the Wolves lads, but this is what Wolves would call a good row, a hundred Vs ten.

A couple of weeks later, a huge mob of the Trooper now thought they would pay the Wolverhampton lot a visit, so the old ambulance is on the road with a few more vans and cars all tooled up to fuck. Birmingham had now taken a huge mob of skins from Chelmsley Wood and landed in Wolverhampton centre. Birmingham bowled into The George pub and asked the bar man, "Where are the lads from The Lafayette?" NO SIGN ATALL ALL NIGHT...!!!

Wolves away December 26th 78

Birmingham had spread the word that Wolves were tooled up and out numbered them a few weeks ago ten to one with tools, so when Birmingham had the chance of going to Wolverhampton again, the devils arse had turned up also. 350 skinheads and lunatics from all over Birmingham, had marched into a hardware shop in Birmingham, and stripped the place. Tools have to be used when in places like Wolves, because they have no real concept of man-to-man fighting. A few Birmingham would slash you up if they had the opportunity, but most preferred fists and feet unless it is called for something else. Birmingham now get off the train in Wolverhampton mob handed, carrying hammers, saws, chisels and knives, and go looking for Wolverhampton. NO SIGN ATALL ALL DAY...!!!

Birmingham won the game 1–0 scored by the 1st million pound player, Mr Trevor Francis.

Wolves away Sept 83

A couple of Birmingham fans are standing on New Street Station listening to a couple of Wolves fans mouthing off about Birmingham City. One Wolves lad was saying he could bring a huge firm into Birmingham, which made everybody yawn because we have heard that bit for years. Two Wolves fans now invite two Blue noses for a straighter down on one of the platforms on the station. As the two Brummies oblige our Yam yams from off the beaten track, a Wolves lad now pulls out a cutthroat razor at speed from the inside of his jacket, and nearly slashes a Brummie lad's throat. It misses him by inches. The two Wolves lads now jump the station barriers and head for the platform back to Wolverhampton being chased by the Birmingham lot. From realising how dirty and underhand Wolves mentality is regarding a fair fight, the Birmingham lot were not about to be caught out again so they went over to the nearest WHSmith store, and stole as many Stanley blades, axes and screwdrivers to take on the journey to Wolverhampton. All of the hardware store was now on the train travelling to Wolves with Birmingham's firm of around 150 at about 12.30pm. Blues get off the train and Wolves are at the station waiting for our arrival. These Wolves fans were the scouts for The Subway Army who were caught out, as they didn't think that a firm of Blues would arrive this early. Blues go straight into Wolves and clatter the ones that stood to fight then also taxed them, the rest ran back into town. Blues now bowl into the shopping precinct looking for the Subway Army. Blues are now walking through the subway mob handed and also had a firm up top but still could not find Wolves firm at all. As Blues couldn't find Wolves, they went to have a drink in one of their pubs right near the ground on the corner. It was a big pub that could easily fit well over 200 lads in there. The police landed outside the pub but Birmingham had already sent out scouts in order to have a mooch up and down the surrounding streets in order to see what they could see. Even though they knew we had landed, no Subway came anywhere near us. Birmingham now enters the ground and the Wolverhampton police were not happy, as they hate Birmingham fans as much as the Subway Army. As Morph has gone to take a quick leek in the toilets, a police officer has grabbed him by the arm and asked him where he was going. Morph says, "I'm going to the bog." The police officer was so hungry for an arrest that he says, "You don't say that word in here." Morph says to the officer, "I'm going to the bog." The officer now says to Morph, "If you say that word again then I will throw you out of the ground. He asks Morph again the same question, "Where are you going?" Morphs says, "I'm going to the bog." Hands were thrown up Morphs back and he was ejected from the ground for answering the police officer and informing him he was going to the toilet. What you also have to understand is that Wolverhampton is a place with aspirations on being a proper good mob, but completely missed the boat in the 80s. Now, years later, they throw bottles and bricks at away fans and kick them in when given the opportunity to perform, but they are a completely different breed to Birmingham, as they have never reached the dizzy heights of the Zulu's firm. This is the main reason they hate our guts. Childish I know, but that's just how it is.

Morph is now standing outside the ground when the police officer says, "If you hang around outside the ground, then we will arrest you." As a black face in Wolverhampton you can get away with one or two black lads here or there, but they all know each other, so you stand out like a sore thumb. The police are standing outside the ground telling Morph to get away from the ground knowing full well that some Wolves always hang around the Subways waiting for away fans to cut to ribbons and rob them. The police are basically in a round about way, trying to send the Blues fan towards the subways to get home, knowing he would not make it. Everyone knows what Wolves have done over the years to away supporters and today, it wasn't going to happen. A guy now approaches Morph with a half Brummie and half Yam yam accent. I think he was from somewhere like Stourbridge. This guy comes up and explains to Morph that he has also been thrown out of the ground and was told to do one by the old bill.

Morph is now walking with this guy, which was, as he has already admitted, a bit naive and they are walking towards the subway. The guy says to Morph when they arrive at the underpass, "Let's go under the subway" This was definitely a no no, as anyone with half a brain would not suggest something so absurd. Morph and this guy are now walking over the subway when there are around six or so lads standing on the other side of the road. As they are getting closer to the other group, Morphs notices there were a few of the Wolves lads wearing a bit of clobber, but they didn't have the garms head to foot. The guy who was walking with Morph was happy just to stroll without even investigating who these other lot were. Morphs slows down behind the lad he's with around three steps. Then all this guy said who had been walking with Morph for the last ten minutes, "Come on, I've got one." The guy pulls a tool out and Morph is well and truly on his toes, with seven Wolves snides chasing him up the road with blades. Morph is now running over hills and across roads with seven Wolves fans chasing him to cut him to ribbons. Morph is now running down a road outside the ground and is stopped by the same police officer who told him to get away from the ground. The officer has seen Morph is being chased by a group of Wolves fans but yet still wanted to get Morph regardless if he was about to be assaulted, wounded or worse.

The chuffed officer now says the words he has wanted to say all day, "Your nicked." Morph was not about to be arrested for running away from shity Wolves fans who wanted to slash him to pieces so instead the old bill checked his and the Wolves fans pockets. The officer searches the Wolves fan and finds a knife still in his pocket. The other Wolves lads scattered as they all had tools also. As this Wolves guy is being arrested he was saying to Morph, "Mate, we're friends, we're friends." This is how some Wolves fans operate then it is no wonder they have never really seen the whole picture. Everybody knows you don't score points for being snide, you're just snide.

The Gilroy Shaw book launch – Running With A Pack Of Fools

On 28th May 05, myself, Morph and a friend of mine called Hilary travelled over to St Thomas Moore Catholic school in Daliston, Wolverhampton.

Gilroy Shaw was having a book launch party and had invited a few hundred of Wolves lads to the book signing which I happened to get an invite to with a couple of friends. I had heard quite a lot of nothing about this character and was interested to see the man to find out where his head was. Bullshitting, and grassing are both in this man's armoury, so I was definitely keen to see the whites of his eyes. Morph, myself and Hilary walked into a football academy sports centre, where the launch was taking place.

We stop at the counter in the hallway and speak to a gentleman who is short, squat, and wide, who looks as though he probably head butted away fans in the days of The Subway Army. He is holding a collection of pint glasses. We ask him if Gilroy was available for the interview, which we had arranged, and the guy wishes to know who we are.

I tell him I'm a freelance journalist writing an article on Gilroy Shaw and his book. The guy looks at me with curiosity and says, "This interview is only for your article, is it, it won't be used for anything else will it?" "No, it's just for my personal use," I said. One of the female bar staff goes into the main room where the book signing is taking place, and informs Gilroy we have arrived. We are called through to the main room where there are around 300 people there for the book signing or for a trip down memory lane. This was Wolves' top firm and it wasn't very big at all. From scanning the room, I would say that if you went to any of the major staunch Blues public houses, either on a Friday or Saturday evening, they would have the same numbers. I walk over to where Gilroy has a queue of overweight skinheads with tight fitting garments to get the man's autograph and a few words.

We have a quick chat, and he explains he should be free in around half an hour, so we head off to the bar and order a round of drinks. As we are walking through the crowd, I noticed there were not many older chaps in the room at all and what you had was mainly lads of around thirty year wearing their best-pressed shirts and new shoes and trainers. We take our drinks outside and we are looked at by a few, as we arrive at a table and place our drinks down.

From looking round the room and checking out the characters, I noticed they didn't seem to have an angle on dressing at all.

If you were to belt out the five most common designer labels known in the country, you would have just described 99% of the clothes worn in this room. Wolverhampton lads had never been known for their dress sense, since claiming themselves to be a top firm only a few years ago.

I pop over to the buffet to look at the food situation and was greeted by a tray of Vidal Sassoon chicken. What I mean by Vidal Sassoon is when you get a load of chicken, and throw it under a tap of water, then bung it into a baking tray and into the oven. It is known as "Wash & Go." There is an assortment of chunky sandwiches with various fillings, which didn't look too appetising. I wondered how many people had been to the toilet and not washed their hands, and then tucked into the spread of food I headed outside to have a rendezvous with my pint of Guinness, and manage a mouthful when I get a tap on my shoulder. A good friend of mine called The General has just turned up with a number of Chelsea Head-Hunters, who are publishing the book. I ask The General how he came to be here, and he replies that he was invited by a Chelsea lad to come out for a couple of cheeky drinks. He then tells me with a raised voice that he fucking hates Wolves, and he is blues through and through. Lifting up the sleeve on his T-shirt revealing a Zulu – BCFC tattoo on his arm and saying, "I come in here Blues, and when I leave, I'll be fucking going out Blues an all." I look at The General with a smile on my face, which turns into us both pissing ourselves laughing. I say to him while laughing, "What are ya doing ya nutter, I'm not in here to bang it off? He replies, "Yeegh well, I hate these cunts," he says, and I don't give a fuck anyway." For some reason, The General reminded me of a close relative of mine. The music was a nice mixture of old and new, playing tracks from The Jam to The Stone Roses. The only thing that made it slightly dodgy was the DJ. If you have ever heard a disc jockey who plays music on the Walzters at a fair ground, then you will be on the money with regards to what we were listening to.

As I'm chatting with The General, Morph and Hilary, I'm called through by one of Gilroy's friends and shown into a changing room to set up my equipment. As I've nearly finished setting up, a couple of lads walk in looking for the toilets. The one guys says in a broad yam yam accent, "Am nu toilets in eya mouight?" Trying to stop myself laughing, I explain that the toilets are next door, and they leave.

I won't mince my words about the Wolverhampton accent, and I'll just say, I think it's so bad it makes Brummies sound posh.

Birmingham has never seen Wolves as a top firm, because they are simply not. In order to establish that you're one of the top firms in the country, you must first have done most of the full firms in the top ten in the UK, home and away. Wolves have clearly not done anything of the kind, and have not hit those heights, as they are some light years behind.

Gilroy's first experience with Birmingham City was in 85, which means he must have completely missed what happened at Molineux when Blues arrived at their ground and embarrassed them. I take a quick look at Gilroy's book and noticed that through its slim 137 pages, there are no decent rows from beginning to end. My advice to Mr Shaw would be to settle down and look after the family, because you are clearly not what is categorised as a top-flight hooligan, as you have been taken on a ride by the media where all you have done is surf the wave. In no particular order, these are the teams who have been there or thereabouts for the past two or more decades, so pay attention and you may learn something.

Portsmouth – Pompey 6.57

Tottenham - N17 Yids.
Westham - Inter City Firm - Under 5's.
Birmingham City -HTBB - Apex - Zulu Warriors - Junior Business Boys.
Manchester United - Inter City Jibbers- Cockney Reds - Red Army - The Men In Black.
Manchester City - Cool Cats - Gov'nors - Main Line Service Crew - Snipers.
Leeds United - Service Crew - Very Young Team + C18 NF.
Cardiff - Soul Crew.
Millwall - Bushwhackers - The Treatment + C18 NF.
Chelsea - Head-hunters + C18 NF.

Others missing from this list have changed positions throughout the years and have the capability to upset most of the top ten, but not consistently.

Arsenal – Gooners – The Herd
Bristol City - Inter City Robins - City Service Firm - Bristol Business Crew
Newcastle United - Newcastle Mainline Express - Gremlins

APEX TO ZULU A2Z!

Middlesborough - Boro Frontline.
Stoke City - Naughty Forty.
Everton - The Scallies - Everton's Charming Men.
Sunderland - Seaburn Casuals - Boss Lads - The Redskins.
Nottingham Forest - Red Dogs - Naughty Forties - Trent End Boot Boys - Forrest Executive Crew.

Gilroy Shaw enters the room; he's around six feet tall with a chubby face with a nervous double eye blink. He takes a seat and prepares himself for the interview. I have twelve questions for him to answer in to find out if this lad was the real deal or not. I personally knew the answer as soon as I met him, but never the less, here is the interview.

Q. Tell me your first experiences meeting Birmingham Citys firm?
A. It was around 85 at St Andrews and around thirty Wolves lad were bashed just outside the ground by about 60 blues, it was a good firm, a proper firm and they smashed us to pieces.

Q. What major firms have you done in London in the last 25 years?
A. We've done Leicester. PAUSE. Oh and we nearly got it on with Tottenham. We had it with West Ham toe to toe in 1990.

Q. What areas do Wolves firm come from?
A. They come from everywhere really, but mainly from Bushby and Wendsfield, Daliston & Dudley.

Q. What major northern firms have you done up north?
A. We done Leeds away in the cup.

Q. Where did this happen and what year?
A. Not sure.

Q. Who would you say are the top firm in the midlands?
A .At the moment? Us I do. Because we are so well organised. Not now, but 2004, yes. I don't mean to blow my own trumpet, but since

DAVID C GEORGE

I've been gone, it's all gone to pot.

Q. What would you say are the main differences are between Birmingham City & Wolverhampton Wanderers?
A. Blues have got a good track record, they were awesome, and you can't knock it.

Q. Did Wolves have a junior firm in the 80s, and if so, what were they called?
A. No they didn't.

Q. Have Wolves ever taken on blues full firm?
A. Yes, Moseley Road.

Q. Do you think that 40 people were blues full firm?
A. Was you there? Well I seen all the faces, I know who they were and it was a lot of Blues proper firm.

Q. Did they get done then?
A. No, but they did hold their own. Personally, I think that we burst your bubble.

Q. How big is the Wolves firm?
A. About sixty to seventy-handed for away games, you get more fun to play up at away games, and I mean you know yourself?

After listening to this information from this so called top-flight hooligan called Gilroy Shaw, I realised the event at Moseley Road had really made olves day. If he thought that was blues full firm at Moseley Road, then what the hell would he think if he ever saw 600 Zulus walking through Wolverhampton city centre? From Wolves exploits up and down the country over the past two decades, it is clear to see that having a fight with West Ham and Leicester in twenty five years in London, automatically sets yourself up to be top drawer in any football casuals list of firms. Twenty-five years and two fights in London, do I have to say more? He's done it all for me really. If you were to ask a

Birmingham lad about fights up and down the country over the last 25 years, you would have to go and get a sleeping bag and a packed lunch, because you would be talking to him for the next 72 hours straight. Before I left, I noticed a minor conversation between The General and Gilroy, which went down like a lead balloon. Gilroy had been saying to numerous people that he knew The General, but this was not the case at all. When The General stood in front of Gilroy, he smiled and put his hand out towards The General and was totally ignored. The reason was simple really, because if you are the dog's swingers, you will get respect for the right reasons and this is clearly not the case when meeting this Bridge Street character. He is another name who has come out of a scene that Wolves have really missed in its heyday.

Wolves Who?

On the 22nd Sept 84, Birmingham Zulus landed in New Street station 500 handed to wait for the train to Wolverhampton. We're standing just behind the barriers in front of the cafeteria, and the concourse is packed. As we are standing they're having a chat, nobody was talking about Wolves at all, and we were discussing which nightclub everyone was going to in the evening. To be honest, in the 80s we thought nothing of Wolves and we had no reason to. We knew that if a few people come unstuck in Wolverhampton, they would probably be kicked to death because when you are a firm looking to get credibility from anywhere you can, then to beat Blues fans unconscious is something for a Wolves fan to look forward to. As we are waiting for the train to Wolverhampton, a voice over the intercom tells us a London train has just arrived and on this day Tottenham were playing West Bromwich Albion, and had to change trains at New Street.

About six Yids walk up the stairs from platform 3 and turn towards the exit, but were confronted by a 500 strong firm of Zulus. From what Tottenham had done in the seats to Blues the season before, Birmingham would have normally let this small amount off the hook, but today, it didn't look as though this was going to happen. The Yids lined up about forty yards from us and their hearts must have been in their mouths because we were blocking their way to get to the next platform, and the only way was through us. One London lad stepped

DAVID C GEORGE

forward a few feet in front of the other Yids, dropped his eyebrows and lifted up his arms on either side as if to invite any of the Zulus to come and have a go. Now at the time I was only fifteen so for me, I thought this guy was either really hard, or just plain mad. Later, when you have had numerous clashes with Cockneys, it becomes more apparent that this particular behaviour is none of the above, but just good old fashioned front.

For instance, if you know you're going to get a hiding, you might as well style it out before you get knocked out, and this is what a lot of London heads introduced to Birmingham. The front, giving it the big one even though your chances of getting a result are non-existent.

The London guy who stepped forward was called Carpel, who seemed to have an I don't give a fuck look in his eyes. He smiled at Blues and then offered the whole 500 for an invitation to knuckle. Another Yid was called Maguire and between the two of them, they had huge reputations in London. At the time, a few British Transport Police were standing with Birmingham's firm, but there were only a hand full of them all radioing for backup. Blues rushed forward about twenty feet, and Tottenham ran down onto the nearest platform. Blues had no intention of going after the six Yids, but they did want to shit them up before they went to play the Baggies.

The train now arrives to Wolverhampton and Blues all get on. Wolverhampton police escort us straight to the ground. Blues firm all pay into the seats where the Wolverhampton firm sat, and are now sitting right next to them as the game starts. Blues are playing well and mount an attack just missing the crossbar, and as this occurs, one of Blues lads sitting in the middle of the Wolves firm stands up and shouts, "Oooooh" with his hands up to his face. We all turn to see Fat Errol in the middle of the Wolves, having it bang off on his own. He gets out of his seat and runs down the stairs being smacked over the head by Wolves fans with those push handle umbrellas. Errol now steps over the advertising boards, turns round bouncing his head, and invites the whole of the Wolves firm onto their pitch. The Wolves don't move and just sit there looking at Errol, when the whole of Blues firm stands up in the seats, runs down the steps and onto the pitch to back Errol. Blues firm are now in front of the Wolves end inviting them to come onto the pitch, but they still don't move. The police are called with extra reinforcements and horses, which now chase the Birmingham fans off the pitch and back into the seats. The Wolves firm were saying absolutely nothing and for them it was a lesson in what the difference is between a wanna be, and a big bee. Wolves got stung.

Many occasions years later, some of Wolves' lads used to annoy Blues fans season after season by continually phoning them up and suggesting places to meet for knuckle and most of this was a wind up. Sometimes Wolves used to walk through Birmingham fifty handed after a game, and go in search of Blues, and beat up any small numbers they could find, but this is the main difference between a wanna be, and the real deal. When you have numbers of at least 120 lads tooled up and you fight 40 Blues fans with no tools, you should get a result, but if anyone wishes to check the details of all of the head injuries and lads hospitalised on that day, they were all from Wolverhampton. Check the archives, as I don't tell porkpies. One of the Wolverhampton lads was put into a coma for a month.

West Bromwich Albion Vs Birmingham City Oct 29th 83

Section 5 are another Midlands firm that seem to be able to do a bit of damage occasionally when they play at home matches, but have never been in the same category as Birmingham City. Birmingham has come unstuck once in West Bromwich in the eighties, but it is really just one of those things. A number of West Broms' black lads turned into mercenaries, and would travel with Birmingham City to away matches because they knew Blues would have a proper good day, whether in Blackburn, or Portsmouth. For Blues, West Brom is a short distance from Birmingham City, and a lot of people could never be arsed to go because on a scale of 1–10 of violence with West Brom, this place was number two. On this particular day, Blues took only a small firm up to Smethwick to have a mooch for Section 5. We got off the train 60 handed and came out of the station and walked towards their pub, which is called The Talbot. West Broms lads were standing outside about thirty handed and ran back into the pub as we approached.

This didn't feel like a buzz you get when you are fronting a top firm, in fact it just felt as though we were sightseeing.

DAVID C GEORGE

Blues now walk straight past The Talbot and start to walk up the hill, but as they are doing this, the pub starts to empty into the street behind them. Blues nonchalantly carry on walking up the short hill, and at the top, turn and beckon the now hundred-handed West Brom up the hill. Blues now turn right and walk down a short road and stand at the bottom waiting for West Brom, and one of the Blues lads is telling us about a cracking chip shop up the road that does mini fish and chips. West Brom are now running down the hill at Blues who have now lined up in the road in straight lines.

As West Brom approach, their strategy goes all wrong because they expected Blues to scatter, but Blues stood firm waiting for them to arrive. Hands up and fists clenched, stance correct and ready for a minor workout. If you have ever seen people who are running too fast trying to slow down when there are at least three lines of Blues fans ready to punch your face in, it makes for good TV. West Brom are now running straight at Blues and being put flat on their arses. At least six people were put on their backsides before they turned and ran back to The Talbot. Blues walked off to find that chippy and went to the game which we won 2–1.

Birmingham City Vs West Bromwich Albion 28th Feb 84

Standing outside the Grapes public house on Hill Street having a drink and a chat with McCormick, at the bottom of the road we could see a number of chaps walking towards us up from the Crown. They were scruffily dressed and obviously were part of West Bromwich Section 5 firm. There must have been around 70 of them at the time and they were keen on banging it off with Blues on our doorstep. I have to tip my hat to West Brom, because in those days to walk up to the Grapes public house and call it on to Blues was an act of insanity or true courage.

West Brom now mobbed up outside the Grapes and were calling it on to Blues who gladly obliged. A few heads were looking out of the window of the pub, then they all vanished and the doors came flying open with Blues' Zulus spilling into the road to confront West Brom.

West Brom had a little go, but get bashed, so they then turned and ran back down Hill Street.

APEX TO ZULU A2Z!

Blues now chase Section 5 down Hill Street and past The Crown pub, where West Brom's lads are bashed again, leaving a few people on the floor. Blues now are still chasing Section 5 past the Old Rep theatre, where a West Brom lad manages to lose his balance, and falls on his face. He is then introduced to a claw hammer on the back of his head by a Blues lad, but is pulled off by another Blues fan, because this situation was totally unnecessary, as this skirmish was already in the bag. West Brom are now chased through the old bus depot, and through the Bull Ring market where in the film called The Firm, starring Gary Oldman. West Ham's ICF come a cropper.

The West Brom lads are now running straight to Digbeth police station and up the stairs, and this is where all blues lads turn and run back into the Bull Ring market and scatter.

Stoke – The 90s Firm

From reading the Stoke Naughty Forty book I have in my opinion put together all you need to know about Stoke City. I will always give credit and respect to firms up and down the country who are deserving of it; this is why Stoke only has a paragraph. When we played Stoke away, we smashed them to pieces, and at our ground, our old bill ran us. If Birmingham are walking in front of your escort and you charge at us with the police in front of you running at us also with their truncheons out, then I'm honest enough to say that Blues did run, but if you are deluded enough to think you run us, you cannot be helped. From looking at the pictures they have in their book of over three thousand Birmingham fans on the pitch inviting Stoke to come and play, and for them still to say they did Blues on the fences, begs belief. You were bloody lucky that the fences were there. One more thing, when you show a picture of your little firm walking round an industrial estate in Birmingham telling the country you are hunting Zulus in the nineties, please tell the truth. Blues don't drink in the industrial estate lads; you have to come into town. If you're in Birmingham in the eighties or nineties, you know where we are and you wouldn't need to hunt for us at all. Nuff said. Have a nice day in Walt Disney, chaps. Keep taking the tablets.

PS Your mum works where?

DAVID C GEORGE

Birmingham City Vs Stoke City 92
J. Pedley

On match day a group of us from Billeslley were drinking around town ending up in the Kaleidoscope club, when some lads came in and said there were Stoke lads in the Stevenson's Hotel opposite the Midland Red bus garage.

So around 40 of Blues walked round to the hotel and clocked about 100 Stoke lads in the bar reception. Five of us now entered the bar and as soon as they clocked us walking in, they started throwing glasses and chairs through the windows at us outside. We threw the chairs back and left quickly, waiting outside for them to now, we thought to start piling out of the doors, but they wouldn't come out. The police now arrive and Blues are chased through the midland red bus depot and then through the fish market. Some blues lads got nicked on the escalators but around fifteen of us now made our way to the ground through Digbeth. As we got to the then Watering hole public house where McDonalds now stands at the bottom of Cattle Road, a riot van lands on us and starts asking where we are going, where did you just come from. I said that was going to the game so the officer nicked me. The other Blues lads carried on walking after a few minutes and I was driven up the Coventry Road towards Small Heath. The van now stops and the one officer says to me, "We're busy, but if we see you again later on today, you're nicked. This was a system that is still used by police up and down the country to football fans in order for you to behave yourself, but a lot of the time the police never arrest the right person who is at it, just anybody in a crowd. I quickly made my way back up to the ground and met up with the lads. Inside the ground we sat in the paddock area towards the railway end, the Blues were winning 1–0 when Stoke City scored. The reason Birmingham city fans went berserk was that the Stoke player produced a two-footed challenge on the Birmingham keeper into his chest causing the ball to roll away with Stoke then scoring a simple tap in. The Ref who said the goal stands ignored the foul on the keeper. This decision caused a pitch invasion from the railway end and the paddock area of the ground by Blues lads, but also the taunting of our fans from the Stoke end of the ground was unbearable. I was jogging towards the

Tilton corner where the Stoke were, when the Ref was running past me heading towards the tunnel. I gave him a left hook as I jogged past still heading towards the Stoke fans who were now up on the fences fighting blues fans with one especially giving it loads. I made a beeline towards him and gave this guy an almighty left hook, which Henry Cooper would have been proud of, and it was goodnight from him. The police now charged us back into the lower paddock area where a guy jumped on me from the crowd. With this, a number of Birmingham lads thought it was a very keen Stoke fan wanting a bit of a play-up. Blues fans attack the guy who grabbed hold of me until more police come through the crowd and the fighting stops. The guy who grabs me now shows his police badge, talking through his bruised face, "Arrest this man, he's just knocked out the Ref." Hooli- coppers sat behind us throughout the whole game which was unknown to us. In court I was sentenced to 6 months for assaulting the Ref, and 6 months for knocking out the Stoke fan who was never found. The rest is history. Respect to the Yardley Wood/Billseley lads, you know who you are.

Keep Right On!

Stoke City Vs Birmingham City FA Cup 5th Round 19th Feb 2006
Travelling up to Stoke with some friends of mine, Bram, Kingy, Stones, Mitch and myself. We stopped off in Stafford for a quick drink in a pub near the station down by the river, and met up with a good mob of Birmingham's younger firm. They were around 150 handed with a few older chaps combined in the crew. My friend who is a journalist had a spare ticket for me to sit in the John Smiths Upper Tier at the Britannia Stadium and after a quick pint, we carried on with our journey to Stoke.

We have had a good few run-ins with Stoke where they have had a right hiding from us, including us going to their main pub and giving them a slap. I was looking forward to going to see how Stoke's mentality has changed towards Birmingham, and also to see if they are still in cloud cuckoo land.

Birmingham fill the south end stand and proudly sing throughout the game, even though everybody knows we haven't played real football since the 1960s.

As the battery has gone on my mobile phone, myself and Kingy couldn't call over to Bram who was sitting in the away end for us to meet up after the game and all drive home in the one car. The Stoke firm are below us in the John Smith Lower Tier singing to the away end about, "Where are your famous Zulus?"

I thought this was hilarious, as I was sitting in their end watching the game.

It was very difficult to keep our mouths shut as Birmingham were looking for a goal, but we managed it quite well except for one young Stoke kid who kept on looking at me biting my lip and making squeaky noises under my breath anytime Birmingham came close to scoring in the game. The lad must have thought I had Torettes syndrome.

At half time we went downstairs to have a drink and watched the highlights of the first half on a TV screen. On our left we could see around seven of Stoke's firm who never even batted an eyelid at us, even though I was the only black geezer in that particular stand. As we are talking to a local Stoke fan about the view outside the Britannia Stadium, he was informing us that the whole area around the stadium was where the coalmines were situated way back in the day. A loud groan is heard throughout the Stoke end, as Mikael Forsell scores, putting the Blues one nil up. I rushed around the crowd of Stoke fans asking who scored, knowing full well it was Forsell, as I just wanted to see how upset the locals were. I'm now standing there pretending to frown at the TV screen listening to Stoke fans swearing all around me. Kingy and i decide on a plan of action to get us to the other side of the ground before the end of the game. The plan fails and we go back to our seats thinking of another idea when the stadium louder speaker is heard. "Bing Bong"

Important message for Mr David George, David George could you please come down to reception as your wife has just gone into labour. I looked at Kingy with a huge smile on my face as we both burst out laughing. Kingy turns round and starts pointing at me saying, "It's him." I stood up in my seat smiling and holding my hands in the air greeting the Stoke crowd who are now clapping and cheering me.

APEX TO ZULU A2Z!

As I'm walking down the stairs in the John Smith stand I get a little carried away and start shouting at the Skoke crowd saying, " I think it's fucking twins?"

As we get down to one of the stewards and explain the situation, he congratulates me and then personally escorts us both past Stoke's firm in the lower tier and onto the touchline at the side of the pitch. We are now escorted round the pitch to the south stand away end where the Birmingham fans are now cheering me. The steward now walks us through the Birmingham crowd until we find our friends, Stones Bram and Mitch. Bram is the genius that arranged our tour around the ground, and for thinking that quickly on his feet, I have to give him maximum respect for his skills. At the end of the game, we were leaving the stadium when we could see that to our left, a fight was taking place with Birmingham fans and Stoke. Stoke had walked down a small embankment to taunt the Blues through two fences. Now being a casual for a considerable amount of time, I found it extremely disappointing that Stoke couldn't even manage to come round to the car park where Blues were being held. They instead decide on using swear words through a couple of fences but obviously didn't think anyone was going to react. With Blues proper firm now congregated outside in the car park, a handful of Birmingham now rushes the fence to get at the Stoke. The first fence is demolished instantly then Blues rush the next fence intent on showing Stoke what was what. Stoke ran from the second fence, even though it hadn't come down yet, but when they saw what they faced, all of them beat a hasty retreat. Stoke are youngsters who enjoy wearing Berghaus cagoules, and stand outside chip shops swearing and smoking cannabis. What they faced was 300 grown men who didn't take too kindly to a bunch of kids calling it on through two fences, which blocked their way. It would have been men against boys. These Stoke fans are the new breed that have come through after the overrated Naughty Forty era but didn't really have a clue on what they were supposed to be doing. We jumped back into our car and headed into the city centre where Stoke where congregated around their main pub on the outskirts of town. We drove right into the centre and saw a huge mob of kids who were waiting to supposedly have it with Blues, but there was no way that this was going to happen

DAVID C GEORGE

as the police had escorted a firm of Birmingham into town on a bus with vans in the front and back, including a helicopter hovering above the bus. Another firm were also all escorted to their vehicles and then out of town without a single incident. What Stoke fail to realise is that Birmingham have consistently had the same firm for over twenty years respectively and are not about to run from a bunch of kids who want to make a name for themselves.

APEX TO ZULU A2Z!

Stoke vs. Blues after running from fence – 2006

Blues in Stoke – 1986

Stoke running – 2006

CHAPTER 17

Operation Red Card

OPERATION RED CARD was in full swing, with Birmingham lads being dragged out of their houses early in the morning. I was arrested a week later after being grassed on by my so-called mate called Boomer from Chelmsley Wood, of all fucking places. This guy had put so many people in the picture that we thought Fuji Film had sponsored him. The night before my arrest, I was in my friend's house called Toads. There, a good few of us were having a good drink and smoking some good shrubs. One of the lads had a bag of magic mushrooms, which he boiled up and made into hot cups of coffee, which tasted like coffee and dirt. After ¾ hour, I found myself in Never Never Land, where the wallpaper moves and the patterns jump out at you. Even the carpet was now increasing in length and decreasing every time I looked at it. I was well and truly ripped to the tits. After leaving Toads gaff at stupid o'clock, I ended up trundling home and going to sleep, but the only problem was that every time I closed my eyes I was skydiving off the side of the Grand Canyon. What a fucking night. After the mushroom situation had calmed down, I got my head onto my pillow and got some serious kip, but it was short lived as there was a heavy duty knocking on the front door, which could only be the dibble at this hour of the morning. It had just gone 6.00am when I looked out of the window and saw six police officers standing on the path outside the front door. I then went and took a look out of the bathroom window, which covers the back garden and the same situation there as well. I heard a little of the conversation at the door between my mother and one of the officers, and I knew that The Price Was Right and it was time for me to, "Come On Down." They drove me to Steelhouse Lane Police station, where I met up with numerous other proper lads from all over Birmingham who had experienced the same early morning wake up call as myself. I'm now sitting in a cell with Elvis, Fat Errol, Stig and many other chaps who were all half awake at the time. Also within our cell was the Bass player from the group Musical Youth called Patrick, who seemed to have problems more complicated than the ones we were about to face. He ended up showing us how many press-ups he could do on the floor, with hardly anybody in the cell paying attention. I was later convicted of conspiring to commit violent disorder, and assaulting a police officer, but these were two different incidents with one taking place outside the Crown public house, and the other in The Southern Cross public house on Chelmsley. After a number of us being sentenced to 9 months, we were taken to Winson Green prison and as we entered the wing, the inmates were all standing on the balcony clapping and cheering shouting Zulu. It was quite funny to walk through a prison holding a pile of folded blankets, receiving a round of applause, but the smiles soon left my face when I entered my cell and the door shut behind me which didn't have a handle for me to open it back up again. Oh shit, I can't go home. This is when it really dawned on me that the whole idea of people doing time was mostly ridiculous. For instance, the Tottenham fans that came to fight Birmingham on this particular day numbered around 300, with Birmingham numbering around 30–40.

I defended myself against foe that came with the vowed intent of wiping us out. You put the idea of being wiped out to any group of people who have courage, honour, respect, pride, tenacity, gaul, and then you will see people who will fight with more passion and belief than ever before.

Keep Right On!

DAVID C GEORGE

Keith Holmes Vs Robert McCracken 2000-2001
Sooty

Blues arranged to meet up with Manchester Utd in London before the boxing match. Most Blues fans drove down to the capital and a number caught the train. The previous season we played Manchester City and it really did kick off up there, and the Saturday we supposed to be playing Manchester City away. A guy at the Evening Mail knew Blues were playing away and it was a high profile game. The word went out that Birmingham were going to Manchester firm handed, but before that they are going into Blackpool for a good drink up. McCracken didn't want a full firm down in London as he knew there is a strong possibility it would go right off, as on the same bill were a number of Londoners from south of the river. Birmingham are now in London in Leicester Square 500 handed and having a good time. Birmingham had London to themselves. Manchester Utd were playing at Watford and they were allegedly supposed to make a show sometime in the day near a pub called The Torch. Birmingham went over to The Torch and waited for Manchester Utd who never showed but I'm sure they would have been surprised by a firm of Birmingham 500 handed when everybody thought Birmingham were up north at Man City. The police were told Birmingham were going to Blackpool then onto Manchester and they were waiting in both parts of the country for a huge mob of Brummies to arrive, but Birmingham's proper firm was in London, soaking up the watered down lager and the arrogance that naturally exude from Londoners personalities.

The Marvin Haggler Meeting

In a Hotel on Edgware corner, Fishheads spots marvellous Marvin Haggler and asks for an autograph for his mother. Haggler says, "No, I don't give autographs." A group of blues fans heard what Haggler said and now stood up and surrounded him because they were not happy with this sporting hero who had just snubbed some of his fans. When Haggler saw the looks on the disgruntled Brummies faces standing around him, he said wisely, "Alright you can have a couple of photographs lads." What Haggler knew was he had just been threatened by one of the Blues lads, and realised it would be best to play ball than get jumped for being an arrogant old boxer.

Birmingham entered the arena and had a huge section for themselves. They sang throughout the evening with their voices echoing around the arena. Birmingham fans were singing Zulu, Zulu Warrior.

It was a great night for Birmingham fans with McCracken wining the fight in the...... round.

The NBC sports channel & the NEC battle. Don King quote: They are Warriors.

Robert McCracken Vs Steve The Viking Foster or Red Army Vs Zulu Warriors.

<u>Round 1.</u> Horses Shoes pub, Cov Rd – Man Utd taking the piss in pub.

Around ten blues fans who were going to watch a well known local boxer called Robert McCracken, but before they went to the NEC arena, they stopped to have a drink in the Three Horse Shoes on the Coventry Road, when a coach load of around fifty mean looking Manks who were obviously supporting their man Steve Foster, entered the same pub. Some of the blues lads had been taking LSD and at the time were tripping their faces off, while having a quick drink. A few words were exchanged back and forth and the Manchester lads were taking the piss out of the Brummy lad's big time. The Blues lads decide to leave the pub and make their way over to The NEC, as the situation was moody as hell. They decide to go for another cheeky drink, and then head off to the NEC.

<u>Round 2.</u>

As they arrive at the NEC, the Manks are already there in numbers of around a hundred strong and proceed in bullying and picking blues fans off in small numbers and bashing them as they entered the arena.

Some time later, the main firm of Zulus turn up at the arena 200 hundred handed and are told by numerous other Blues fans that the Manchester lot are looking for trouble, big time. Birmingham mobbed up and went in search of Man Utd.

Round 3.

With numbers of around 250 strong, Birmingham marched to the refreshments kiosk and steamed into Man Utd's Salford firm, some wearing Viking hats in homage to Steve Foster. Man Utd's firm was made up of many ugly looking steroid freaks who had over the years, drunk too much ale. One Brummy guy said it was like a scene from the movie Platoon, when the VC had over run the Americans. People were being cancelled all over the place and nobody was backing down. The Manchester lads ran at first, and then decided to make a stand. They kept fighting, even though they were being individually bashed as time went on. As the fight continued, more and more Blues fans were getting involved which swelled the numbers to over 300 easy. It was like hundreds of people were cage fighting with no rules. Tables were broken over people's heads, and chairs were wrapped around many faces on both sides. Birmingham kicked and punched the Manchester lads all around the arena, with the Manchester lot getting a taste of their own medicine, but the fighting hadn't finished just yet. More and more Manchester lads were joining in and the fighting was getting well out of hand. The security at the NEC bottled it and announced that the fighting is all on CCTV, and the police were on their way. This was a total lie, as the fighting went on for around half an hour before they arrived. Manchester were surrounded by Birmingham's Zulus, and fair play to them, they did put up a bloody good battle, but in no way shape or form did Birmingham get done as this is total fantasy on their behalf.

Round 4.

A Birmingham lad was now getting grief from some Manks within the seated area, and this is when all hell broke loose. The fighting had now spilled into the seated arena where the boxing was taking place and this was beamed all round the world.

I sat at home watching the fight on the TV, and couldn't believe how long it went on. Man Utd rush Blues in the seats and at first back Blues off. Blues then let out the battle cry, ZUUUUUUUUUUULU! And rush forward hurling chairs and punching any Manks that still had teeth. Nigel Benn, who was boxing in the ring at the time had to come and speak to the crowd on the intercom system to calm them down. Don King, who was commentating on the fight at the time, and was heard saying. "Who are these guys fighting in the seats?" "Black and white fighting together." "They're like Warriors." An English reporter who was working with Mr King at the time is heard to say to Don King, that the people fighting are known as the "Zulu Warriors." I have read a few reports on the Internet saying that some people thought that the fighting was a black Vs white thing, but you couldn't be further from the truth. The fact is that Steve Foster is a well respected lad from working class Manchester who has a strong following of local supporters who just happen to be football casuals as well as Birmingham supporting their local hero. Most of the injuries were to Manchester people, except one Brummy lad who lost an eye from a chair leg being smacked in it. The fighting did carry on but in smaller numbers around the arena, but not as bad as earlier in the evening. The fact of the matter is that Manchester never turned Birmingham over as they claimed in the Red Army General book, but they did give Blues a fucking good run for their money. People were badly injured on both sides but Birmingham didn't get turned over by Manchester at all.

Man Utd's monsters were intent on trouble from the get go, but Blues are not about to be turned over at the NEC, as Man City found out in the early eighties at the 5-aside Atari football tournament, when they got a right hoofing. I was 13 at the time and witnessed Man City get bashed outside the arena by Birmingham City; they then ran into Birmingham International. A Birmingham lad called Adam Felli gets drunk in one of the bars in the arena and we decide on putting him head first into a giant plastic bin, with his legs hanging out of it. Nottingham Forrest were playing in the tournament and their manager at the time was Brian Clough. He comes stumbling out of a bar and starts ranting at us to stop messing about, when our friend's legs are hanging out of a giant plastic bin. At first we all stopped and our faces were that of shock. "Look, it's Brian fucking Clough pissed as a fart!"

It's not very often you end up having an argument with one of the most influential football managers this country has ever known. Sod that, he was a rowdy piss head who got a verballing from a bunch of school kids that went, "Well why don't you fuck off back to Nottingham, and get drunk over there then, you miserable old spunk up?"

Arrested Double Murder

Sunday evening in Stetchford, I'm standing at a bus stop ready to visit my mother on Chelmsley Wood. I check my change, and stand and wait for the bus. A man comes from nowhere and enters the bus stop and asks me for the time then leaves, later on, I find it was this person who gave the word for me to be landed on. As I'm looking up the main road, I see a police car coming towards me, but I think nothing of it. The lights are on in the car, and it is moving quite slowly. I look at my watch, and then in a split second, the police have skidded in the road in front of me and are now both holding machine guns pointing at me. There are a group of rowdy black teenagers in the bus stop opposite, who are standing there with their jaws dragging on the floor. Thinking I was dreaming, I kept looking behind me, and searching for the other person who they were after.

I looked round the bus stop and nobody was there, then realising after pointing at myself at least four times saying, "Me? "Do you mean me?" "It can't be me?"

As the police move closer towards me, I drop my Paul Smith hat in the rain, due to nerves, but as I go to pick it up, I hear the sound of guns being prepped for firing.

I look at my chest and it's covered in red dots, which brings on breathing difficulties and I hit the floor. I'm grabbed by two burly coppers who throw me around on the floor and slap the handcuffs on me. "We are arresting you for double murder, you don't have to say anything, but anything you say will be taken down and used as evidence." I'm thrown into a car by armed police, and taken to Stetchford police station at high speed, escorted by a car in front and behind. As we drive from the bus stop, the guys at the opposite side of the road are still standing there with their mouths wide open. I'm sitting in the back of a police car with two of the henchest officers from the serious crime squad. As we get to the desk, I'm trying to explain they have the wrong person, but my speech isn't working to well due to me still having flashbacks of machine guns and red dots pointing at me. They place me in a room on a chair with a copper must have been 6ft 5 &20stone. This guy was a fucking monster. The kind of guy who could hold a basketball with one hand very easily. The copper is walking round me trying to be intimidating and asking me why I shot two people! He couldn't get past the idea he might have the wrong person sitting in front of him. I then started thinking some unlucky people get put into prison for years before they realise they have the wrong person, that is when I started to get worried about the situation, as people from ethnic backgrounds never do well in circumstances like this. Another police officer enters the room and whispers in the other officer's ear, and it turns out to be the same person who asked me for the time in the bus stop. The burly police officer now has no choice but to be nice to me, as he has just been told I am completely the wrong person, which I'm sure he was finding difficulty in dealing with. This guy normally deals with armed criminals, but today, he and his fellow officers have managed to apprehend a blackman going for Sunday dinner at his moms. The guy who they have now arrested looks nothing like me anyway. After doing some research, I find out the person who has now been arrested for the crime was mixed race and over six feet tall. How the hell can a 5ft 8ins black lad all of a sudden turn into a 6ft mixed race lad? Answers on a postcard please.

I'm now driven to an off licence and given 4 cans of Stella's and 20 Benson & Hedges by the burly copper who says with a smile on his face, "You'll have something to tell your grandkids now won't ya?"

Arriving at my mothers I found that my appetite had completely vanished, and all I kept thinking was that if I had made the wrong move in the bus stop, I would not be here anymore. The police would come and see my parents and explain that they made a mistake, and they are sorry for the loss. I jumped into a taxi to Dorridge and went to see a good friend of mine called Debbie who is always a ray of sunshine. I poured a huge glass of wine and explained what had happened to me, but I now know I was still in shock as I kept laughing and imagining me been taken away in a body bag.

Later that decade Hip Hop took to the charts. Many thought this was a phase. But it gave young black & white people of my generation a real 'modern' music to identify with. Artists such as 'African Bambata' that Hip Hop did have legs, could run, walk and even shout with the rest of the styles.

Acid House, 1988. Youths hugged each other a lot and gave you bubble gum, bubble gum was important. The warehouse parties, 'Sunrise', 'Biology' will never be forgotten.

The Manchester scene was another strong movement. Innovative bands such as the 'Stone Roses' and 'New Order' and The Happy Mondays, brought us into the nineties with some really strong groundwork.

Hip Hop, Dance, and Indie all had a strong influence on the nineties, which continued to be a development of three musical styles. I for one, am proud to remember what kicked it all off.

Birmingham has always had a reputation for having groups of people who are willing to fight at the drop of a hat, just as many of the other Midland cities do. The only difference is that Birmingham has a proper reputation for the right reasons without making up stories or exaggerating incidents to make particular situations distorted in the favour of somebody else. The camaraderie is not as strong as it was twenty years ago, but it still has the same ethos that has kept the firm friends for over two decades. When people normally speak of the Zulu Warriors it is usually something negative from a person who knows nothing about how the Zulu operate, and would be a comment made by a supporter of our local rivals. Admittedly, there are a sizeable amount of knuckle draggers and slab eaters who follow the cause, but to create a tidy firm you need many different types of people to make the whole thing work. If everyone was a nutter, it wouldn't work, if everybody was good at planning but couldn't fight, then it just wouldn't work. Many different types of people under one banner, and the banner or name is Zulu. The Birmingham meaning for the word Zulu is together and some who follow Birmingham have now forgotten this and tend to separate themselves from the full crew. I have and always will be a Bluenose till the day I die, but I have now moved into other areas bringing out my dormant creative side that has been itching to come to the forefront for a considerable. It's still in me to bowl down the road and perform, but what now stops me is that I have something else in my life that has given me more of a buzz than banging it right off at Tottenham or Pompey ECT. There is still that aaaaaaagh in me, which will never go away, but this is not something to be ashamed of as every human being has this feeling inside him or her. If you can imagine going to an away match at the age of fourteen and being chased up the road by youths carrying knives and iron bars who are wanting to smash you to pieces and then rob your clothes. This was our reality as young dressers and we knew the risks but were willing to take them many times over. I salute Birmingham's defensive skills and their capabilities to get the job done, many must admire this, but not many would admit this to be fair. Birmingham are good at what they do and sometimes it is just to show others that we are nothing like what some perceive us to be, but we can also be everything you never wanted us to be.

The name of the Zulu is respected throughout the British Armed forces, and has been for decades due to their bravery and courage when in battle. The African Zulu attacked the British in order to protect their own land from invaders, and were willing to fight against gattling guns and rifles, and die for the cause. In 2005, the British Elite force that operates in Basra is known as Zulu Company. Need I say more? If you have a gun, and another man has a spear, and both of these people are ready to fight to the death, then who would you say is brave? The man with the gun, or the man with the spear who is defending his land? Answers on a postcard please.

These days in 2006 on Chelmsley Wood, the togetherness is not there anymore just as many other areas are feeling the same overwhelming passion, that of Heroin and Crack cocaine.

I've have seen so many soldiers and good people fall into this murky world and never to come back at all which does makes me sad for the future of youths in areas such as ours. ¬(The Trooper Nippa Posse) took heavy casualties from this drug, and a lot of them are still in that same place. I wish that there was a way of reversing the clock and for people not to have chosen this route but unfortunately it is done, and will take a hell of a long time to fix. If it can be fixed at all?

I'd like to thank all of the people up and down the country who have assisted me in putting these memories together and hopefully you have been taken on an adventure that is still ongoing for Birmingham who are still active and very much alive and kicking. From bowling through London 600 handed only last year, and making sure London know when we are about, Birmingham have consistently had it all over the capital with anyone who wants it for decades. There is only one firm in the Midlands that can still go to London or the North, and land heavy. For this reason, the rest of the top firms in the U.K rate Blues because they admire firms that are not all talk. In writing this book and doing my research over the past year, I was only refused an interview by one person who told me he didn't want to talk to me as he is writing his own memories, and didn't wish to be associated with myself and what I was producing. I have not mentioned this character within the book, as he didn't want to be mentioned at all. The Birmingham Zulu story however, is bigger than everybody in Birmingham and could go on and on for years if someone were willing to put in the work that goes with it. Myself, I'm not sure how many more rows and scuffles you can mention without people falling asleep.

The 80s were some of the best times of my life and I have to thank all the Birmingham fans and the Zulu family of their patience and assistance in completing this book. Also, a thank you goes out to Gary from Doncaster for helping me out with the Leeds end. Thank you to Gilroy from Wolverhampton; even though he has been the biggest tool I had spoken to all year, trust me. Thank you goes out to Eddie Kelly and China for the Leeds info. Black Danny for giving me another angle come in from. Gerry and Wogga from the Cardiff sides, and also Nikola from Red Star Belgrade Zulu Warriors.

Thank you to the new Juniors at Birmingham City who have made me smile on numerous occasions when listening to them speaking about scuffles, as I can see myself in all of them. All in all, human beings are capable of many different things including some good and some bad. The way in which the government and the police have categorised people who venture down the football, as no good is ridiculous and will continue. Mindless hooligans who do not support their local team and are only interested in causing a fight. Well I hope someone in the future changes this attitude, as it is total rubbish.

There you are folks, those are only some the stories from the band of

APEX TO ZULU A2Z!

Brummies who have hot up the spot for a considerable and it is a story that had to come out linking up with the first best seller written by Caroline Gall. Thank you to one and all and I bid you all a good day.

The End, or is it?

Final Word

Jim Brown spits flavour

RECENT REPORTS OF FIGHTING between blacks and Asians are the cause of both depression and bewilderment. How can it be, that people have lived alongside each other, fairly harmoniously for half a century, should suddenly

See as mortal enemies. How could an area immortalised by Steele Pulse on their ground breaking number one album "Handsworth Revolution," have lost the very thing that defined it, its diversity. But perhaps we can only understand the loss by explaining what it is we once had.

I was borne in Yardley Wood maternity hospital in Birmingham. My father worked on the production line at BSA factory for over twenty years, polishing chrome for the world famous motorbikes. Some of my earliest memories are of Sunday nights at the Works social club, the Works fishing trip and the annual pantomime and holidays with the families of men who worked alongside him on "The Track." I was brought up fully immersed in the working class Brummie culture of the time. The very thing that Thatcher would destroy and Blair would later bury and deny.

(Judas anyone?) Even my mother worked evenings occasionally at the local factory (1). Although the popular perception at the time was that working class men were bigoted abusive drunkards, the reality contradicted that image. My father may have liked a drink, but he always looked after his family and treated his mother with total respect. To him, keeping his family safe and happy was part of being a man.

He had little time for men who failed to live up to that expectation.

Much of the Union activism of the time was specifically designed to facilitate family life for men who paid their dues and worked hard for a little financial reward. History may have been written by management (And The Media Barons), but anyone who lived through that period will know just how poor management were in those days (And still are today) (2).

I spent the first fourteen years of my life living in a Victorian terrace house in an inner city area of Birmingham called Small heath. Everything was so far- so ordinary, but in the sixties something amazing started to happen. The cultural landscape of the area started to transform in a time of expansion, the government of the day-recruited workers from the colonies to fill vacancies in the British Public sector. They were to do the jobs that we didn't want. (3) my street would change from elderly English to multi-cultural in what seemed like the blink of an eye. (4).

A typical class of twenty Whites, Blacks, Asians and Arabs in a fairly equal amount. The white and back kids may have teased the Asian more, but there was no real sense of a dominant culture. We were all just kids who learned together and played together. (5)

By the late sixties the effect of social change on youth culture was starting to show. Skinheads had superseded Mods as the latest working class fashion movement and skinheads having grown up alongside the first generation of Black English, adopted Reggae as their music of choice (6). Skinhead fashions with their trademark signature Crombies, sta press and Harrington's were worn by both black and white.

The local youth clubs and dances would be controlled by Jamaican style sound systems with their wardrobe speakers and Do It Yourself ethos (7).

Within a decade, the transformation from post war austerity to modern day melting pot was complete. That generation of youth would form relationships with each other, independent of their parent's experiences that would strengthen and last right up until today. A natural integration born of shared personal experience.

Before you accuse me of looking through rose tinted glasses, I have to point out that I am aware of the more sinister side of the Brummie psyche. Any Irishman or woman who lived there in the weeks and months after the infamous Birmingham pub bombing can attest to a viciously xenophobic, vengeful streak that can rear it's ugly head from time to time. Another example came late one Friday night of 1974 when a policeman was stabbed outside a reggae club called "The Rainbow," situated just off New Street in Birmingham city centre. (8)

What passengers witnessed that evening on the night service buses would be talked about for years afterwards. The first hint of something unusual came when all night buses were made to make an unscheduled stop at their local police station.

The main station on Digbeth Street was a favoured location, but most of the inner city stations that rang the centre were used. What happened next was unprecedented. Passengers watched as police boarded each bus and frogmarched every black male aged between fifteen and thirty, off the bus and into the local police station. Followed by twelve hours of what can only be described as organised torture as black men hung out of fourth-story windows, asphyxiated and beaten, subjected to various acts of violence at the hands of the police. In an effort to find the guilty man. Not many black men were spared a kicking that night and most have a story to tell of their treatment while in custody. This was happening at a time when support was for the National Front (NF), a British right wing party that believed in forced repatriation was as high as 16%. Even today, one of the reasons the phoenix consortium found manipulating the workers so easy during the recent Rover debacle was that they could tap into the anti-German attitude of the workforce.

But this is the other side of the coin and does not represent the majority of opinion in Britain today. As is the way of these things, its the white English who have benefited the most. To be brought up in the world at your doorstep is an enormous privilege and is surely one of the few benefits of Empire. We owe a debt to foreigners who in one way or another have helped build a life for themselves and their children and coincidentally, prepared this country to face the future.

APEX TO ZULU A2Z!

Where did it all go wrong? We are afraid to talk of repatriation and we continue to be in denial. Marlborough school is now 100% Asian. Blacks and Asians are fighting each other in Handsworth. We have "New Labour," Tony Blair and the politics of tolerance. (11)

Single faith schools lead to segregation, not integration. American style ghettos have replaced the diverse melting pot of my youth and society is less integrated.

I'm very lucky to have a job that involves a lot of travelling. I've been to every continent, and most major cities, but the thing that has most prepared me for life has been my upbringing in that inner city area of Birmingham. It taught me the importance of treating others, as I would like to be treated myself, no matter what they look like, or where they come from. It's an experience I would like my own children to have, as my wife is half Jamaican and half Irish, so they have a pretty good head start. Unfortunately, we are further from that ideal than we were 30 years ago.

1. My father would have to do his share of domestic chores like getting the kids to bed. He never once made us feel like we were too much trouble, or that his masculinity was threatened. It needs to be done, so he did it.
2. In Germany the proportion of the workforce that are management is around 6%. In Britain it's more like 14%. We have the least efficient and most expensive management in Europe.
3. We need bus drivers, labourers, nurses, sanitation workers ect.
4. An Irish family on one side, and Asian family on the other, and a black family next door but one.
5. I used to think that my childhood was normal, later I would discover just how wrong that assumption was.
6. It's only later that skins would come to be associated with Nazis.
7. Through many of the families from the Caribbean came from the smaller islands like St Kitts, Antigua or Trinidad, it was Jamaican culture that would have the biggest influence on British life.
8. This was a time when anyone could open up a club in Birmingham city centre.... So long as your name was Fewtrell.
9. This support would fall away within a year or two. With the introduction of race relations, legislation many institutions slowly

DAVID C GEORGE

began to change. Only the police have been allowed to continue their culture of racism. This institutionalised racism exposed by the McPherson report in the wake of the Stephen Lawrence enquiry, has been forgotten since 9/11. Many people shudder when they hear the police have given powers to harass minorities.
10. It is no coincidence that many of our Stately Homes were built at the height of the slave trade.
11. I find this vaguely insulting. I want to be respected, not tolerated. Typically our leaders are trying to disguise a weakness as strength.

Thank you goes out to Nino Cerutti, Slazenger, Pierre Cardin, New Balance, Christian Dior, Le coq sportif, Valentino, Fred Perry, Reebok, Hugo Boss, Valentino, Daniel Hechter, Fila, Helly Hanson, Lutha, Versace, Adidas, Puma, Pringle, Lyle & Scott, La Coste, Jaeger, Daks, Nike, Farah, Belstaff, Pierre Cardin, Ellesse, Fila, Hugo Boss, Slazenger, Gabicci, Ellesse, Sergio Tachini, Nino Cerutti, and Giorgio Armani for helping me with the information from their websites.

Acknowledgements to British History Online, John Lerwill and Virtual Brum for information on the beginnings of historical Birmingham.

Printed in the United Kingdom
by Lightning Source UK Ltd.
124549UK00001B/22-45/A